# Indiana

## Scott Foresman
# Science

*See learning in a whole new light*

PEARSON
Scott Foresman

Editorial Offices: Glenview, Illinois • Parsippany, New Jersey • New York, New York
Sales Offices: Needham, Massachusetts • Duluth, Georgia • Glenview, Illinois •
Coppell, Texas • Sacramento, California • Mesa, Arizona
www.sfsuccessnet.com

## Series Authors

**Dr. Timothy Cooney**
*Professor of Earth Science and Science Education*
University of Northern Iowa (UNI)
Cedar Falls, Iowa

**Dr. Jim Cummins**
*Professor*
Department of Curriculum, Teaching, and Learning
The University of Toronto
Toronto, Canada

**Dr. James Flood**
*Distinguished Professor of Literacy and Language*
School of Teacher Education
San Diego State University.
San Diego, California

**Barbara Kay Foots, M. Ed**
*Science Education Consultant*
Houston, Texas

**Dr. Shirley Gholston Key**
*Associate Professor of Science Education*
Instruction and Curriculum Leadership Department
College of Education
University of Memphis
Memphis, Tennessee

**Dr. M. Jenice Goldston**
*Associate Professor of Science Education*
Department of Elementary Education Programs
University of Alabama
Tuscaloosa, Alabama

**Dr. Diane Lapp**
*Distinguished Professor of Reading and Language Arts in Teacher Education*
San Diego State University
San Diego, California

**Sheryl A. Mercier**
*Classroom Teacher*
Dunlap Elementary School
Dunlap, California

**Dr. Karen L. Ostlund**
UTeach
College of Natural Sciences
The University of Texas at Austin
Austin, Texas

**Dr. Nancy Romance**
*Professor of Science Education & Principal Investigator*
NSF/IERI Science IDEAS Project
Charles E. Schmidt College of Science
Florida Atlantic University
Boca Raton, Florida

**Dr. William Tate**
*Chair and Professor of Education and Applied Statistics*
Department of Education
Washington University
St Louis, Missouri

**Dr. Kathryn C. Thornton**
*Professor*
School of Engineering and Applied Science
University of Virginia
Charlottesville, Virginia

**Dr. Leon Ukens**
*Professor of Science Education*
Department of Physics, Astronomy, and Geosciences
Towson University
Towson, Maryland

**Steve Weinberg**
*Consultant*
Connecticut Center for Advanced Technology
East Hartford, Connecticut

ISBN: 0-328-14961-6
Copyright © 2006, Pearson Education, Inc.
All Rights Reserved. Printed in the United States of America.
This publication is protected by Copyright, and permission should be obtained from the publisher prior to any prohibited reproduction, storage in a retrieval system, or transmission in any form by any means, electronic, mechanical, photocopying, recording, or likewise. For information regarding permission(s), write to: Permissions Department, Scott Foresman, 1900 East Lake Avenue, Glenview, Illinois 60025.

3 4 5 6 7 8 9 10 V063 12 11 10 09 08 07 06 05

**Photographs**

Every effort has been made to secure permission and provide appropriate credit for photographic material. The publisher deeply regrets any omission and pledges to correct errors called to its attention in subsequent editions.
Unless otherwise acknowledged, all photographs are the property of Scott Foresman, a division of Pearson Education.
Photo locators denoted as follows: Top (T), Center (C), Bottom (B), Left (L), Right (R), Background (Bkgd)

**Earth Science:** 1 ©Ron Leonetti; 2 (CL) Bruce Coleman Inc., (B) ©Jennifer Shepard /AP/Wide World Photos; 3 (C) ©Darron Cummings/AP/Wide World Photos, (B) ©Ron Leonetti; 4 ©Christopher Jordan/CJ Photography

**Life Science:** 1 (C) ©Aflo/Nature Picture Library, ©DK Images; 2 (CL) ©Tiffany M. Hermon/The Image Works, Inc., (CL) ©Silvestre Machado/SuperStock, (BR) ©Gay Bumgarner/Alamy Images; 3 ©Fred McConnaughey/Photo Researchers, Inc., 4 (BR) ©Michael O'Neill/Grant Heilman Photography, (CL) ©JS SIRA/Alamy Images, (TR, CR) ©Royalty-Free/Corbis

**Physical Science:** 1 ©Bill Friel/AP/Wide World Photos; 2 (B) ©Jan Halaska/Photo Researchers, Inc., (CL) ©Francis Miller/Getty Images; 3 NMAH / Transportation Collections/Smithsonian Institution; 4 ©Michael Kim/Corbis

**Space and Technology:** 1 ©Banayote Photography; 2 (C) ©Don Marvel/WonderLab Museum, (BR) Ron Dye/Photo Dyenamics, (TL) ©Patrick Bennett/Corbis; 3 Culver Pictures Inc.; 4 ©Kim Karpeles/Alamy Images

## Consulting Author

**Dr. Michael P. Klentschy**

*Superintendent*
El Centro Elementary School District
El Centro, California

## Science Content Consultants

**Dr. Frederick W. Taylor**

*Senior Research Scientist*
Institute for Geophysics
Jackson School of Geosciences
The University of Texas at Austin
Austin, Texas

**Dr. Ruth E. Buskirk**

*Senior Lecturer*
School of Biological Sciences
The University of Texas at Austin
Austin, Texas

**Dr. Cliff Frohlich**

*Senior Research Scientist*
Institute for Geophysics
Jackson School of Geosciences
The University of Texas at Austin
Austin, Texas

**Brad Armosky**

*McDonald Observatory*
The University of Texas at Austin
Austin, Texas

 **Content Consultants**

**Adena Williams Loston, Ph.D.**

*Chief Education Officer*
Office of the Chief Education Officer

**Clifford W. Houston, Ph.D.**

*Deputy Chief Education Officer for Education Programs*
Office of the Chief Education Officer

**Frank C. Owens**

*Senior Policy Advisor*
Office of the Chief Education Officer

**Deborah Brown Biggs**

*Manager, Education Flight Projects Office*
Space Operations Mission Directorate
Education Lead

**Erika G. Vick**

*NASA Liaison to Pearson Scott Foresman*
Education Flight Projects Office

**William E. Anderson**

*Partnership Manager for Education*
Aeronautics Research Mission
Directorate

**Anita Krishnamurthi**

*Program Planning Specialist*
Space Science Education and
Outreach Program

**Bonnie J. McClain**

*Chief of Education*
Exploration Systems Mission
Directorate

**Diane Clayton Ph.D.**

*Program Scientist*
Earth Science Education

**Deborah Rivera**

*Strategic Alliances Manager*
Office of Public Affairs
NASA Headquarters

**Douglas D. Peterson**

*Public Affairs Officer,
Astronaut Office*
Office of Public Affairs
NASA Johnson Space Center

**Nicole Cloutier**

*Public Affairs Officer,
Astronaut Office*
Office of Public Affairs
NASA Johnson Space Center

# Reviewers

**Dr. Maria Aida Alanis**
Administrator
Austin ISD
Austin Texas

**Melissa Barba**
Teacher
Wesley Mathews Elementary
Miami, Florida

**Dr. Marcelline Barron**
Supervisor/K-12 Math
and Science
Fairfield Public Schools
Fairfield, Connecticut

**Jane Bates**
Teacher
Hickory Flat Elementary
Canton, Georgia

**Denise Bizjack**
Teacher
Dr. N. H. Jones Elementary
Ocala, Florida

**Latanya D. Bragg**
Teacher
Davis Magnet School
Jackson, Mississippi

**Richard Burton**
Teacher
George Buck Elementary
School 94
Indianapolis, Indiana

**Dawn Cabrera**
Teacher
E.W.F. Stirrup School
Miami, Florida

**Barbara Calabro**
Teacher
Compass Rose Foundation
Ft. Myers, Florida

**Lucille Calvin**
Teacher
Weddington Math &
Science School
Greenville, Mississippi

**Patricia Carmichael**
Teacher
Teasley Middle School
Canton, Georgia

**Martha Cohn**
Teacher
An Wang Middle School
Lowell, Massachusetts

**Stu Danzinger**
Supervisor
Community Consolidated
School District 59
Arlington Heights, Illinois

**Esther Draper**
Supervisor/Science Specialist
Belair Math Science
Magnet School
Pine Bluff, Arkansas

**Sue Esser**
Teacher
Loretto Elementary
Jacksonville, Florida

**Dr. Richard Fairman**
Teacher
Antioch University
Yellow Springs, Ohio

**Joan Goldfarb**
Teacher
Indialantic Elementary
Indialantic, Florida

**Deborah Gomes**
Teacher
A J Gomes Elementary
New Bedford, Massachusetts

**Sandy Hobart**
Teacher
Mims Elementary
Mims, Florida

**Tom Hocker**
Teacher/Science Coach
Boston Latin Academy
Dorchester, Massachusetts

**Shelley Jaques**
Science Supervisor
Moore Public Schools
Moore, Oklahoma

**Marguerite W. Jones**
Teacher
Spearman Elementary
Piedmont, South Carolina

**Kelly Kenney**
Teacher
Kansas City Missouri
School District
Kansas City, Missouri

**Carol Kilbane**
Teacher
Riverside Elementary School
Wichita, Kansas

**Robert Kolenda**
Teacher
Neshaminy School District
Langhorne, Pennsylvania

**Karen Lynn Kruse**
Teacher
St. Paul the Apostle
Yonkers, New York

**Elizabeth Loures**
Teacher
Point Fermin
Elementary School
San Pedro, California

**Susan MacDougall**
Teacher
Brick Community Primary
Learning Center
Brick, New Jersey

**Jack Marine**
Teacher
Raising Horizons Quest
Charter School
Philadelphia, Pennsylvania

**Nicola Micozzi Jr.**
Science Coordinator
Plymouth Public Schools
Plymouth, Massachusetts

**Paula Monteiro**
Teacher
A J Gomes Elementary
New Bedford, Massachusetts

**Tracy Newallis**
Teacher
Taper Avenue Elementary
San Pedro, California

**Dr. Eugene Nicolo**
Supervisor, Science K-12
Moorestown School District
Moorestown, New Jersey

**Jeffrey Pastrak**
School District of Philadelphia
Philadelphia, Pennsylvania

**Helen Pedigo**
Teacher
Mt. Carmel Elementary
Huntsville Alabama

**Becky Peltonen**
Teacher
Patterson Elementary School
Panama City, Florida

**Sherri Pensler**
Teacher/ESOL
Claude Pepper Elementary
Miami, Florida

**Virginia Rogliano**
Teacher
Bridgeview Elementary
South Charleston, West
Virginia

**Debbie Sanders**
Teacher
Thunderbolt Elementary
Orange Park, Florida

**Grethel Santamarina**
Teacher
E.W.F. Stirrup School
Miami, Florida

**Migdalia Schneider**
Teacher/Bilingual
Lindell School
Long Beach, New York

**Susan Shelly**
Teacher
Bonita Springs Elementary
Bonita Springs, Florida

**Peggy Terry**
Teacher
Madison District 151
South Holland, Illinois

**Jane M. Thompson**
Teacher
Emma Ward Elementary
Lawrenceburg, Kentucky

**Martha Todd**
Teacher
W. H. Rhodes Elementary
Milton, Florida

**Renee Williams**
Teacher
Central Elementary
Bloomfield, New Mexico

**Myra Wood**
Teacher
Madison Street Academy
Ocala, Florida

**Marion Zampa**
Teacher
Shawnee Mission
School District
Overland Park, Kansas

# Science

## See learning in a whole new light

# Unit A Life Science

**How do the different parts of a plant help it live and grow?**

Life Science in Indiana

# Chapter 2 • How Animals Live

## How do different animals live, grow, and change?

# Unit A Life Science

How are ecosystems different from each other?

# Chapter 4 • Plants and Animals Living Together

## How do plants and animals interact?

# Unit B Earth Science

## How does water change form?

## How does weather follow patterns?

Earth Science in Indiana

## Chapter 7 • Rocks and Soil

Why are rocks and soil important resources?

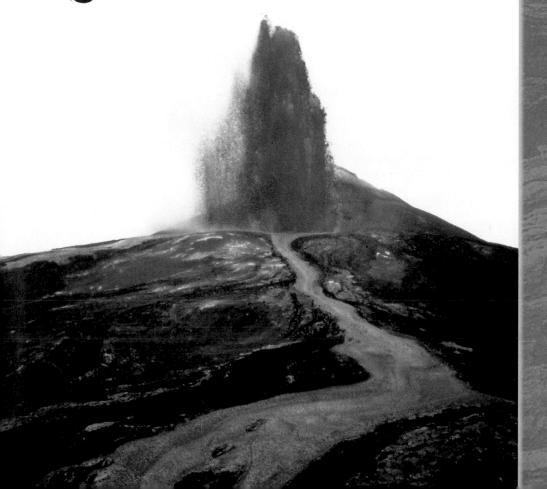

# Unit B  Earth Science

How do forces cause changes on Earth's surface?

## Chapter 8 • Changes on Earth

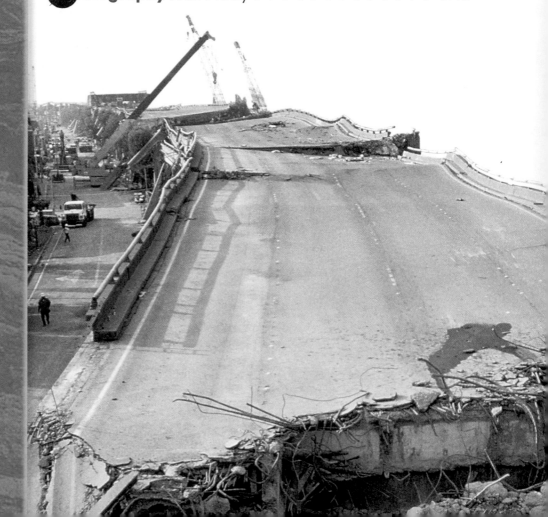

# Chapter 9 • Natural Resources

How can people use natural resources responsibly?

# Unit C  Physical Science

## Physical Science in Indiana

**What are the properties of matter?**

**What are physical and chemical changes in matter?**

# Chapter 12 • Forces and Motion

## How do forces cause motion and get work done?

# Unit C Physical Science

How does energy change form?

## Chapter 13 • Energy

# Chapter 14 • Sound

## How does energy produce the sounds we hear?

# Unit D Space and Technology

Space and Technology in Indiana

## Chapter 15 • Patterns in the Sky

What patterns do the Earth, Sun, Moon, and stars show?

## Chapter 16 • The Solar System

How are the planets in the solar system alike and different?

# Chapter 17 • Science in Our Lives

## How does technology affect our lives?

# How to Read Science

A page like the one below is found near the beginning of each chapter. It shows you how to use a reading skill that will help you understand what you read.

## Before Reading

Before you read the chapter, read the Build Background page and think about how to answer the question. Recall what you already know as you answer the question. Work with a partner to make a list of what you already know. Then read the How to Read Science page.

**Target Reading Skill**
Each page has one target reading skill. The reading skill corresponds with a process skill in the Directed Inquiry activity on the facing page. The reading skill will be useful as you read science.

**Real-World Connection**
Each page has an example of something you might read. It also connects with the Directed Inquiry activity.

**Graphic Organizer**
A useful strategy for understanding anything you read is to make a graphic organizer. A graphic organizer can help you think about the information and how parts of it relate to each other. Each reading skill has a graphic organizer.

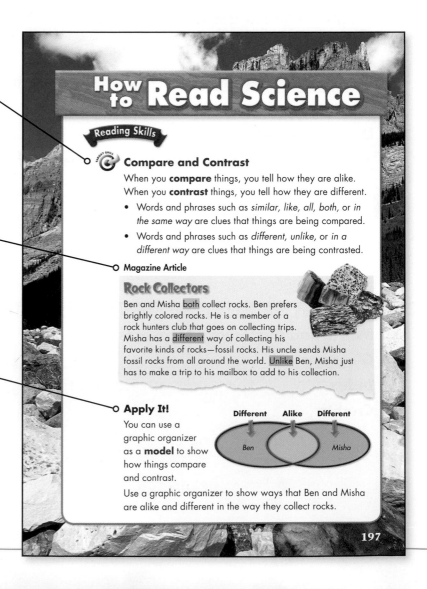

How to Read Science

### Reading Skills

**Compare and Contrast**
When you **compare** things, you tell how they are alike. When you **contrast** things, you tell how they are different.
- Words and phrases such as *similar, like, all, both,* or *in the same way* are clues that things are being compared.
- Words and phrases such as *different, unlike,* or *in a different way* are clues that things are being contrasted.

Magazine Article

#### Rock Collectors
Ben and Misha both collect rocks. Ben prefers brightly colored rocks. He is a member of a rock hunters club that goes on collecting trips. Misha has a different way of collecting his favorite kinds of rocks—fossil rocks. His uncle sends Misha fossil rocks from all around the world. Unlike Ben, Misha just has to make a trip to his mailbox to add to his collection.

**Apply It!**
You can use a graphic organizer as a **model** to show how things compare and contrast.

Different | Alike | Different
Ben | Misha

Use a graphic organizer to show ways that Ben and Misha are alike and different in the way they collect rocks.

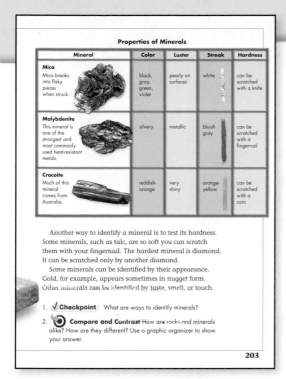

**Properties of Minerals**

| Mineral | Color | Luster | Streak | Hardness |
|---|---|---|---|---|
| **Mica** Mica breaks into flaky pieces when struck. | black, gray, green, violet | pearly on surfaces | white | can be scratched with a knife |
| **Molybdenite** This mineral is one of the strongest and most commonly used heat-resistant metals. | silvery | metallic | bluish gray | can be scratched with a fingernail |
| **Crocoite** Much of this mineral comes from Australia. | reddish-orange | very shiny | orange-yellow | can be scratched with a coin |

Another way to identify a mineral is to test its hardness. Some minerals, such as talc, are so soft you can scratch them with your fingernail. The hardest mineral is diamond. It can be scratched only by another diamond.

Some minerals can be identified by their appearance. Gold, for example, appears sometimes in nugget form. Other minerals can be identified by taste, smell, or touch.

1. ✓ **Checkpoint** What are ways to identify minerals?
2.  **Compare and Contrast** How are rocks and minerals alike? How are they different? Use a graphic organizer to show your answer.

203

**Process Skills**

13. **Predict** Which would dry faster after it rains: a sandy beach or a grassy field? Give a reason for your answer.

14. **Model** Make a model or a drawing that shows the different layers of soil.

15. **Infer** You observe that a mineral sample can be scratched with a coin. What do you infer about the hardness of the mineral?

**Compare and Contrast**

16. Make a graphic organizer like the one below. Fill it in to compare and contrast sandy soil and clay soil.

Sandy soil    Both types of soil    Clay soil

**Test Prep**

Choose the letter that best completes the statement or answers the question.

17. All rocks contain
   Ⓐ loam.
   Ⓑ minerals.
   Ⓒ water.
   Ⓓ sediments.

18. In what rocks are fossils most often found?
   Ⓕ sedimentary
   Ⓖ igneous
   Ⓗ metamorphic
   Ⓘ all of the above

19. The layer of soil just below the topsoil is
   Ⓐ loam.
   Ⓑ decayed matter.
   Ⓒ rock.
   Ⓓ subsoil.

20. **Writing in Science**
   **Persuasive** Write a letter to a member of a city council that discusses why rich farmland is valuable to everyone in the community.

215

## During Reading

As you read the lesson, use the Checkpoint to check your understanding. Some checkpoints ask you to use the target reading skill.

## After Reading

After you have read the chapter, think about what you found out. Exchange ideas with a partner. Compare the list you made before you read the chapter with what you learned by reading it. Answer the questions in the Chapter Review. One question uses the target reading skill.

### Graphic Organizers

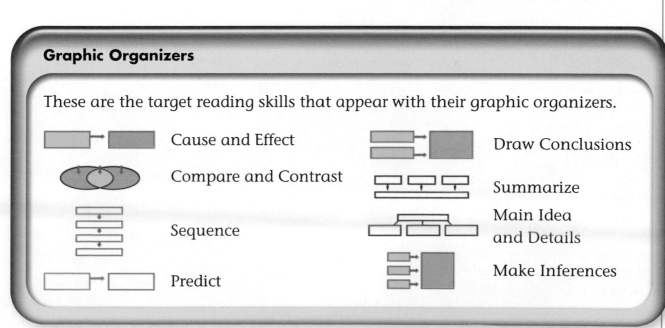

These are the target reading skills that appear with their graphic organizers.

Cause and Effect

Compare and Contrast

Sequence

Predict

Draw Conclusions

Summarize

Main Idea and Details

Make Inferences

# Science Process Skills

# Investigating Weather

Scientists use process skills when they investigate places or events. You will use these skills when you do the activities in this book. Which process skills might scientists use when they investigate weather?

## Observe

A scientist who studies weather observes many things. You use your senses too to find out about other objects, events, or living things.

## Classify

Scientists classify clouds according to their properties. When you classify, you arrange or sort objects, events, or living things.

## Estimate and Measure

Scientists estimate how much rain will fall. Then they use tools to measure how much rain fell.

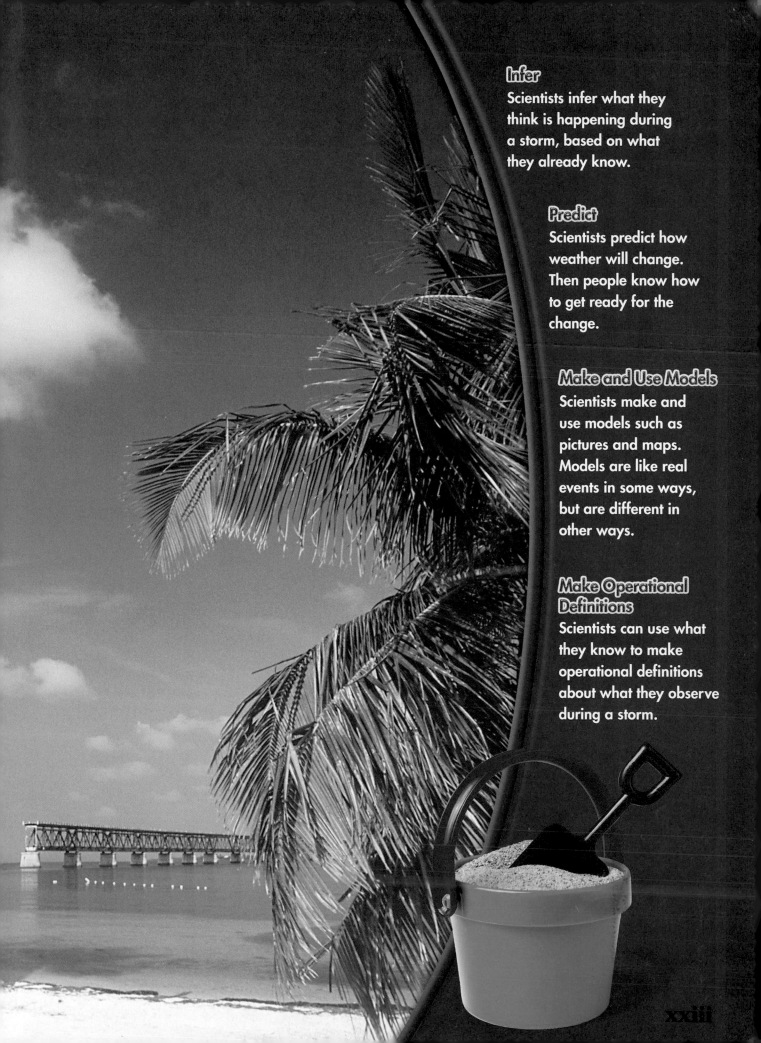

### Infer
Scientists infer what they think is happening during a storm, based on what they already know.

### Predict
Scientists predict how weather will change. Then people know how to get ready for the change.

### Make and Use Models
Scientists make and use models such as pictures and maps. Models are like real events in some ways, but are different in other ways.

### Make Operational Definitions
Scientists can use what they know to make operational definitions about what they observe during a storm.

# Science Process Skills

## Form Questions and Hypotheses

Think of a statement that you can test to solve a problem or answer a question about storms or other kinds of weather.

## Investigate and Experiment

As scientists observe storms, they investigate and experiment to test a hypothesis.

## Identify and Control Variables

As scientists perform an experiment, they identify and control the variables so that they test only one thing at a time.

If you were a scientist, you might want to learn more about storms. What questions might you have about storms? How would you use process skills in your investigation?

**Collect Data**
Scientists collect data from their observations of weather. They put the data into charts or tables.

**Interpret Data**
Scientists use the information they collected to solve problems or answer questions.

**Communicate**
Scientists use words, pictures, charts, and graphs to share information about their investigation.

# Using Scientific Methods for Science Inquiry

Scientists use scientific methods as they work. Scientific methods are organized ways to answer questions and solve problems. Scientific methods include the steps shown here. Scientists might not use all the steps. They might not use the steps in this order. You will use scientific methods when you do the **Full Inquiry** activity at the end of each unit. You also will use scientific methods when you do Science Fair Projects.

## Ask a question.

You might have a question about something you observe.

What material is best for keeping heat in water?

## State your hypothesis.

A hypothesis is a possible answer to your question.

If I wrap the jar in fake fur, then the water will stay warmer.

## Identify and control variables.

Variables are things that can change. For a fair test, you choose just one variable to change. Keep all other variables the same.

Test other materials. Put the same amount of warm water in other jars that are the same size and shape.

## Test your hypothesis.

Make a plan to test your hypothesis. Collect materials and tools. Then follow your plan.

## Collect and record your data.

Keep good records of what you do and find out. Use tables and pictures to help.

## Interpret your data.

Organize your notes and records to make them clear. Make diagrams, charts, or graphs to help.

## State your conclusion.

Your conclusion is a decision you make based on your data. Communicate what you found out. Tell whether or not your data supported your hypothesis.

*Fake fur did the best job of keeping the water warm.*

## Go further.

Use what you learn. Think of new questions to test or better ways to do a test.

Ask a Question

State Your Hypothesis

Identify and Control Variables

Test Your Hypothesis

Collect and Record Your Data

Interpret Your Data

State Your Conclusion

Go Further

# Science Tools

**S**cientists use many different kinds of tools. Tools can make objects appear larger. They can help you measure volume, temperature, length distance, and mass. Tools can help you figure out amounts and analyze your data. Tools can also help you find the latest scientific information.

You should use **safety goggles** to protect your eyes.

You use a **thermometer** to measure temperature. Many thermometers have both Fahrenheit and Celsius scales. Scientists usually use only the Celsius scale.

You can use a **telescope** to help you see things that are very far away, such as stars and planets.

**Binoculars** make far-away objects appear larger, so you can see more of their details.

A **hand lens** doesn't enlarge things as much as a microscope does, but it is easier to carry.

Scientists use **rulers and metersticks** to measure length and distance.

A **balance** like this one can be used to measure mass.

**Microscopes** use several lenses to make objects appear much larger, so you can see more detail.

# Science Tools

**Magnets** can be used to test if an object is made of certain metals such as iron.

Pictures taken with a **camera** record what something looks like. You can compare pictures of the same object to show how the object might have changed.

A **graduated cylinder** can be used to measure volume, or the amount of space an object takes up.

**Calipers** can be used to measure the width of an object.

You can figure amounts using a **calculator**.

Scientists use **computers** in many ways, such as collecting, recording, and analyzing data.

You can talk into a **sound recorder** to record information you want to remember.

A **spring scale** measures the force of gravity on an object. It is a type of **force meter**.

**Clocks** and **stopwatches** are used for measuring time.

**Hot plates** are often used by scientists as a heat source in experiments.

**Collecting nets** are used by scientists who study living things. They are used to collect organisms.

A **microscope** uses several lenses to make objects appear much larger, so you can see more detail.

# Safety in Science

**Y**ou need to be careful when doing science activities. This page includes safety tips to remember:

- Listen to your teacher's instructions.

- Read each activity carefully.

- Never taste or smell materials unless your teacher tells you to.

- Wear safety goggles when needed.

- Handle scissors and other equipment carefully.

- Keep your work place neat and clean.

- Clean up spills immediately.

- Tell your teacher immediately about accidents or if you see something that looks unsafe.

- Wash your hands well after every activity.

# Unit A

# Life Science

## in Indiana

Did you know that Indiana changed its state flower three times? Today the peony is the state flower. Peony flowers grow all over the state. They are usually red, white, or pink.

# Field Trip

## Purdue University Horticulture Gardens

At the Purdue University Horticulture Gardens in West Lafayette, visitors can see hundreds of different kinds of plants. Purdue's gardens have many special collections of flowers, including a collection of Indiana's state flower, the peony. The pictures on this page show all of Indiana's state flowers, from 1913 to the present.

**Carnation, 1913–1931**

**Zinnia, 1931–1957**

**Dogwood blossom, 1957**

## Find out more:

Research to find out more about plants that can be found at Purdue University Horticulture Gardens.

- Draw a picture of the plant.
- Write a paragraph about the characteristics of the plant.
- Draw a simple map of Indiana showing where the plant grows in the state.

**Peony, 1957–present**

EC IN 10 9 8 7 6 5 4 3

## You Will Discover

- ways parts of a plant help it survive.
- different types of plants.
- different ways plants make more plants.
- that plants have changed over time.

# Chapter 1
# Plants
## and
## How They
## Grow

online
Student Edition
sfsuccessnet.com

1

# How do the different parts of a plant help it live and grow?

system

coniferous

pollinate

seed leaf

germinate

2

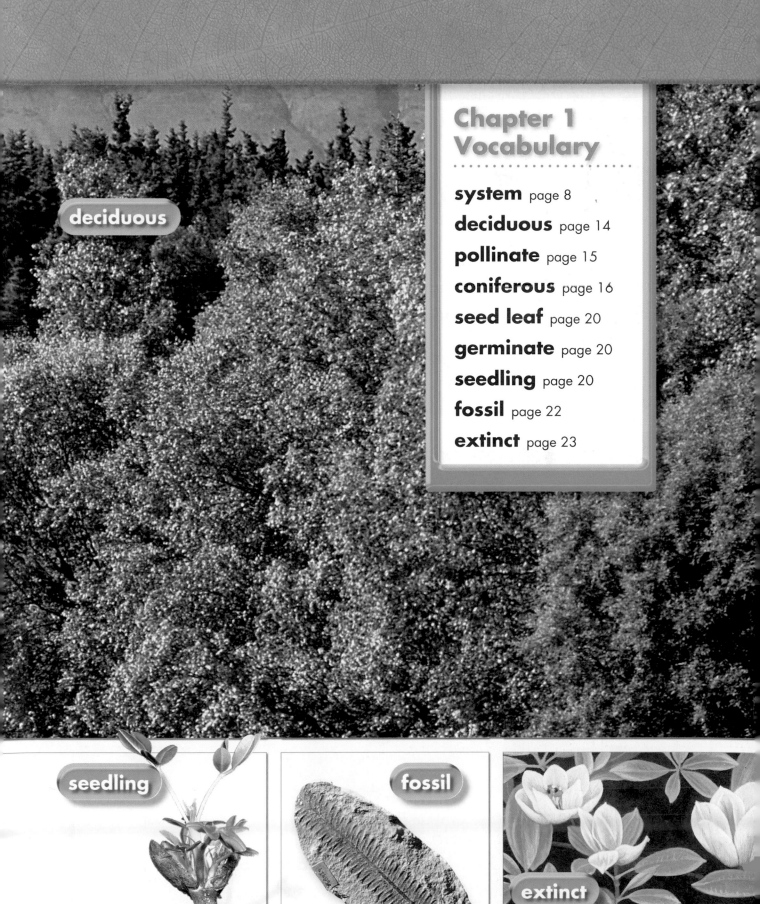

deciduous

seedling

fossil

extinct

3

# Explore How are plants alike and different?

**Materials**

grass

radish

hand lens

## What to Do

**1** **Observe** each plant with a hand lens. Notice the characteristics of their leaves and roots.

**2** Look for the places where the leaves grow from the stems of the plants.

**3** Look at the roots that grow from the stems of the plants.

root

root

**Process Skills**

You used your **observations** to explain how the plants are alike and different.

## Explain Your Results

Use what you **observed** to explain how the two plants are alike and different.

# How to Read Science

## Compare and Contrast

Knowing how to compare and contrast can help you understand what you read and the things you **observe.**

- We **compare** when we say how things are alike. We **contrast** when we say how things are different.
- Words and phrases such as *similar, like, all, both,* or *in the same way* are used to compare.
- Words and phrases such as *unlike* or *in a different way* are used to contrast.

**Science Article**

### Plants and Animals

Both plants and animals are living things that need food, air, water, and space to live. Unlike most plants, most animals don't stay in the same place. They move around. Unlike animals, most plants have roots that keep them in the same place.

| Plants | Both | Animals |
|--------|------|---------|
| Ways that plants are different from animals | Ways that plants and animals are alike | Ways that animals are different from plants |

## Apply It!

Make a graphic organizer like the one shown. Use the information from the science article to fill it in.

# 🔊 You Are There!

It's a cool **spring** day and you are walking along a river in Alaska. Tall trees rise above the river. Why do some have flat, broad leaves, while others have sharp needles? Lots of other kinds of plants are growing here too. Even though they may look different, every plant needs the same things to live and grow. Listen. You hear a splash. An Alaskan brown bear bounds out of the trees into the river. The bear needs certain things too.

# What are the main parts of a plant?

*Most plants have four main parts. These parts are leaves, roots, stems, and flowers. In different kinds of plants, these parts may look similar. They may also look very different.*

## What All Living Things Need

Most living things, including plants and animals, need food, air, water, and space to live and grow. Animals find and eat plants or other animals to get their food. Unlike animals, plants can make their own food. To make their food, plants need energy from the Sun. Most plants also need soil.

Most plants have four main parts. These parts are leaves, roots, stems, and flowers.

**Black-eyed Susans are one of the many plants you might see in a prairie.**

1. ✓**Checkpoint** What do plants and animals need to live?

2. **Writing** in Science **Descriptive**
Choose an animal and a plant and describe in your **science journal** what each needs to survive.

7

## Why Plants Need Leaves

A plant's leaves make up its leaf system. A **system** consists of parts that work together. Leaves come in many shapes and sizes. They help green plants because they make food. The food they make is a kind of sugar.

To make food, leaves use air, water, and the energy of sunlight. Carbon dioxide is a gas in air. It enters the plant through tiny holes on the underside of leaves. Water passes from soil through roots and stems and into each leaf. The leaves change the carbon dioxide and water into sugar and oxygen. Oxygen goes out from the plant through the same tiny holes on the lower surface of the leaves. The plant uses the sugar to live and grow.

**Gas**
Carbon dioxide enters the leaf through tiny holes on its underside.

**Water**
Water enters the leaf from the roots and stem.

**Sugar**
The leaves make sugar for food that passes through the stems to the rest of the plant.

**Oxygen**
Plants make and let out oxygen gas when they make sugar.

**Sun**
Plants need energy from the Sun to change carbon dioxide and water into sugar and oxygen.

**Leaf Veins**
Tiny tubes called leaf veins deliver water to the leaf. They also carry sugar made in the leaves to the rest of the plant.

## Other Ways Leaves Help Plants

Leaves help plants in other ways. They help plants to balance the amount of water plants take in. If there is too much water in the plant, leaves will let some water out through the tiny holes on their underside. Plants in dry places may have leaves with waxy or fuzzy coatings to help keep water in.

A plant's leaves may also help to protect the plant from being eaten. Leaves might be poisonous, sharp, or tough to chew. Hungry animals will leave the plant alone.

### ✓ Lesson Checkpoint

1. List the main parts of most plants.

2. How does a leaf help a plant live?

3. **Compare and Contrast** Describe ways that leaves are alike and different. Use a graphic organizer.

## Types of Leaves

Some trees have leaves that look like needles.

A pecan tree leaf is made up of many smaller leaflets that grow across from each other.

This oak leaf is more like the pecan leaves than the needle-like leaves. Yet observe how different it is.

9

# Why do plants need roots and stems?

*Along with their leaves, plants need their root and stem systems to live and grow.*

## How Roots Help Plants

The root system of a plant is often below the ground where you cannot see it. The roots hold the plant in the ground. Roots take in water and materials called minerals from the soil. The roots also store food made by the plant.

Many plants, such as carrots and dandelions, have a large root called a taproot. The taproot grows deep into the soil. The taproot stores food for the plant. Have you ever tasted a carrot or a beet? If your answer is "yes," then you've eaten the taproot of a plant!

A young fir tree has a tangled root system.

Water and minerals travel up the root through tubes to the stem and leaves.

*Root hair*

Water enters root through the root hairs.

*Growing tip of root*

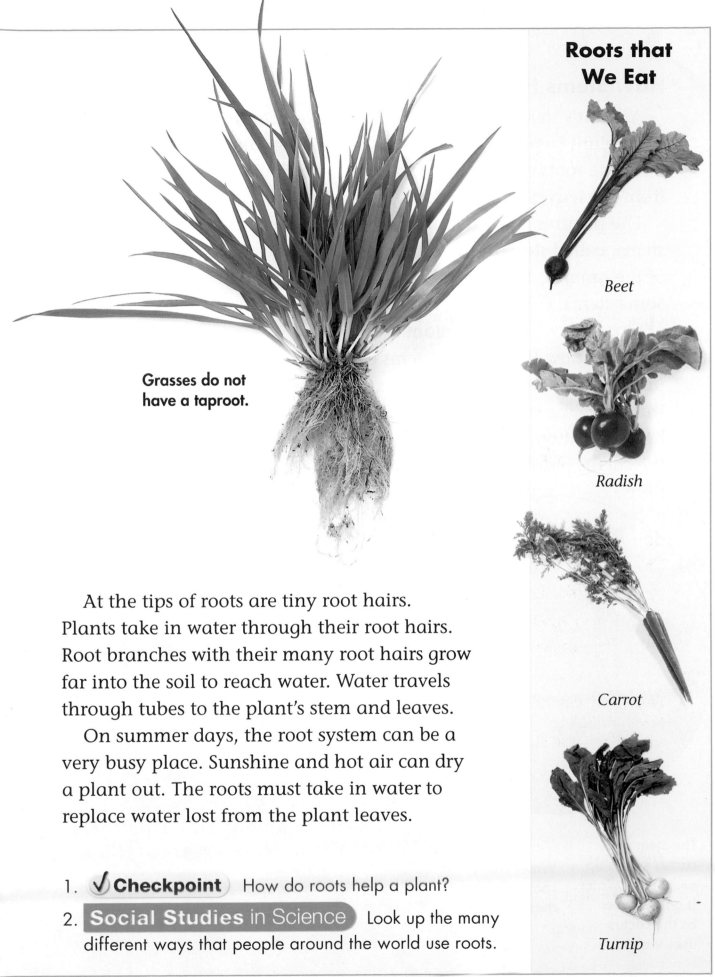

## Roots that We Eat

*Beet*

*Radish*

*Carrot*

*Turnip*

**Grasses do not have a taproot.**

At the tips of roots are tiny root hairs. Plants take in water through their root hairs. Root branches with their many root hairs grow far into the soil to reach water. Water travels through tubes to the plant's stem and leaves.

On summer days, the root system can be a very busy place. Sunshine and hot air can dry a plant out. The roots must take in water to replace water lost from the plant leaves.

1. ✔**Checkpoint** How do roots help a plant?
2. **Social Studies in Science** Look up the many different ways that people around the world use roots.

**11**

## How Stems Help Plants

A plant's stems hold up its leaves, flowers, and fruits. Most plant stems have tubes that move water and minerals from the roots of plants to the leaves. Other tubes carry food from the leaves of plants to the stems and roots.

The pictures show some different kinds of stems. Some stems, called stolons, are thin and grow along the surface of the ground. These stems can grow roots and a new plant. Some stems, called vines, grow parts that wrap around objects that support the plant.

Notice how thick cactus stems can be. Cactus stems swell up as they store water. The stems shrink as the plant uses water. Cactus stems also have a thick, waxy covering to help keep them from losing water. This type of stem helps the cactus plant survive in a desert.

More water makes stem walls swell outward.

Water from roots is stored in this area.

The stem of a cactus swells up as it stores water. It gets smaller as the cactus uses water.

Water from roots passes up these tubes.

Stolons of this strawberry plant are for growing new plants.

*Potato*

Parts of some stems grow underground. When you eat a potato, you eat a stem part that stored food underground. Underground stems can sprout new stems from buds such as the potato's "eyes." These parts grow upward and become new plants.

Some plants have stems with special features to help them survive. For example, some stems have thorns or stinging hairs to keep hungry animals from eating them.

*Vine*

The thorns growing out of this cactus stem are a special kind of leaf.

*Tree (wood)*

### ✓ Lesson Checkpoint

1. How do stems help a plant?

2. How are roots and stems alike and different?

3. **Writing** in Science  **Expository**
   Write a paragraph in your **science journal** that describes the special features of a cactus. Explain how these features help the cactus.

*Rhubarb*

13

# How are plants grouped?

*Plants can be grouped by the kinds of parts they have.*

## Flowering Plants

An apple tree, a grass, and a cactus are flowering plants but each is in a different group. Plants in each group have different kinds of roots, stems, leaves, and flowers. Look at the examples below. Both plants grow flowers with seeds. But the dogwood tree can grow tall with the help of a stiff, woody stem. Many flowering plants, such as grasses and the trillium below, do not have wood. They grow low to the ground.

The dogwood tree survives winter because its leaves die and fall off in the fall. The tree then grows new leaves in the spring. Trees that lose their leaves are **deciduous.** The dogwood tree is a deciduous tree. Many grasses and plants like the trillium die all the way down to the roots instead. In the spring, they grow back again from the roots.

Flowering trees and small flowering plants are similar and different.

## Making Seeds

Flowering plants grow flowers that make seeds. Flowers have parts that make pollen or seeds. Bees, other animals, or wind **pollinate** a flower when they move pollen to the flower part that makes seeds.

After a flower is pollinated, seeds form near the center of the flower. A fruit often grows to surround and protect the seeds.

A flower's petals attract insects and other animals that pollinate the flower.

Pollen sticks to the bodies of bees as bees look for food. They carry this pollen to the part of the flower that makes seeds.

The tip of this part of the flower makes pollen.

Pollen put on the tip of this part helps form seeds down here.

1. ✔**Checkpoint** Describe how a flower makes a seed.

2. **Writing** in Science **Narrative** Write a story in your **science journal** about a flower that invited a bee over for a visit. Be sure to describe the bee's thank-you gift.

## Coniferous Trees

**Coniferous** trees do not lose all their leaves in the fall. The leaves of coniferous trees look like needles or brushes. These trees also grow cones instead of flowers to make their seeds. Coniferous trees include pine, fir, spruce, and hemlock.

## Two Types of Cones

Coniferous trees make two kinds of cones. They make small pollen cones and large seed cones. Wind blows pollen from the small pollen cones to the large seed cones. When pollen attaches to the seed cone, seeds begin to grow. A seed grows under each scale of the seed cone. When the seeds are ripe, they fall to the ground. If conditions are right, each seed can start growing into a new plant. Over time, the seeds may become trees.

## Kinds of Cones

Cones form on branches near the top of conifers.

Wind blows pollen from these small cones to larger cones on other trees.

Seeds are made under the scales of this Douglas fir cone. This cone is about as big as your fist.

Larger cones grow with seeds inside.

Coniferous seeds glide to the ground.

### ✓ Lesson Checkpoint

1. What are two ways to group plants?

2. Describe two kinds of plant parts that can make seeds.

3. **Writing** in Science **Expository**
Write a paragraph in your **science journal** that explains different ways flowers can be pollinated.

# How do new plants grow?

*Most plants make seeds that grow into new plants.*
*Sometimes a stem or root grows a new plant.*

## Scattering Seeds

When seeds are scattered, they are moved away from the plant. Then they have more room to grow.

Seeds are scattered in many ways. Some seeds are spread from one place to another by wind or water. Other seeds are carried to new places by animals that eat fruit with seeds. The seeds pass through the animal's body. Then they are dropped to the ground far from the plant. Some seeds are carried along when they stick to an animal's fur.

**Ways That Seeds Scatter**

| | | |
|---|---|---|
| **Wind** | | Wind scatters seeds that have parachutes or wings. |
| **Water** | | Water scatters seeds that float, such as coconuts. |
| **Carried by animals** | | Animals scatter seeds that can stick to fur. |
| **Eaten by animals** | | Animals scatter seeds when they eat fruit. |

You've probably seen seeds drifting through the air. Wind scatters seeds that are very light. Many of these seeds have special parts that act like tiny wings or parachutes. The seeds can drift for long distances if the wind is strong.

## Special Ways of Releasing Seeds

Some types of pine cones need to be heated in a forest fire to release their seeds. The fire also removes other plants around the trees and clears space for the seeds to grow.

Each of these seeds has a tiny parachute. Wind can carry these seeds long distances where they can grow into new plants.

1. ✓**Checkpoint** What are two ways that animals scatter seeds?

2. **Art** in Science Draw pictures of two groups of seeds. Draw one group of seeds that are scattered by animals. Draw another group of seeds that are scattered by wind. Describe how the parts of these seeds are different.

## Germinating and Growing

Seeds come in many different shapes, sizes, and colors. But they all have the same parts. Every seed has a tiny plant inside it that can grow into a new plant. Every seed also has a seed coat to protect the young plant inside the seed. And, finally, every seed has either one **seed leaf** or two seed leaves to provide food for a sprouting new plant.

Seeds need certain things to start to grow, or **germinate.** They need the right temperature, the right amount of water, and air. When conditions are right, a seed begins to sprout and a root grows from it. The seed then breaks open and a young plant, or **seedling,** begins to grow. The seedling uses food stored in the seed to grow.

As it grows, the seedling's stem rises out of the soil and grows leaves. The seedling's leaves use sunlight to make sugar for food. Soon the seedling grows into an adult plant that has flowers. The flowers are pollinated and new seeds are formed. If the seeds germinate, they grow into new plants. Then the cycle begins again.

Seed coat

Tiny plant

Seed leaf

# Life Cycle of a Plant

**1** **Seeds in Fruit**
The part of a peanut you eat is a seed.

**2** **Germinating Seed**
When a peanut germinates, a stem grows upward and a root grows downward.

**3** **Seedling**
As the small peanut plant grows leaves, it can begin making sugar for food.

**4** **Adult Plant with Seeds**
Adult flower stalks grow downward. The peanut flowers make their seeds underground. When the adult plant dies, it becomes part of the soil.

## ✓ Lesson Checkpoint

1. What are the parts of a seed?
2. Describe the life cycle of a plant starting with a seed being planted.
3. **Social Studies** in Science  Choose a vegetable that is grown in your state. Find out what farmers do to grow the vegetable and get it to market.

# How are plants from the past like today's plants?

*Fossils show the kinds of plants that lived long ago. In some ways today's plants are similar to plants from the past that have disappeared.*

## Plants That Lived Long Ago

We learn about plants that lived long ago by studying fossils. A **fossil** is the remains or mark of a living thing from long ago.

Look at the fern and horsetail fossils in the pictures on page 23. How did they form? Each plant died and was pressed into mud. Next, the plant rotted away. But the mud kept the form of the plant. Over time the mud hardened into rock. The flat imprint of the plant is seen when the rock cracks open.

Another kind of fossil is made when rock replaces the parts that make up a plant. The drawings below show how it might have formed. This rock is called a petrified fossil.

### Formation of Petrified Wood

| Stump is buried in mud. | Minerals replace wood as time passes. | Rock surrounding the fossil is removed. |

# Plant Fossils

The fern that made this fossil lived about 350 million years ago.

This fossil shows a kind of fern that is extinct.

The fossil of this horsetail shows a plant that is extinct.

This log is a fossil trunk of an extinct tree fern.

Petrified wood can form when trees are buried in the ground. Minerals replace wood in the trees. At the same time, water breaks down the wood and carries it away. Over a long period of time, the wood becomes stone with exactly the same shape and markings as the original wood.

Many kinds of plants that lived long ago are no longer alive. They are **extinct.** For example, ferns that live today look different from the ferns that lived long ago. Plants related to the extinct ferns and horsetail fossils shown in the photos live on Earth today.

These petrified wood fossils in Arizona look like wood, but they are made of rock.

1. **✔ Checkpoint** What can scientists learn by studying fossils?

2. **Writing in Science** **Expository** In your **science journal**, write a paragraph that explains how a plant leaf can become a fossil.

23

## Plants Change Over Time

Plant fossils tell us that the first plants did not have flowers or cones. Many were like today's ferns and horsetails. As Earth changed over time, however, plants changed too. Trees that made cones appeared. Then plants with flowers appeared. Many of these kinds of plants have completely disappeared.

Magnolias are an example of a group of flowering plants that has survived. The world was warm and wet year-round when magnolias first appeared. Dinosaurs were everywhere. Big flowers dotted the branches for months. Magnolias grew thick leaves that they kept year-round. Magnolias just like this are alive today. The flower of the magnolia has remained unchanged for 100 million years.

As forms of life continued to change, so did the magnolias. Some magnolias now are deciduous. They lose their leaves in fall. Their flowers grow all at once before the leaves appear in the spring. Even so, their leaves and flowers are similar to those of magnolias that lived long ago.

Fossils of magnolia leaves from long ago look similar to today's magnolia leaves.

Flowers of deciduous magnolias grow all at once in the spring. After flowering, the trees grow new leaves for the summer.

The first magnolia trees were similar to many magnolias alive today. The feathered dinosaur is extinct.

✓ **Lesson Checkpoint**

1. What is an extinct plant?

2. How do scientists learn about plants that are extinct?

3. **Compare and Contrast** How are extinct magnolias alike and different from magnolias alive today? Use a graphic organizer to show your answer.

## Investigate How fast do different kinds of seeds germinate?

Seeds from some kinds of plants germinate faster than seeds from other kinds of plants. Even seeds from just one kind of plant may germinate faster than other seeds from the same kind of plant.

### Materials

paper towel and paper plate

waxed paper and masking tape

5 radish seeds

5 corn seeds

5 pinto bean seeds

5 sunflower seeds

cup with water

metric ruler

### Process Skills

By **interpreting the data** you **collected** in your chart, you can analyze how different seeds grow.

### What to Do

**1** Fold a paper towel in half. Fold it again.

**2** Make 2 lines to divide the folded towel into 4 parts. Label each part.

**3** Put the waxed paper on the plate. Put the folded towel on the waxed paper. Put on the seeds. Wet the towel.

5 radish seeds    5 corn seeds
5 pinto bean seeds    5 sunflower seeds

**4** Put the plate in a warm, bright place.

**5** **Observe** and record changes for 1 week. Describe or draw the plants as they begin to grow and develop.

After the first day, keep the paper towels moist, but not wet.

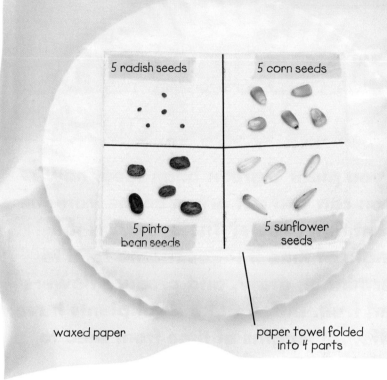

5 radish seeds

5 corn seeds

5 pinto bean seeds

5 sunflower seeds

waxed paper

paper towel folded into 4 parts

| Kind of Plant | Description (write or draw) | Day the First of the 5 Seeds Germinated (Day 1, 2, 3, 4, or 5) | Order in Which Different Kinds of Plants Germinated (1st, 2nd, 3rd, or 4th) | Length of Longest Stem on Day 7 (mm) |
|---|---|---|---|---|
| Radish | | | | |
| Corn | | | | |
| Pinto | | | | |
| Sunflower | | | | |

## Explain Your Results

1. **Interpret the data** you **collected**. Compare the radish and sunflower seeds. How did they grow and develop differently?
2. Were all the radish plants the same? Explain.

## Go Further

Collect more data. Every day count and record the number of each kind of plant that has germinated. Graph your results.

# Math in Science

# Elapsed Time
## from Seed to Fruit

If you plant a green bean seed, how soon can you eat green beans from the plant that grows? The answer is the length of time it takes for the seed to germinate, grow, and produce flowers and fruit. Different kinds of plants have different lengths of time from seed to fruit that is ready to eat.

Green bean

Cucumber

Sweet corn

Tomato

If you plant green bean seeds on May 10, you can start eating green beans 58 days later, on July 7.

| Days from planting seeds or seedling to picking ripe fruit | |
| --- | --- |
| green bean seeds | 58 days |
| cucumber seeds | 55 days |
| sweet corn seeds | 75 days |
| tomato seedling | 59 days |

Use the table and calendars to answer the questions.

**1** If you plant cucumber seeds on May 21, when could you start eating cucumbers?

**2** If sweet corn seeds are planted on May 19, when will the corn be ready to eat?

**3** When could you start eating ripe tomatoes if the seedling was planted on May 31?

## Lab zone Take-Home Activity

Look at the back of seed packets or go to the library or Internet to search for seed catalogs. Find out how long it takes different kinds of seeds to grow and make fruit. Use a calendar to find what dates the fruit might be ready to pick.

# Chapter 1 Review and Test Prep

## Use Vocabulary

| | |
|---|---|
| **deciduous** (page 14) | **pollinate** (page 15) |
| **coniferous** (page 16) | **seed leaf** (page 20) |
| **extinct** (page 23) | **seedling** (page 20) |
| **fossil** (page 22) | |
| **germinate** (page 20) | **system** (page 8) |

Use the vocabulary word or words from the list above that best completes each sentence.

1. When conditions are right, a seed will start to grow, or _____.

2. A tree that makes cones is a(n) _____ tree.

3. Bees, wind, and water can _____ flowers.

4. All the leaves and their parts make up a plant's leaf _____.

5. A(n) _____ tree loses all its leaves in the fall.

6. A new plant that has just grown out of the soil is a(n) _____.

7. A new plant uses food stored in a(n) _____.

8. A(n) _____ plant no longer lives on Earth, but a(n) _____ of its remains might be found.

## Explain Concepts

9. How do scientists learn about plants that are extinct?

10. Explain why all of a plant's roots and their parts are called a system.

11. What do a plant's leaves need to make sugar?

### Process Skills

12. **Classify** Choose one way that plants can be sorted into two groups. Explain how the plants in the two groups are alike and different.

13. **Infer** Bees visit the flowers on apple trees to get food. How might a disease that kills bees affect the number of apples the trees make? Explain your answer.

##  Compare and Contrast

**14.** Make a graphic organizer like the one shown below. Fill in the correct information.

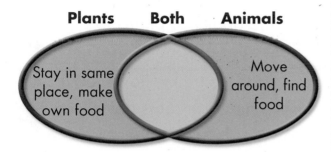

**Plants**    **Both**    **Animals**

Stay in same place, make own food

Move around, find food

## Test Prep

Choose the letter that best completes the statement or answers the question.

**15.** Before a seed can become a plant, the seed must

   Ⓐ germinate.
   Ⓑ be pollinated.
   Ⓒ make food.
   Ⓓ flower.

**16.** A cactus stores the most water in its

   Ⓕ roots.
   Ⓖ leaves.
   Ⓗ stems.
   Ⓘ flowers.

**17.** What fossil is made when minerals replace plant parts, while water breaks the parts down and carries them away?

   Ⓐ imprint
   Ⓑ petrified wood
   Ⓒ extinct fern
   Ⓓ magnolia flower

**18.** Which of the following is an example of scattering seeds?

   Ⓕ pollen sticking to a bee
   Ⓖ wind blowing pollen
   Ⓗ apples growing on a tree
   Ⓘ burs sticking to a dog's fur

**19.** Explain why the answer you chose for Question 18 is best. For each of the answers you did not choose, give a reason why it is not the best choice.

**20.** **Writing in Science**

**Expository** Write a paragraph that describes the life cycle of a plant.

## Plant Researcher

**Do you like plants? Plant researchers study how plants live and grow.**

What if food that astronauts need during long space missions runs out? Grow more aboard ship! Dr. Stutte of NASA tests ways to grow wheat aboard the International Space Station. He also tests the ability of plants to clean the air and water that astronauts use.

Growing plants in space is tricky, however. When seeds germinate on Earth roots grow down and stems grow up. In space, there is no up or down. As a plant researcher you might be called upon to solve problems like this one.

Plant researchers look for ways to grow more or stronger plants. Researchers at NASA are studying how plant seeds might grow better in space. Better traits from seeds grown in space could help farmers grow stronger plants on Earth.

Plant researchers have college degrees.

Dr. Gary Stutte

**Lab zone Take-Home Activity**

Draw a machine that would grow cucumbers in space where there is little gravity. Label the parts that supply the plants with water, fertilizer, carbon dioxide, and light. Write a paragraph explaining how it would work.

# Chapter 2

## You Will Discover

- ways that animals are grouped.
- how an animal's body and its behavior help it survive.
- how animals grow and change.
- that many animals today resemble animals that lived long ago.

# How Animals Live

online
**Student Edition**
sfsuccessnet.com

Discovery Channel School
**Student DVD**
DISCOVERY CHANNEL SCHOOL

# How do different animals live, grow, and change?

vertebrate

trait

inherited

migrate

hibernate

34

adaptation

larva

pupa

It's early morning in the forest and the birds are singing. You look down at your feet and notice ants marching by. You stand very still, listening and watching. Suddenly, you spot what looks like two dogs walking through a grassy field in the distance. As you focus your eyes you realize they are not dogs. You've spotted a wolf and her pup! Animals come in many shapes and sizes. Even though they may be different, do animals need the same basic things to live?

## Lesson 1

# How are animals grouped?

*All animals have the same basic needs. Animals might be grouped by how they look, where they live, or how they act.*

### What All Animals Need

Nearly all animals need water, oxygen, food, and shelter to live. Animals can get water from drinking or from the foods they eat. All animals also need the gas oxygen. They get oxygen from the air or from water. Most animals that live on land have lungs to breathe in oxygen. Many animals that live in water, such as fish, breathe with gills.

Animals also need food and shelter. They get their food by eating plants or other animals. Shelters protect animals from the weather and from other animals. While some animals build or seek shelters, others use their own hard shells as their homes.

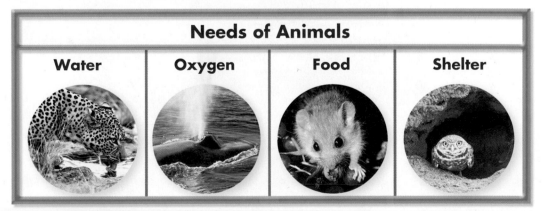

**Needs of Animals**

| Water | Oxygen | Food | Shelter |
|-------|--------|------|---------|

1. ✓**Checkpoint**   What do all animals need?

2. **Writing** in Science   **Descriptive** In your **science journal,** write about how your favorite animal meets its basic needs.

## Ways of Grouping Animals

How we group animals depends on what we want to learn about them. Sometimes animals are grouped by where they live or how they act. They also may be grouped by how they look. A body feature passed on to an animal from its parents is called a **trait.** Traits sometimes include things an animal does.

One animal might be placed into different groups. For example, a group of animals that eat mice can include snakes, hawks, and owls. A group of animals that fly would also include hawks and owls, but not snakes.

## Animals with Backbones

Another way to group animals is by whether or not they have a backbone. An animal with a backbone is called a **vertebrate.** Cats, dogs, and birds are vertebrates. So are fish and snakes. Even though all these animals look very different, each one has a backbone. And that backbone grows as the animal grows.

This lynx is
a vertebrate.

# Groups of Vertebrates

## Fish
These vertebrates spend their entire lives in fresh water, ocean water, or both. Most fish have slippery scales and breathe through gills.

## Amphibians
Frogs, toads, and salamanders belong to a group called amphibians. Many amphibians spend part of their lives in water and part on land. Most young amphibians live in water. They get oxygen through gills and through their smooth, moist skin. As they grow, most amphibians develop lungs that they use to breathe air.

## Reptiles
Snakes, lizards, turtles, crocodiles, and alligators are reptiles. They mostly have dry, scaly skin. These vertebrates breathe air through lungs.

## Birds
Birds are vertebrates with feathers and bills that do not have teeth. They breathe air through lungs. Wings and light bones help most birds fly. Their coats of feathers help them stay warm.

## Mammals
The vertebrates that you probably know best are called mammals. Mammals have hair at least during part of their lives. The hair keeps them warm. Mammals breathe air through lungs and feed milk to their young.

1. ✓**Checkpoint** Should reptiles and amphibians be grouped together? Explain your answer.

2. **Art** in Science Think about two animals that share some of the same traits. Draw a picture of each animal "in action" using a shared trait.

## Animals Without Backbones

In addition to a backbone, vertebrates also have other bones. Their bones give them strong support for their bodies. This allows many vertebrates, such as elephants, to be very big.

Most animals, however, do not have skeletons made of bone inside their bodies. These are the animals without backbones, or invertebrates. Examples include sea stars, butterflies, and spiders.

A soft sac filled with liquid supports worms and sea jellies. A hard shell supports clams and lobsters. These structures would be bulky and weigh too much on big animals. For this reason invertebrates do not get as big as vertebrates can get.

It's hard sometimes to notice invertebrates because they usually are so small. But invertebrates are everywhere on Earth. In fact, there are many more invertebrates than vertebrates. For instance, several million roundworms, each too tiny to see, may live under a square yard of soil. There are also many more kinds of invertebrates than vertebrates, as the chart at the top of the page shows.

### Kinds of Animals

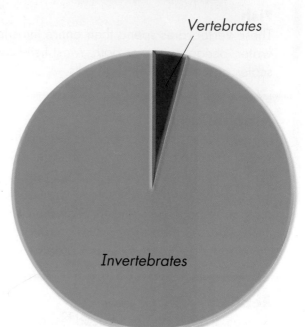

The whole circle stands for all kinds of animals. The small piece shows that kinds of vertebrates are only a small part of the total.

### Kinds of Invertebrate Animals

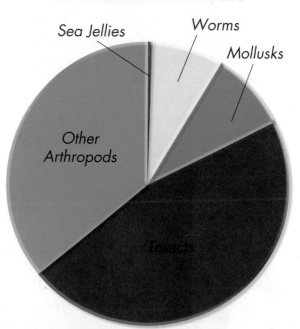

Most kinds of invertebrates are insects.

## Major Kinds of Invertebrate Animals

| Sea Jellies | Sea jellies have soft bodies and long, stinging body parts. The body of a sea jelly is made mostly of water. A sea jelly uses its stingers to stun its prey before pulling it into its stomach. Most sea jellies live in the ocean. |
| --- | --- |
| Worms | Worms are animals with long, soft bodies and no legs. You've probably seen an earthworm in the soil. These invertebrates help keep soil healthy. |
| Mollusks | Mollusks are animals with soft bodies. Some mollusks include the octopus, squid, clam, and snail. Many mollusks have a hard shell. |
| Arthropods | These animals are members of the largest group of invertebrates. They wear their skeletons outside their bodies. The bodies of arthropods are made up of more than one main part and they have legs with joints. Insects, spiders, and crabs are all arthropods. |

## ✔ Lesson Checkpoint

1. If a rattlesnake and a black widow spider both make poison, why are they put in different groups?

2. Explain why most invertebrates are small in size compared to most vertebrates.

3. **Math in Science** There are 5 vertebrates in someone's backyard. There are 20 times as many invertebrates as vertebrates there, too. How many invertebrates are there?

# Lesson 2

# How do animals grow and change?

*Different animals have their young in different ways. But all animals grow and change during their life cycle.*

## Life Cycles

An animal's life starts out as an egg. Sometimes the egg develops into a young animal inside the mother. Then the mother gives birth to a live young. For other animals, the mother lays an egg outside of her body. Then the young develops in the egg and hatches when it is ready.

When some animals hatch or are born, they look like their parents. Many other animals change a lot before they look anything like their parents.

**Adult butterflies lay eggs.**

**❶ Egg**
This is a close-up view of a very small egg. The picture has been magnified, or made to look bigger.

| Life Cycle Stages | |
|---|---|
| **Birth** | Animals are born or hatch. |
| **Growth** | Animals get bigger. |
| **Development** | Animals change into adults. |
| **Reproduction** | Animals produce young. |
| **Death** | Animals' lives come to an end. |

## ④ Butterfly
The adult butterfly comes out of the chrysalis.

## A Butterfly's Life Cycle

The butterfly's life begins in an egg so tiny it is hard to see.

A caterpillar hatches from the egg, the first stage in its life cycle. It is now a **larva.** In order to survive and continue in its life cycle, the caterpillar must eat a lot. It starts munching on the plant where it lives.

As the caterpillar grows, it sheds its skin several times. Then the larva spins a covering around itself. Then a hard covering, or chrysalis, forms. The larva is now called a **pupa.**

The caterpillar's body changes a lot while a pupa. It grows wings and jointed legs. It finally begins to look like an adult butterfly. Soon it breaks out of the chrysalis and crawls out. The adult butterfly dries its wings and flies away. After laying eggs, the butterfly's life cycle is nearly complete. It will soon die, the last stage in its life cycle.

## ③ Pupa
Inside a hard covering, the larva's body changes.

## ② Larva
The butterfly larva is called a caterpillar.

1. ✓**Checkpoint** What is the purpose of the pupa?

2. 🎯 **Sequence** List the sequence of steps in a butterfly's life cycle. Use the signal words *first, next, then,* and *finally.*

## Some Vertebrate Life Cycles

Vertebrates have different kinds of life cycles. Some vertebrates, like frogs, go through many changes as they grow and mature. Other vertebrates, like pandas or monkeys, do not change as much.

## A Frog's Life Cycle

Just like insects, many amphibians change quite a lot as they become adults. Did you know, for instance, that a very young frog looks and acts a lot like a fish?

Look at how a frog changes during its life cycle. This frog completes all the stages of its life cycle in one summer. All frogs do not develop in the same way. In colder places, a developing frog may dig into the mud during the winter. It will not become an adult frog until the following spring or summer.

A panda cub gets a gentle nudge.

Even though it's very small, a new-born panda pup has the same body form and the same number of legs as its parents.

## A Mammal's Life Cycle

Unlike amphibians and insects, young mammals do not change very much as they become adults. Many mammals look like their parents when they are born. Like you, they grow as they get older.

Most mammals develop inside their mother's bodies. When they are born, the babies drink milk from their mothers. They also have hair or fur.

It will be many years before you become an adult. A young rabbit, however, is ready to leave its nest and live on its own when it is less than three weeks old. It will be an adult at about six months.

# Frog Life Cycle

**① Eggs**
Mother frogs often lay hundreds or thousands of eggs in the water.

**② Tadpole**
Tadpoles hatch from the frog eggs. Tadpoles live underwater and breathe with gills.

**③ Growing Tadpole**
As the tadpole grows, it starts to change. Its tail becomes shorter. Legs begin to grow. The back legs grow first.

Before a tadpole becomes an adult frog, it has to grow lungs so it can breathe on land.

**④ Adult Frog**
The adult frog lives on land and in the water. It will need to return to the water to lay its eggs.

## ✓ Lesson Checkpoint

1. Before a frog can live on land, how must its body change?

2. How is a mammal's life cycle different from a frog's or a butterfly's life cycle?

3. **Writing in Science** **Expository** Think about how mammals care for their young. In your **science journal,** describe why this kind of care might be helpful for most mammals.

# How do adaptations help animals?

*Animals have special body parts, features, and ways of doing things that help them survive in their environments.*

## Adaptations

Animals live in many different places on Earth. An animal needs food, water, oxygen, and shelter. A trait that helps an animal meet its needs in the place where it lives is called an **adaptation.**

The webbed feet of a pelican are an adaptation. They help the pelican swim and survive in the water where it finds its food. Adaptations, such as webbed feet, are **inherited,** or passed on, from parents to their young.

Body parts, such as feet and bills, are important inherited adaptations. There are many different kinds of adaptations. Most kinds, such as body color, differ between members of even closely related groups.

This porcupine skull shows adaptations of a plant-eating animal. Sharp front teeth cut off parts of plants. Flat teeth in the back of the jaw move from side to side, grinding tough plant material.

This hyena skull shows adaptations of a meat-eating animal. Sharp front teeth tear off meat and back teeth shred it.

The bill of a pelican has a pouch that hangs from it. When a pelican swoops into the water for food, the pouch acts like a net to help the bird catch fish.

## Adaptations for Getting Food

Animals have many special adaptations for getting food. Prairie dogs and moles have feet that are especially good for digging. Hawks and eagles have feet that can hold tightly onto their food when they swoop down to catch it. Animals may also have the kind of teeth that can handle the foods they eat. Many birds have bills that help them catch and eat their favorite foods. Sometimes you can tell what a bird eats by the shape of its bill.

A long, curved bill helps the flamingo filter food from shallow water.

A short, strong bill helps the cardinal break open seeds.

A small, thin bill helps the warbler pick out insects for food.

1. ✓**Checkpoint** Give two examples of adaptations and tell how they help the animal survive.

2. **Art** in Science Think about an animal that wades into ponds and spears fish for food. Draw a picture of this animal. Include the special adaptations you think it would need to live and get food.

## Adaptations for Protection

The way an animal looks and the way it acts can help it survive. Some animals protect themselves by blending into their surroundings so they are hard to spot. This is called *camouflage*. Other animals protect themselves by looking like a dangerous or poisonous animal. This adaptation is called *mimicry*. The animals mimic or copy another animal. The animal being copied is usually more dangerous. Many animals will climb, run, hop, jump, fly, or swim away from danger.

Animals may also use poison to protect themselves. Animals such as skunks and weasels will spray a bad odor at their enemies. Special body parts such as shells, teeth, claws, hooves, bills, or pointed body parts also protect animals from danger.

For example, the porcupine is covered in quills. These special hairs have sharp hooks on their tips. When the porcupine is scared or threatened, it uses special muscles to make the quills stand up. Then it turns around and swings its tail. If the porcupine hits an attacker with its tail, the quills can let go as they pierce the attacker's skin. The hooks on the quills keep them attached to the attacker.

Porcupines have loose, barbed quills to protect them from their enemies.

# Ways Animals Protect Themselves

| Camouflage | Armor | Mimicry | Poison |
|---|---|---|---|
| Animals that can harm or be harmed by this crab spider cannot see it. | Spikes and horns protect this horned lizard. | A harmless hover fly looks like a dangerous hornet. | Lion fish have poisonous spines. |
| These fish blend in with the bright sea fans. | Pillbugs roll into a ball for defense. | A viceroy butterfly looks like a bad-tasting monarch butterfly. | Monarch butterflies taste bad because of the food they eat. |
| The fur color of this arctic fox changes with the seasons. | A cassowary has a tough helmet to protect its head as it runs through brush. | This king snake looks similar to the deadly coral snake. | Coral snakes bite with poisonous fangs. |

1. ✔ **Checkpoint**  What are some ways that animals protect themselves from their enemies?

2. **Sequence** List in the correct sequence what happens when a predator attacks a porcupine. Be sure to use the signal words *first*, *next*, and *finally* in your list of steps.

51

Baby birds are born knowing how to open their mouths for food.

## Behaviors That Help Animals

Behaviors are things that animals do. Animals are born being able to do some things. These behaviors are inherited. You inherit your ability to do many things such as walk and talk.

You do not inherit your ability to read and write. You need to learn these behaviors. You do inherit your ability to learn these behaviors, though.

Monarch butterflies have an instinct to migrate.

## Instincts

An instinct is a behavior an animal is born able to do. One instinct is an animal's response to hunger. Baby birds, for example, open their mouths when they sense a parent with food is near. Some animals have an instinct to move, or **migrate,** when the seasons change. Some butterflies migrate thousands of miles to warmer weather to survive the winter.

Other animals have an instinct to **hibernate** during the cold winter months. When animals hibernate, their body systems usually slow down to save energy. Then they don't need as much food to survive.

Bats hibernate during the winter months when food is hard to find.

An adult chimp shows a young chimp how to dig for insects.

## Learning

Animals learn some behaviors from their parents and other animals. For example, chimpanzees can learn how to use tools like sticks to catch insects to eat. Chimpanzees are not born knowing how to use sticks as tools. They learn how to do this by watching other chimpanzees. Young chimpanzees also learn which foods are safe to eat from their mothers and other adults.

Some young animals learn hunting behavior from their parents.

### ✓ Lesson Checkpoint

1. Name two types of adaptations having to do with an animal's actions.

2. Why do some animals migrate or hibernate?

3. **Social Studies** in Science
   Chimpanzees live in groups and learn how to behave from other chimpanzees. Describe how humans and chimpanzees are alike in the ways that they learn.

This trilobite fossil is a cast. It shows what the trilobite looked like.

A cast, such as this bird-like dinosaur, is in the shape of the original fossil. It formed when a mold was filled in with rock matter over time.

This fossil cast is of a dinosaur skull about 125 million years old! It looks like the skull of a modern-day crocodile.

# How are animals from the past like today's animals?

*Fossils show the kinds of animals that lived long ago. Today's animals are similar in some ways to animals of the past that have disappeared.*

## Animals That Lived Long Ago

Signs of past life are called fossils. Usually only the hard parts of animals become fossils. A fossil is usually not the actual bone or part. Instead, it is rock in the shape of the part.

A space in the shape of an animal in rock is called a fossil mold. Soft earth covers the remains of the animal, which wears away. This leaves a cavity or mold in the shape of the animal's parts. The earth then turns to rock over time. If the mold gets filled in with other rock materials over time, the fossil is called a cast.

Long ago, this spider got trapped in sticky tree sap that hardened into amber.

Unlike the fossil remains of most dinosaur bones, the bones of this fossil saber-toothed tiger are actual bone.

## Ancient Insects

Some small animals, or parts of animals, have been found in hardened tree sap called amber. Long ago, an insect might have become trapped in the sticky sap. Soon the sap would have completely covered the insect. Over a long period of time, the sap turned into a hard, yellow or reddish-brown substance called amber. Thin pieces of amber are usually clear enough to see through. What you see is the animal's actual body covering kept together for millions of years.

One other type of fossil is found in tar pits. Saber-toothed tigers and other extinct animals fell into these oily pools many thousands of years ago. The soft parts of their bodies broke down and left only the bones. These fossils are the actual bones of these animals.

1. ✓**Checkpoint**  What are some ways that fossils form?

2. **Math** in Science  If a modern-day lizard is 10 meters long and a dinosaur skeleton is 3 times as long, how long is the dinosaur skeleton?

## How Animals Today Compare to Those of Long Ago

Fossils can tell us how animals have changed over time. Dinosaurs are extinct. An extinct animal is a kind of animal that no longer lives on Earth. As you can see from the pictures, some animals today look like animals of long ago.

Fossils also tell us how Earth has changed over time. The drawing on the next page shows what the Badlands of South Dakota probably looked like more than 65 million years ago. At that time, dinosaurs like *Tyrannosaurus rex* roamed the area. Plant fossils found in layers of rocks near *T. rex* fossils tell scientists that the climate was hot and wet when *T. rex* lived. Plants could grow year-round. That is why you see plants in the drawing of the *T. rex*.

*T. rex's* habitat has changed a great deal. The photo in the drawing shows what the Badlands look like today. Only animals that are adapted to hot, dry conditions can live there now.

Although this collared lizard is a tiny, modern-day reptile, it resembles dinosaurs of long ago.

Dinosaurs like this T. rex became extinct about 65 million years ago.

Today the Badlands in South Dakota are almost like a desert.

This is one artist's view of how a *T. rex* might have looked. It also shows its habitat.

✔ **Lesson Checkpoint**

1. Describe four kinds of fossils.

2. What can fossils tell us about extinct animals?

3. **Writing in Science** **Expository** In your **science journal,** write about what might have happened to *T. Rex* when its environment changed.

# Investigate What can you learn from an imprint?

Imprints fossils are one type of fossil. Scientists can learn about animals that lived long ago by studying the imprints they made.

imprint made by a dinosaur

## Materials

cup with prepared plaster of Paris

spoon

paper plate and paper towels

bowl of water

## What to Do

**1** Put plaster of Paris onto a plate.

Spread the plaster of Paris around with a spoon.

Be careful!

**2** Wet one of your hands.

Do not put plaster of Paris into a sink. It can clog the drain.

**3** Spread the fingers of your wet hand. Press the palm side of this hand into the plaster of Paris.

**4** Remove your hand from the plaster. Let the imprint dry.

Wipe the plaster of Paris off your hand. Use paper towels. Wash your hands thoroughly.

**5** Make a chart to record what you **observe** about your hand and its imprint.

| Appearance | |
|---|---|
| **Imprint** | **Hand** |
| | |

## Explain Your Results

1. How is your imprint like your hand that made it? How is it different?

2. **Infer** How might an imprint fossil of an animal be like the animal that made it? How might it be different?

## Go Further

Use a hand lens to observe and study tiny details. If you wish, make sketches or diagrams. Use your ruler to measure your hand and its imprint.

# Comparing Speeds of Fish

**There is a great difference in the swimming speeds of fish. Generally, larger fish can swim faster than smaller fish. The bar graph below shows the greatest swimming speeds of six different fish.**

**Greatest Swimming Speeds**

Fish

- Barracuda
- Southern Bluefin Tuna
- Marlin
- Salmon
- Sailfish
- Swordfish

0 5 10 15 20 25 30 35 40 45 50 55 60 65 70 75 80 85 90 95 100 105 110

**Kilometers per hour**

**1** Which of the six fish is the fastest swimmer?

    A. Salmon                   B. Marlin

    C. Barracuda            D. Sailfish

**2** Which of the six fish is the slowest swimmer?

    F. Swordfish            G. Barracuda

    H. Southern Bluefin Tuna      I. Marlin

**3** Use the data in the graph to list the six fish in order from slowest to fastest.

## Lab zone Take-Home Activity

Use an almanac, the Internet, or other sources to find the most recent Olympic records for swimming. Make a graph or a chart showing the record times for each swimming event.

## Use Vocabulary

| | |
|---|---|
| **adaptation** (page 48) | **migrate** (page 52) |
| **hibernate** (page 52) | **pupa** (page 45) |
| **inherited** (page 48) | **trait** (page 40) |
| **larva** (page 45) | **vertebrate** (page 40) |

Use the vocabulary word from the list above that best completes each sentence.

**1.** An animal with a backbone is called a(n) _____.

**2.** In an early stage of life, when a butterfly eats and grows, it is called a(n) _____.

**3.** Some animals need much less food to survive when they _____.

**4.** Something that helps a living thing survive is called a(n) _____.

**5.** If something passes on from a parent to its offspring, it is _____.

**6.** The stage in the life cycle of a butterfly during which it changes into an adult is called the _____.

**7.** Sometimes animals move to another place, or _____, to find better food or shelter.

**8.** A feature passed on to an animal from its parents is a(n) _____.

## Explain Concepts

**9.** Explain why different animals can be grouped in more than one way.

**10.** Why does inheriting an adaptation help offspring survive?

**11.** What is the difference between instinct and learned behavior?

**12.** Describe the changes a frog goes through during its life cycle.

### Process Skills

**13. Infer** If a fossil skull has flat teeth, what do you think this animal probably ate?

**14. Predict** A hawk has feet with sharp claws on them to help it catch small animals to eat. What kind of feet would you predict a bird that swims would have?

**MindPoint** Quiz Show

## Sequence

**15.** Use the signal words to put the stages of the life cycle of a frog in the correct sequence.

| **First** |
| **Next** |
| **Finally** |

## Test Prep

Choose the letter that best completes the statement or answers the question.

**16.** Fossils tell us

   (A) about animals that lived in the past.

   (B) about how Earth has changed.

   (C) how today's animals are similar to past life.

   (D) all of the above.

**17.** The earliest stage in a frog's life cycle is a(n)

   (F) pupa.

   (G) egg.

   (H) chrysalis.

   (I) tadpole.

**18.** Which of the following is an animal without a backbone, or invertebrate?

   (A) insect

   (B) bird

   (C) mammal

   (D) amphibian

**19.** Explain why the answer you chose for Question 18 is best. For each of the answers you did not choose, give a reason why it is not the correct choice.

**20.** **Writing** in Science

**Descriptive** Suppose a hungry fox comes upon a porcupine. Write a paragraph describing what happens between the two animals.

# Paul Sereno:
# Expert Dinosaur Hunter

**Paul Sereno**

When he was a boy, Paul Sereno liked to go on nature hikes with his brothers. He brought home insects to add to his collection. Paul went to college to study art. However, while he was in college, Paul decided he wanted to become a paleontologist—a scientist who studies ancient life.

Paleontologists like Dr. Sereno try to find fossils to piece together the story of what life was like long ago. Dr. Sereno and his team have found many new kinds of dinosaurs.

Dr. Sereno's team made a discovery in Africa. A giant claw lying in the desert was the first clue. Dr. Sereno and his team carefully dug for more bones. They found a huge skeleton of a dinosaur. Its skull was long with crocodile-like teeth. Dr. Sereno named the new dinosaur *Suchomimus* which means "crocodile mimic."

It sometimes takes years for paleontologists to make sense of what they find. But their hard work often leads to new discoveries.

## Lab zone Take-Home Activity

Using library resources and the Internet, research newly discovered dinosaurs. List them by name, type of dinosaur, and where found.

**You Will Discover**

- what an ecosystem is.
- different kinds of land ecosystems.
- different kinds of water ecosystems.

# Chapter 3

# Where Plants and Animals Live

online
**Student Edition**
sfsuccessnet.com

# How are ecosystems different from each other?

environment

ecosystem

desert

grassland

66

# Chapter 3 Vocabulary

population

community

tundra

wetland

## Explore In which soil do grass seeds grow best?

How will you know in which soil grass seeds *grow best*? Should *grow best* mean the most blades of grass grow, the tallest blades grow, or the greenest blades grow? You decide. **Make an operational definition** of *grow best*. Begin with the words "Grow best means. . . ." Then say what you will observe that will tell you which *grows best*.

### Materials

3 paper cups and a pencil

sandy, clay, and loam soils

grass seeds and cup with water

spoon and masking tape

### Process Skills

You explained how you would decide in which soil the seeds *grow best.* When you told what you would **observe** to make this decision, you **made an operational definition**.

### What to Do

**1** Make 4 holes in the bottom of each cup with a pencil. Half fill the cups with soil. Put 2 spoonfuls of water in each cup.

Label the cups.

**2** Sprinkle $\frac{1}{2}$ spoonful of grass seeds in each cup. Lightly cover the seeds with more soil. Set the cups in a warm place with bright light.

sandy soil

clay soil

loam soil

**3** Add 1 spoonful of water to each cup daily for 2 weeks. **Observe** each cup daily.

### Explain Your Results

What is your **operational definition** of *grow best*? In which soil did the seeds *grow best* according to your definition?

# How to Read Science

## Main Idea and Details

A number of different things might all be connected to a **main idea**. These are called **details.** Learning to find the **main idea and details** helps you understand what you read. Look at the graphic organizer. The main idea is at the top. The details help support the main idea.

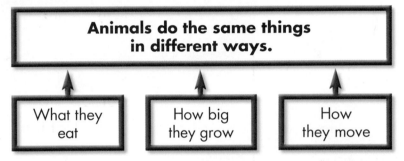

**Animals do the same things in different ways.**

| What they eat | How big they grow | How they move |

**Science Article**

## Home Address

Animals live in different places. Some live in forests. Others live in lakes or oceans. Different animals have different body coverings. Some have fur or feathers. Others have scales. The animals' body coverings help them live where they do.

## Apply It!

Make a graphic organizer like the one shown above. Use it to help you **make an operational definition** about what you read and what you have observed. Write the main idea at the top. Fill in the missing details that support the main idea from the science article.

## You Are There!

You are standing where the ocean meets the land. You can feel the warm sunlight on your face. You hear the waves rush onto the shore. You wiggle your toes in the cool, damp sand. Birds circle above you. This is a terrific place for you to visit. What makes it a perfect place for certain plants and animals to live?

AudioText

## Lesson 1

# What are ecosystems?

*Plants and animals meet their needs in the place where they live. Living things depend on other living things and nonliving things around them.*

### Places for Living Things

Each living thing needs a certain environment. A living thing's **environment** is everything that surrounds it. An environment has living parts and nonliving parts. The living parts include plants, animals, and other living things. The nonliving parts include the Sun's rays, air, water, and soil.

The Sun's rays are necessary for life. They warm the air, water, and soil to the temperature that living things need. Sunlight helps plants make food.

Climate shapes each environment. Climate is the weather in a place all year. For example, one place might have cold, wet winters and hot, dry summers. Another place might be cold and dry all year long.

Water and soil are important parts of each environment. Water falls as rain and snow, and enters the soil. Soils differ in the way they hold this water. Each type of plant needs a certain amount of water and a certain kind of soil.

1. ✔ **Checkpoint** Name four nonliving things that are part of a plant's or animal's environment.

2. **Art** in Science Draw a picture that shows the things that you need that your environment provides. Write labels on your drawing of what these things are.

## Parts of an Ecosystem

In an environment, living and nonliving parts act on each other or interact. These interacting parts make up an **ecosystem.**

The living parts of an ecosystem depend on nonliving parts. For example, coastal redwood trees need sunlight, soil, and air. They also need a lot of water. There is plenty of rain in winter, but no rain falls in the summer. So, in the summer, the trees get water instead from fog that rolls in from the ocean.

The living parts of an ecosystem also depend on one another. For example, some sea birds scoop up fish from the ocean. Then they fly inland to nest in the redwood trees.

## Special Homes

The place where a living thing makes its home is its habitat. A habitat has all the things that a plant or animal needs to live. For example, a habitat can be a branch of a redwood tree in which a bird builds a nest. The habitat gives plants light, air, water, living space, and pollinators. It gives animals food, water, shelter, and living space. If any of these things is missing, something will change. The habitat might no longer be able to support some plants or animals. These plants or animals may struggle to survive, die, or try to move to a new habitat.

| Interacting Parts of an Ecosystem | |
|---|---|
| **Living** | **Nonliving** |
| plants | light/heat |
| animals | air/water |
| other living things | rocks/soil |

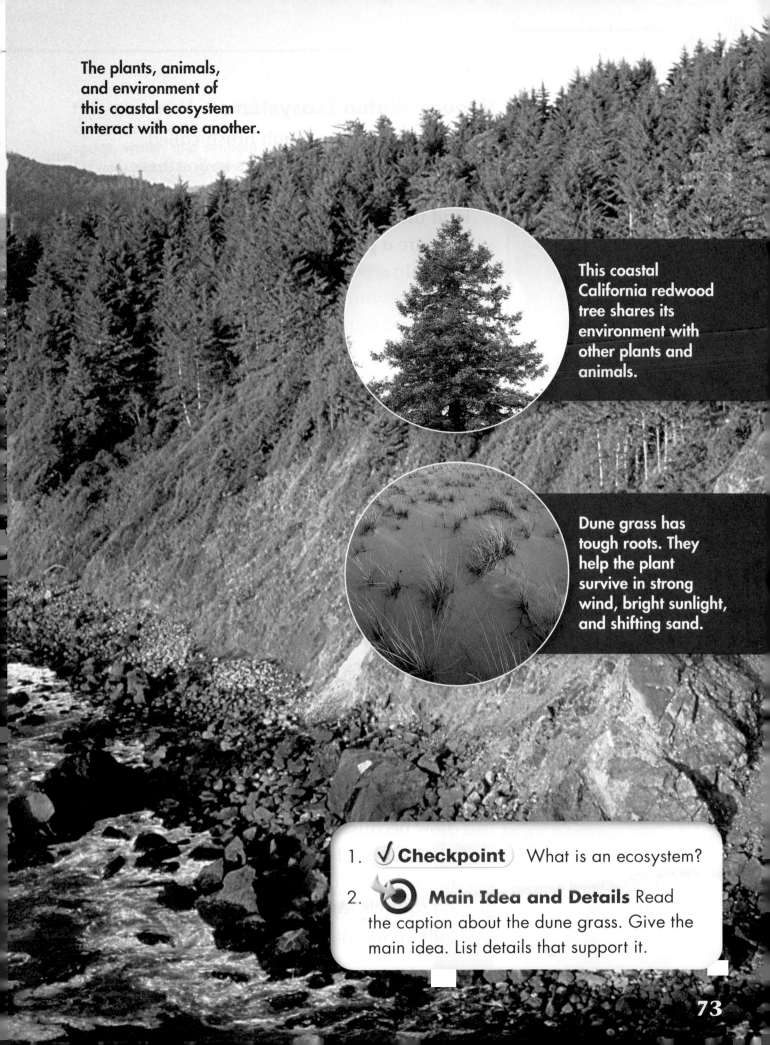

The plants, animals, and environment of this coastal ecosystem interact with one another.

This coastal California redwood tree shares its environment with other plants and animals.

Dune grass has tough roots. They help the plant survive in strong wind, bright sunlight, and shifting sand.

1. ✔ **Checkpoint** What is an ecosystem?

2. 🎯 **Main Idea and Details** Read the caption about the dune grass. Give the main idea. List details that support it.

73

# Which ecosystems have few trees?

*Different places on Earth have different climates. Some land ecosystems have climates that support only a few trees.*

## Grassland

Think about looking out over a wide, grassy field. A strong summer breeze makes the tops of the grasses move like waves on the ocean. A **grassland** is a kind of land ecosystem. It has many grasses and flowering plants, but few trees. A climate of cool or cold winters and hot summers supports grasslands. The climate includes little rain, so the soil is dry. Trees cannot grow well in this soil. They need more water. The trees grow mostly in the wetter soil along rivers and creeks.

Many grasses grow well in this kind of habitat. They survive because they have deep roots. These roots help the plants in many ways. When grazing animals, fire, or the cold winters kill the plants above ground, the roots survive. Deep roots also help the plants find water in the dry, hot summers.

Some grasslands get more rain than others. Tall-grass prairies grow in the wetter eastern parts of the Midwest. Short-grass prairies grow farther west where less rain falls.

| Climate in the Kansas Grassland | | |
|---|---|---|
| Average Temperature (°C) | | Average Yearly Rainfall (cm) |
| Summer | Winter | |
| 20 | 2 | 90 |

This is the Konza Prairie in Kansas. Like other parts of the Midwestern United States, it is grassland.

Winters are cool or cold in the grasslands. Deep roots help the plants store food for winter.

Many kinds of insects, such as this grasshopper, live in grasslands.

Once huge herds of bison roamed the grasslands. Now, only a few herds remain.

1. ✓**Checkpoint** What is a grassland?

2. 🎯 **Main Idea and Details** Tell the main idea about grasslands. Give supporting details.

77

## Desert—A Surprising Ecosystem

A **desert** is an ecosystem that gets very little rain. Days are often hot, but the nights are cool or even cold. Many people think of deserts as nothing but sand. However, most desert ecosystems are full of life. Desert plants and animals can live with little rainfall. Some plants, including cactuses, store water in their leaves or stems.

During the day, you might see a lizard warming itself on a rock. But many desert animals rest out of sight during the hottest time of day. Some stay in underground tunnels. Others find a shady spot under a plant. At night the desert comes alive. Animals come out of their hiding places to search for food.

| Climate in a Desert | | |
| --- | --- | --- |
| Average Temperature (°C) | | Average Yearly Rainfall (cm) |
| Summer | Winter | 30 |
| 30 | 10 | |

Yucca plants provide shade and cover for small animals like snakes and lizards. Small birds eat the fruits.

This sidewinder rattlesnake usually hunts at night. It kills small animals for food.

This desert bobcat warms itself on a sunny rock in winter. At night, it hunts for birds and other small animals.

## Map Fact

Joshua Tree National Park is a desert ecosystem in southern California. Joshua trees are a kind of yucca plant, which grows only about 6 centimeters a year. More than 78 kinds of birds nest in the park.

1. ✓ **Checkpoint** Why do certain plants do well in deserts?

2. **Writing** in Science **Expository**
Write a newspaper article about desert animals. Explain why they are active at night.

## Tundra—Land of Long Winters

The **tundra** is a cold, dry, land ecosystem. It is in the very northern part of the world. Parts of Alaska are tundra. Winters there are long and cold. Snow falls and cold winds blow. Summers are short and cool. The snow melts in summer, but the soil below the surface does not become soft. It stays frozen all year.

Summer days are very long in the tundra. In some places, the summer Sun shines 24 hours a day. Winter days are very short. Some places get no sunlight at all in winter.

Many plants cannot grow in this climate. For example, few trees grow in the tundra. Their roots cannot grow in frozen soil. Small plants grow here instead. These include grasses and wildflowers.

In summer, the melting snow forms ponds in the tundra. Many ducks, geese, and swans nest near these ponds. Other birds also nest in the tundra. In summer, there are millions of insects for them to eat. Most tundra birds travel to warmer places during winter.

| Climate in the Tundra | | |
|---|---|---|
| Average Temperature (°C) | | Average Yearly Rainfall (cm) |
| Summer | Winter | |
| 6 | 30° below 0 | 10 |

Caribou travel in large herds. In winter, they find food by digging through the snow with their front hooves.

What type of plant is missing in this tundra? Trees! Their roots cannot grow into the frozen soil. Grasses and wild flowers grow close to the ground.

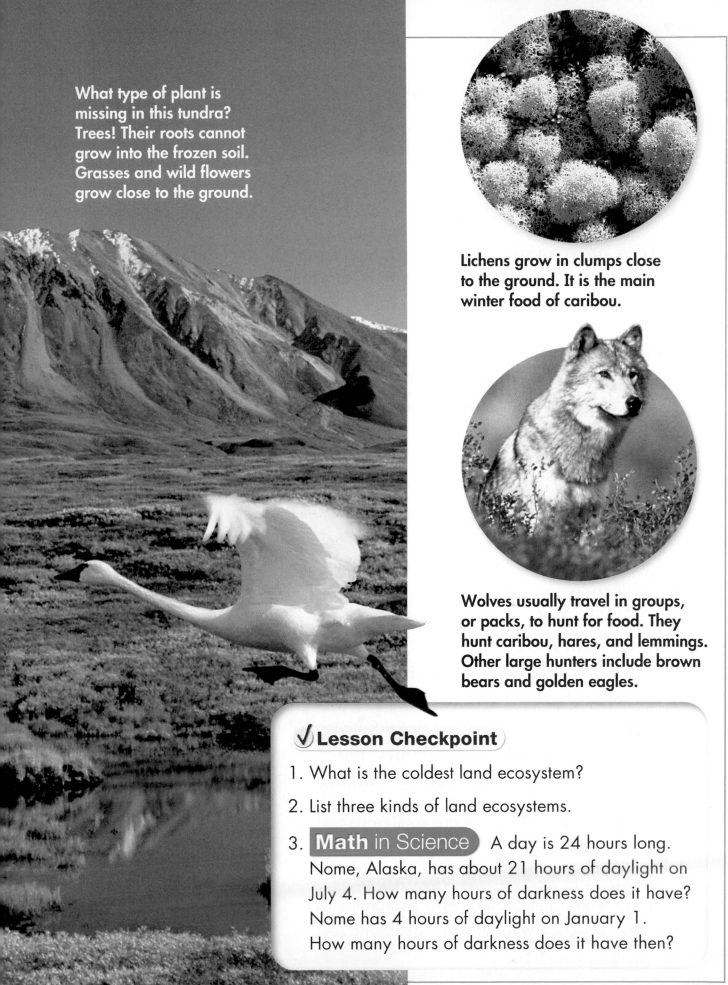

Lichens grow in clumps close to the ground. It is the main winter food of caribou.

Wolves usually travel in groups, or packs, to hunt for food. They hunt caribou, hares, and lemmings. Other large hunters include brown bears and golden eagles.

## ✓ Lesson Checkpoint

1. What is the coldest land ecosystem?

2. List three kinds of land ecosystems.

3. **Math** in Science   A day is 24 hours long. Nome, Alaska, has about 21 hours of daylight on July 4. How many hours of darkness does it have? Nome has 4 hours of daylight on January 1. How many hours of darkness does it have then?

# What are some forest ecosystems?

*There are ecosystems that have different kinds of thick forests. Each kind of forest ecosystem has its own plants and animals.*

## Coniferous and Deciduous Forests

Coniferous forests grow mainly in northern North America, Europe, and Asia. They grow in places that have cold, snowy winters. They grow where summers are warm and dry. These forests have many conifers such as spruce, fir, and pine. The tree leaves look like needles.

Few plants grow under coniferous trees. Mosses are a common type of plant that grows there. Lichens also grow under the conifers. Still, many animals live in coniferous forests. They can find food and shelter.

Climates where deciduous forests grow are generally warmer than those of coniferous forests. Deciduous forests get rain in summer and snow in winter. Deciduous forests can have oak, maple, and beech trees. They drop their leaves in the fall. For part of the year, sunlight reaches the forest floor. Many shrubs and other plants can grow there. These plants provide habitats for animals.

1. ✔ **Checkpoint** How are coniferous and deciduous forests alike and different?

2. **Writing** in Science **Descriptive** Write a short story about walking through an evergreen forest or a deciduous forest. Describe what you see, hear, and feel.

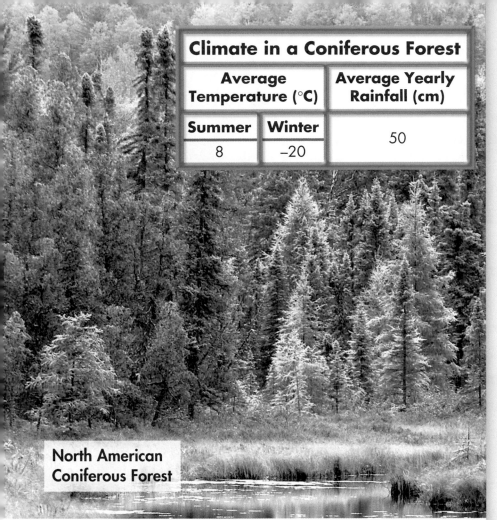

| Climate in a Coniferous Forest | | |
|---|---|---|
| Average Temperature (°C) | | Average Yearly Rainfall (cm) |
| Summer | Winter | 50 |
| 8 | −20 | |

North American Coniferous Forest

Moose eat twigs, bark, roots, and young stems of woody plants. In summer, they feed on water plants like water lilies.

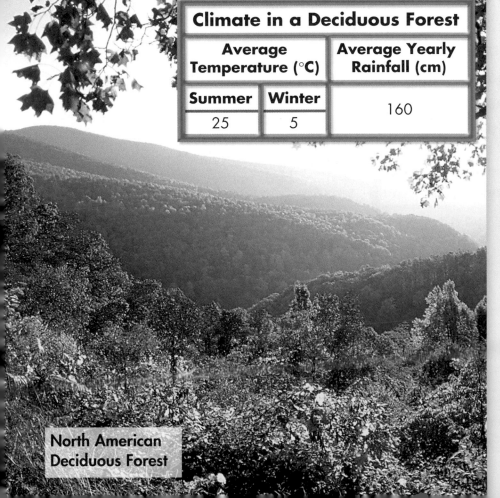

| Climate in a Deciduous Forest | | |
|---|---|---|
| Average Temperature (°C) | | Average Yearly Rainfall (cm) |
| Summer | Winter | 160 |
| 25 | 5 | |

Many insects and birds live in deciduous forests. Woodpeckers eat beetles that dig into tree trunks.

Beavers use their sharp teeth to cut forest trees and branches. They build dams of sticks and mud across streams.

North American Deciduous Forest

83

## Tropical Forests

Where could you find a spider so big that it eats birds? These spiders live in a tropical forest. These forests grow near the equator. Tropical forests can have a climate that is warm and rainy all year long. The many tall trees let little sunlight reach the forest floor. Some of the trees can be 35 meters tall—taller than a ten-story office building. Plants such as orchids grow on the trees.

Most animals of the tropical forest live in the trees. Some spend their whole lives there.

Some of these animals, such as bats, can be found in many different tropical forests. Others live in only certain forests and not in others. For example, many kinds of beetles live in only one forest in Brazil. They are found nowhere else. The tropical rainforest has huge numbers of insects. No one has ever named them all.

**Woolly monkeys live in South America. They live in trees and eat fruits, leaves, seeds, and some insects.**

**Rainbow lorikeets live in the tropical forests of eastern Asia and Australia. These noisy birds eat nectar, flowers, seeds, and fruit.**

| Climate in a Rainforest | | |
|---|---|---|
| Average Temperature (°C) | | Average Yearly Rainfall (cm) |
| Summer | Winter | 300 |
| 25 | 25 | |

**These red stinkbugs live in tropical forests.**

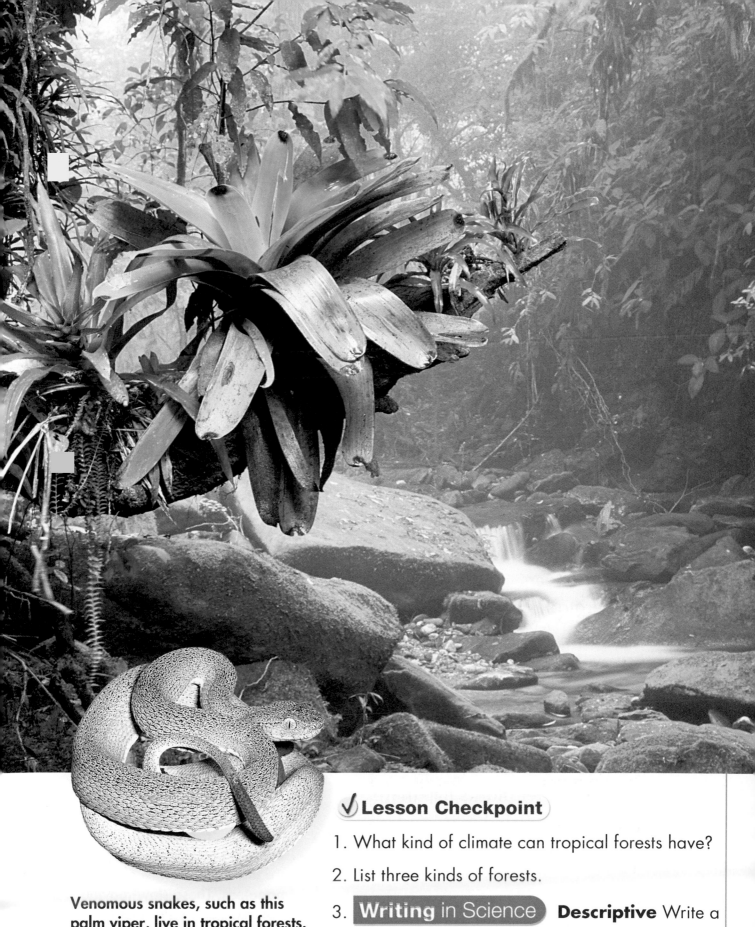

Venomous snakes, such as this palm viper, live in tropical forests. Most snakes eat frogs, lizards, and other small animals.

## ✓ Lesson Checkpoint

1. What kind of climate can tropical forests have?

2. List three kinds of forests.

3. **Writing** in Science **Descriptive** Write a paragraph in your **science journal** describing how climate affects different kinds of forests.

# What are water ecosystems?

*Water ecosystems can have fresh water, salt water, or both.*

### Freshwater Ecosystems

Freshwater ecosystems include lakes, ponds, rivers, and streams. Lakes and ponds are water surrounded by land. Rivers and streams are moving water. Rain or melting snow supplies water for most lakes and rivers. Springs that flow from underground supply water for others. Many plants and animals live in lakes and rivers.

The Everglades in south Florida is a large wetland. A **wetland** is low land that is covered by water at least part of the year. Water flows very slowly through the Everglades south to Florida Bay. This "river of grass" is very wide. But its water is very shallow. Trees, grasses, and water plants live there. Animals such as fish, bears, and birds live there, too.

Florida Everglades

Many large Florida springs are the winter homes of manatees. These slow-moving mammals eat water plants.

**Map Fact**

There are hundreds of springs that empty into lakes and rivers in Florida. Weeki Wachee Spring in central Florida supplies the water for the Weeki Wachee River, shown here.

1. ✓**Checkpoint**) Name four kinds of freshwater ecosystems.

2. **Technology** in Science) Use the Internet to find out about the plants and animals that live in the Everglades. Make a list of these plants and animals.

## Saltwater Ecosystems

Oceans cover much of Earth's surface. Ocean water contains salt. The ocean is shallow along the shore. Clams, crabs, kelp, fish, and coral live here. Otters, seals, and sea birds swim and dive for fish.

The open ocean gets very deep, but most life is in the top 200 meters of water. Very small animals feed on tiny algae that make food. Large fish and whales also live here. The deep ocean is dark and cold, and it has little food. Few animals live here.

Many rivers flow into the ocean. Fresh water from the river can mix with salt water from the ocean. Salt marshes can form in these areas. Salt marshes are wetlands that contain special plants and animals. These living things are able to live in salty water and soil. Many plants grow in salt marshes. These wetlands also contain a muddy soup of tiny living animals. Some are too small to see with just your eye. Many kinds of fishes, crabs, and other ocean animals begin their lives in salt marshes.

| Life in the Oceans | |
|---|---|
| Kinds of Living Things | 275,000 kinds |
| Longest Animal | Blue Whale, 33 meters |
| Longest Fish | Whale Shark, 12 meters |
| Fastest Ocean Animal | Sailfish, 30 meters per second |

This reef cuttlefish can squirt a jet of water out of its body. This helps it escape from an enemy.

The Great Barrier Reef is a huge coral reef. It is along the eastern coast of Australia. Australia is in the southern Pacific Ocean.

**Australian Great Barrier Reef**

A coral is an animal about the size of an ant. It builds a hard, rocky skeleton around itself for protection. Millions of corals build a coral reef.

## ✓ Lesson Checkpoint

1. Where do most corals live?

2. Where is most life found in the oceans?

3. **Writing in Science** **Narrative** Find out about an animal that lives in salty water. Then write a story in your **science journal** about that animal. Title your story (Name of your animal)—This Is Your Life!

# Math in Science

# Comparing Data

The major grasslands of North America are located in six areas, as shown on the map. The tall-grass prairie, the mixed-grass prairie, and the short-grass prairie together are known as the Central Prairies.

Intermountain Grassland (30 cm)

Short-grass Prairie (25 cm)

Mixed-grass Prairie (50 cm)

Tall-grass Prairie (90 cm)

California Grassland (20 cm)

Desert Grassland (30 cm)

Average Rainfall/Snowfall in North American Grasslands

eTools Take It to the Net
sfsuccessnet.com

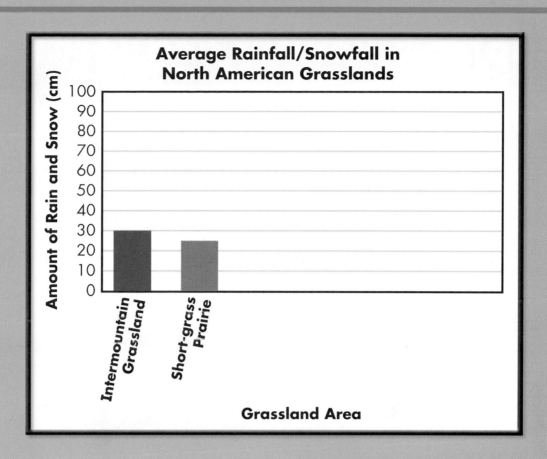

**Average Rainfall/Snowfall in North American Grasslands**

Amount of Rain and Snow (cm)

Grassland Area

Use the map and the graph to answer each question.

**1** Copy the bar graph on grid paper and complete it. Your graph should show the data for all six grasslands.

**2** Which describes how the amount of rain and snow in the Central Prairies changes?

A. increases from west to east     B. decreases from west to east

C. increases from north to south     D. decreases from north to south

**3** Which grassland gets the most rain and snow? Which gets the least?

**Lab zone** **Take-Home Activity**

Use the library or the Internet to find data about rainfall and snowfall amounts in any type of ecosystem in North America. Show the data on a bar graph.

# Chapter 3 Review and Test Prep

## Use Vocabulary

| | |
|---|---|
| **community** (page 74) | **grassland** (page 76) |
| **desert** (page 78) | **population** (page 74) |
| **ecosystem** (page 72) | **tundra** (page 80) |
| **environment** (page 71) | **wetland** (page 86) |

Use the term from the list above that best completes each sentence.

1. Low land that is often covered by water is a(n) _____.

2. All the moose that live in one place are a(n) _____.

3. Everything that surrounds a living thing is its _____.

4. An ecosystem with hot days and little rain is a(n) _____.

5. All the populations living in the same place form a(n) _____.

6. The ecosystem that is coldest and farthest north is the _____.

7. All the living and nonliving things that interact in an area form a(n) _____.

8. An ecosystem with many grasses and few trees is a(n) _____.

## Explain Concepts

9. Explain how dry soil and frozen soil affect the types of plants that grow in them. Give examples.

10. Explain how chaparral, coyotes, and ground squirrels depend on each other.

11. Explain how some desert plants are able to have enough water.

### Process Skills

12. Wheat and oats are cereal grasses. **Infer** in which ecosystem these farm crops would grow best.

13. Desert snakes eat kangaroo rats. **Predict** what would happen to the population of rats if the population of snakes grew larger.

14. **Interpret data** Use the data table below. Find the difference between the greatest yearly rainfall and the least.

| Forest | Yearly rainfall |
|---|---|
| Coniferous forest (Alaska) | 70 cm |
| Deciduous forest (Maryland) | 120 cm |
| Tropical forest (Hawaii) | 1,234 cm |

## Main Idea and Details

**15.** Draw the graphic organizer below. Choose an ecosystem for the main idea. Fill in details that support the main idea.

All _____ ecosystems have similar features.

## Test Prep

Choose the letter that best completes the statement or answers the question.

**16.** A group of trout that live in a river make up a(n)

Ⓐ community.

Ⓑ population.

Ⓒ habitat.

Ⓓ ecosystem.

**17.** Which ecosystem has a warm, rainy climate?

Ⓕ tropical forest

Ⓖ tundra

Ⓗ evergreen forest

Ⓘ desert

**18.** Which populations might live in a wetland?

Ⓐ corals, whales, and fish

Ⓑ coniferous trees, foxes, and woodpeckers

Ⓒ birds, alligators, and grasses

Ⓓ cactuses, rattlesnakes, and bobcats

**19.** Explain why the answer you selected for Question 16 is best. For each of the answers you did not select, give a reason why it is not the best choice.

**20.** Writing in Science

**Expository** Write a paragraph about a plant or animal and how it survives in a desert ecosystem.

# Eric Stolen

Eric Stolen

"Getting wet, dirty, hot, bug-bitten and chased by critters" are things Eric Stolen loves.

Eric Stolen is a wildlife biologist at NASA's Kennedy Space Center, which includes a wildlife refuge. Mr. Stolen studies how wading birds choose a place to live and how they get food.

Mr. Stolen finds ways to study the birds without them noticing he is there. Sometimes he wades through mud. Other times he flies over the birds in a helicopter. He uses binoculars and other tools to see what the birds are doing.

When Eric was growing up, he often went camping, hiking, and boating. He became interested in nature and animals while he was in grade school. Later on, Mr. Stolen studied biology in college. He never tires of studying nature because there are so many interesting things to see and learn.

## Lab zone Take-Home Activity

Spend an hour outdoors. Find a place where you can see birds or other animals. Write in your **science journal** about the animals you see and what they do.

96

EC NTL 109876543

# Chapter 4

# Plants and Animals Living Together

## You Will Discover

- ways that plants and animals interact.
- how food energy moves through an ecosystem.
- what a healthy environment for people includes.

online
**Student Edition**
sfsuccessnet.com

# How do plants and animals interact?

consumer

producer

herbivore

98

# Chapter 4 Vocabulary

decomposer

decay

germs

disease

omnivore

carnivore    predator

competition    prey

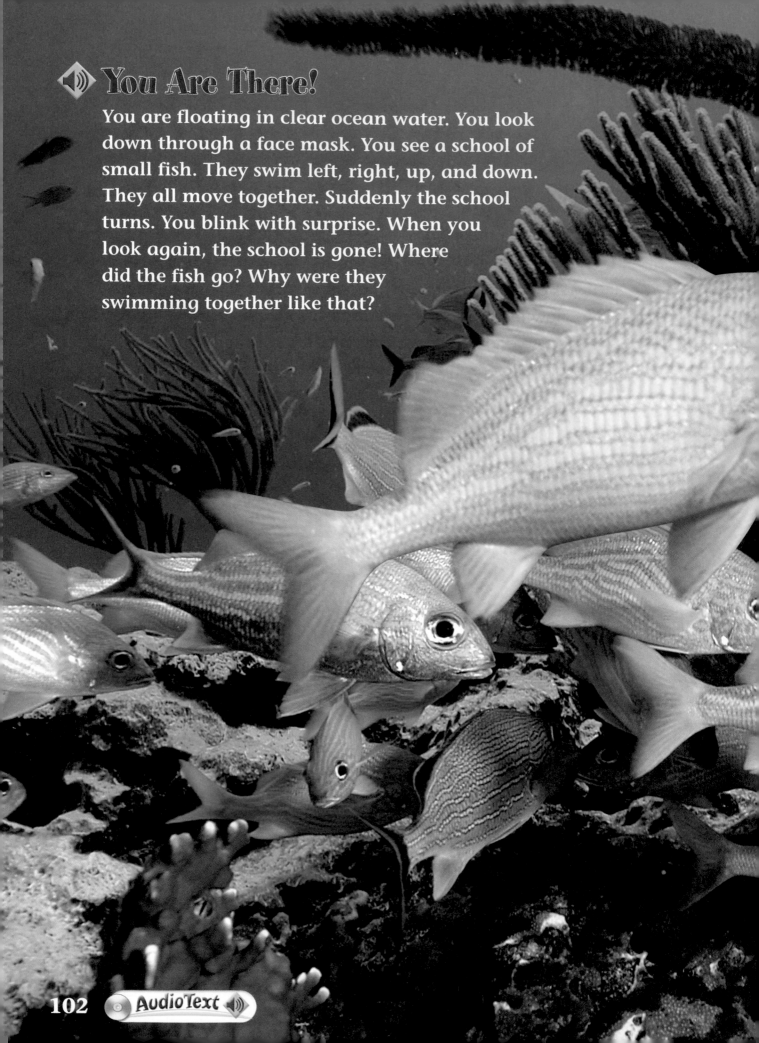

## 🔊 You Are There!

You are floating in clear ocean water. You look down through a face mask. You see a school of small fish. They swim left, right, up, and down. They all move together. Suddenly the school turns. You blink with surprise. When you look again, the school is gone! Where did the fish go? Why were they swimming together like that?

**AudioText** 🔊

## Lesson 1

# How do living things interact?

*Living things may affect each other when they interact. The interactions can be helpful, harmful, or neither.*

**Ways Living Things Interact**

Living things interact in different ways. Their interactions may help them survive. Study the examples in the chart. Those living in groups help each other. One kind of living thing might help another kind without being helped in return. Or different kinds might help each other.

| Ways Living Things Interact | | |
|---|---|---|
| **Helping in Groups** | Members of a herd protect each other. | |
| **One Kind Helping Another** | A tree helps a flower get light. | |
| **Two Kinds Helping Each Other** | While it drinks flower nectar, an insect spreads pollen among the flowers. | |

1. **✓Checkpoint** List three ways in which living things might interact.

2. **Writing in Science** **Narrative** In your **science journal** describe a day during which you helped as a member of a group. Describe how the group helped you.

**103**

One bee may find flowers. Then it will fly back to the beehive and move in a certain way. This "dance" tells the other bees where the flowers are.

A grown barnacle is about 5 cm wide. It grabs food from the water that the whale swims through.

## Living in Groups

Animals that live together might all help protect the group from predators. Together, the animals may be safer than each animal alone. For example, prairie dogs live in groups. Coyotes and golden eagles eat them. Coyotes hunt on the ground. Eagles hunt from the sky. Prairie dogs take turns standing watch at their burrow openings. If any prairie dog senses danger, it whistles. At this sound, the whole group runs and hides. All the prairie dogs stay hidden until the danger has passed.

## One Kind of Living Thing Helping Another Kind

Notice the barnacles on the whale. Some barnacles swim through the ocean and attach to the skin of a whale. A barnacle usually spends its whole life attached to the same whale.

The barnacle opens and closes its shell to catch food as the whale moves through the water. The barnacles do not harm the whales. They don't help the whales either. In this partnership, only one partner is helped— the barnacle.

## Helping One Another

Some kinds of living things help each other. The moth seen here shares its life with only one kind of yucca plant.

The moth helps the yucca by carrying pollen from another yucca. The yucca helps the moth by giving it a habitat and food for its young. The moth lays her eggs in the flower pods. Each larva hatches in the pods and eats some of the seeds the flower pod makes.

The cleaner fish is another example. Several kinds of small fish clean larger fish. They eat pests off the big fish. The cleaner fish gets a meal. The other fish gets clean and stays healthy.

A yucca moth provides a ball of sticky pollen from another yucca. In exchange it lays its eggs in the flower.

This large coral hind fish learns to know the small cleaner fish. It lets the cleaner fish do its work.

### ✔ Lesson Checkpoint

1. Give two examples of how living things benefit from living together.

2. How do yucca moths and yucca plants help each other?

3. **Draw Conclusions** Why do living things interact?

# How do living things get energy?

*Plants get energy from the sun. Animals get energy from plants or from other animals that eat plants.*

## Sources of Energy

Green plants make their own food. A living thing that makes its own food is a **producer.** Producers use energy from sunlight to make food out of matter from the air and soil.

Many living things cannot make their own food. They must get their energy from food that they eat. A living thing that eats food is a **consumer.**

## Kinds of Consumers

Some consumers eat plants, others eat animals, and some eat both. A consumer that eats only plants is a **herbivore.** A consumer that eats only animals is a **carnivore.** A consumer that eats both plants and animals is an **omnivore.**

Cattails produce their own food. Every animal's food energy can be traced back to producers.

The crayfish is a consumer because it must eat food for energy.

Sunlight provides all the energy for an ecosystem.

Sheep are herbivores.
They eat only plants.

A wolf is a carnivore.
It eats only meat.

A bear is an omnivore.
It eats both plants
and animals.

## Food Chains

Energy passes to living things within food chains. Food chains are groups of producers and consumers that interact in a special way. A consumer eats a producer. The producer passes energy to that consumer. That consumer may then become **prey** for another consumer. Prey is any animal that is hunted by others for food.

The prey passes energy on to a **predator.** A predator is a consumer that hunts for food. In this way, energy can move from a producer to a predator. As each living thing uses food energy, some energy is given off as heat.

The raccoon is
an omnivore.
It eats crayfish,
other animals,
and plants.

### ✓Checkpoint

1. Trace the transfer of energy through a food chain that includes raccoons, crayfish, cattails, and sunlight.

2. Art in Science Draw a food chain that shows how grass, a cow, and a person drinking milk are connected.

107

## Energy in a Food Web

A food chain is simple. Energy moves from one type of living thing to another. Real life is not so simple. Energy often moves in many different ways. It might transfer from one kind of producer to many kinds of consumers. One kind of consumer might be prey for more than one kind of predator.

Energy flow in a community forms a web. A food web is made up of more than one food chain. Food webs tie a community together. Each part of a web affects other parts.

An example of a food web is found on the Great Plains. Prairie grasses grow there. They are producers. Energy flows from the grasses to the animals that eat them. These animals include prairie dogs and mice. Prairie dogs are prey for ferrets and golden eagles. Ferrets are prey for badgers. So energy can flow through the food web from grasses to golden eagles and badgers.

Energy from grass flows to cattle.

Energy from grass flows to prairie dogs.

Prairie grasses are producers.

Energy from grass flows to mice.

## A Changing Food Web

If one part of a food web is removed, other parts change. For example, prairie dogs once built large colonies on the grassy plains. Then cattle began to feed on these same plains. This reduced the habitat for prairie dogs. Many prairie dogs also became sick and died. As a result, the number of prairie dogs was reduced.

Removing one part of the food web caused a number of things to happen. The cattle had more food, but ferrets had less. With fewer prairie dogs to eat, ferrets no longer had the food they needed. Ferrets began to die out.

This, in turn, affected predators of ferrets, such as badgers. Now badgers had to look for other food. Golden eagles and foxes also hunt prairie dogs. They too had to get more food energy from other kinds of prey, such as mice. All this can happen when one part of a food web is removed.

Ferrets eat mostly prairie dogs. Energy flows to the ferrets.

Badgers eat ferrets. Energy flows to the badgers.

Golden eagles eat prairie dogs and mice. Energy from these animals flows to the eagles.

### ✓ Lesson Checkpoint

1. How did reducing the number of prairie dogs affect ferrets?

2. How does the loss of prairie dogs affect eagles and foxes?

3. **Draw Conclusions** Tell what happens when a food chain is broken.

The young trees in this forest compete for sunlight and room to grow.

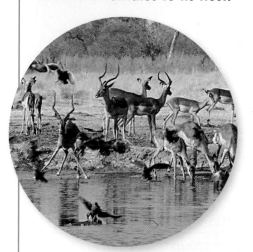

This male bower bird competes with other males to attract females to its nest.

Many different animals compete for water in dry places.

# How do living things compete?

*Maybe you have tried to fit under an umbrella with another person to stay dry. You had to compete with the person for shelter. Living things often compete with one another. Usually they compete for food, water, and room to live.*

## Competing for Resources

Picture yourself in a dark, cool forest. The treetops form a roof high above you. Few small trees are growing. Why? They struggle to get enough energy from sunlight to grow. The small trees are in **competition** with one another. When two or more living things need the same resources, they are in competition. Since the tall trees in this forest get most of the sunlight, the small trees compete for the light that is left.

Living things compete for many kinds of resources besides light. These resources include food, water, and living space. The winners in these competitions survive. The losers might not survive.

SciLinks Take It to the Net
sfsuccessnet.com
keyword: competition
code: g3p110

## Predators and Prey

Many predators may compete for the same prey. Faster, stronger ones might catch more food. For example, some hunting birds may get more food by stealing prey caught by the other birds. Predators with greater ability are more likely to survive and reproduce. They pass these valuable traits on to their young.

Different types of predators may compete with each other. Lions and hyenas might want the same prey, for example. The lions hunt and kill the prey. Then the hyenas fight the lions and try to steal it.

Animals that are prey also compete. Deer that are stronger or healthier than others are more likely to protect themselves. They are better able to escape from predators.

The lions have killed the prey. But the hyenas are not afraid to compete for as much of this food as they can get.

✔ **Checkpoint**

1. What do living things compete for?
2. **Writing in Science** **Expository** Write a short paragraph in your **science journal** explaining why living things compete.

111

## Other Kinds of Competition

Some living things compete for space. Purple loosestrife is a plant that competes in this way. Years ago, someone brought this plant to the United States. It grew well near rivers. Animals here do not eat loosestrife, so it grew and spread. Now purple loosestrife takes space away from other plants. It is winning the competition for space in many places.

Sometimes animals and humans compete for space. People move to places where animals live. Then they see coyotes in their backyards or sea gulls nesting on their beaches.

Living things may compete for oxygen. Algae are like plants. They provide oxygen and food for fish and other living things. If too many algae grow, some will block the light needed by the others. These other algae die. Many tiny consumers of dead algae grow and use up the oxygen in the water. Fish and frogs must then compete for the oxygen that is left.

## A Competition Cycle

Competition can follow a cycle. For example, lemmings are small mammals that live in the tundra. If there is plenty of grass for them to eat, the population grows quickly. Soon, less food is available because so many lemmings are eating it. After three years, too many lemmings are competing for too little food. Many lemmings leave to find food elsewhere. The population of lemmings is reduced. Then the grass can grow back. The cycle begins again.

Purple loosestrife competes with other plants for space.

Sea gulls compete with humans for living space.

Too much algae can lead to too little oxygen that fish and tadpoles need.

Competition between these lemmings for food can follow a cycle over time.

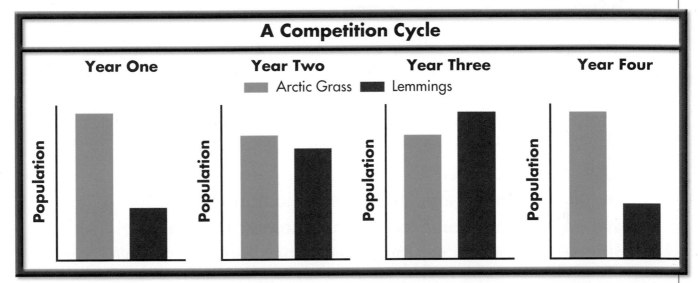

**A Competition Cycle**

| Year One | Year Two | Year Three | Year Four |
|---|---|---|---|

Arctic Grass ■ Lemmings ■

There is plenty of arctic grass for lemmings to eat.

The population of lemmings grows. The amount of grass goes down.

The population of lemmings grows. There is not enough food. Many lemmings leave or die.

With fewer lemmings, the grass grows back. Once again there is enough food.

## ✓ Lesson Checkpoint

1. Why do living things compete with one another?

2. What kind of living thing usually survives in a competition?

3. **Draw Conclusions** Explain the pattern of change in the lemming population over time.

# How do environments change?

*Plants and animals can change their environment. Natural events, such as fire, can change the environment too. These changes affect plants and animals that live in the environment. Changes often occur in patterns.*

## Living Things Cause Change

People often change the environment to better suit their needs, but they are not the only ones. For example, when a beaver builds a dam, many changes occur. Water backs up behind the dam. Then a new wetland habitat grows. Fish, birds, and many other types of animals can now live there.

The dams, however, flood places that were once dry. What do you think happens to the living things that once lived on dry land? Some look for new homes. They might compete for space in nearby places. Others may not survive.

Beavers change the environment when they build their homes and dams of sticks and mud.

This place was once a grassy meadow. How has this beaver dam changed it?

140

## Natural Events Cause Change

Natural events also change environments. For example, hurricanes can change coastlines. They wash away beaches and knock down trees. They can cause terrible floods.

Floods change environments too. They kill plants and wash away birds' nests. Floods spread thick blankets of mud. They also carry rich soil from one place to other places.

Too little water also causes changes. Little rain falls during a drought. Plants die from lack of water. If animals cannot find enough water, then they may die or move to other places.

**The Mississippi River sometimes floods. The floodwater carries rich soil down the river. When floodwater drains off the land, it leaves behind a layer of soil.**

**High winds and water will change this environment.**

**Few plants, animals, or humans can live in a drought area.**

### ✓ Checkpoint

1. Describe ways that living things and natural events can cause an environment to change.

2. **Writing** in Science **Descriptive**
   Write a paragraph or a poem in your **science journal** about one change you have seen in your environment.

## Living Things Return

On May 18, 1980, the volcano Mt. St. Helens erupted in the State of Washington. This eruption was huge. Winds carried clouds of ash around the world.

The blast changed the local environment. It knocked over trees. It burned whole forests. Rivers of mud covered large areas.

There were few signs of life after the eruption. Over time, however, wind carried the seeds of grasses, flowers, and trees to the mountain. New plants began to grow. Soon spiders and beetles arrived. Birds returned to live in the standing dead trees. Each new change allowed more kinds of plants and the animals that depend on them to live there again. Today, even elk live on Mt. St. Helens. The mountain is filled with life once more.

In September 2004, Mt. St. Helens rumbled to life again. An active volcano can bring sudden change at any time.

**Mt. St. Helens erupts.**

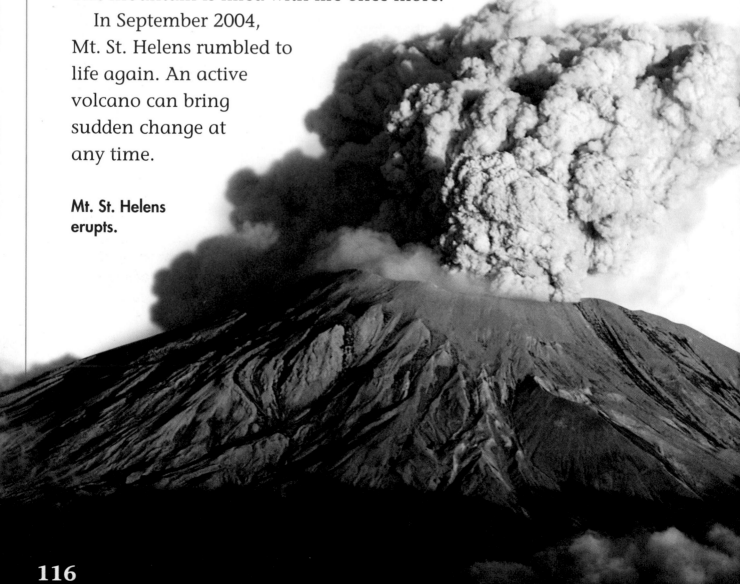

Fires also change environments. Fires happen often in forests and grasslands. Lightning may strike a tree. A burning branch falls to the ground. Then a fire creeps along the forest floor. It removes small plants competing for space to grow. However, the plants that do not burn will have more living space. Also, ash from fires is good for the soil. It helps plants to grow.

Eruptions and fires are examples of events that cause change. The changes often kill plants and destroy animal homes. The changes, however, may improve habitats for other plants and animals.

### ✓ Checkpoint

1. Explain how fire is a change that can improve growing conditions for plants.

2. **Art** in Science Draw a forest before a fire. Then draw the forest on fire. Finally, draw the forest five years later.

Ground fires kill plants but help new plants grow.

This young pine grows fast in an area cleaned by fire.

Very few plants remained after the volcano erupted.

New life has returned to the mountain.

This burnt stump gives a spruce seedling a place to grow.

117

Many years will go by before these Douglas fir seedlings become full-grown trees.

Smaller trees compete for sunlight because they are shaded by tall trees.

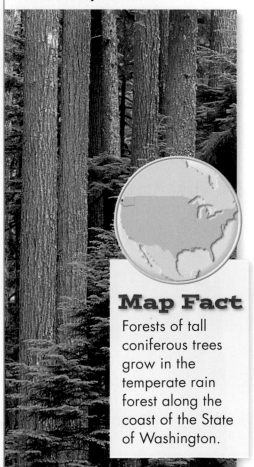

## Map Fact

Forests of tall coniferous trees grow in the temperate rain forest along the coast of the State of Washington.

## Patterns of Change

Living things change together. These changes often happen in patterns. Let's look at one growth pattern. It takes place in a cool, misty forest in the northwestern United States. Douglas firs and western hemlocks are two kinds of trees that live there. Their life cycles are connected.

Douglas fir trees have cones which are often knocked off by squirrels. Seeds from the cones sprout on the forest floor where they compete for sunlight and other resources. A few survive and grow into giant trees. Some of these giants grow old, die, and fall.

Mushrooms and other decomposers feed on the dead trees. A **decomposer** is a living thing that breaks down waste and living things that have died. This action is called **decay.** Decay returns certain materials to the soil. The trees had taken these materials from the soil in order to grow. Decomposers cause the dead tree to slowly crumble into the soil.

Western hemlock trees live in the same forest. Seeds from their cones land on the decaying Douglas fir logs. The decaying nurse logs supply things that help young seedlings to grow. Also, light reaches logs in the open where the giant trees once stood. The hemlock seeds sprout and grow quickly.

In time, the hemlocks become tall trees. They provide homes for squirrels, spotted owls, and many other animals. When the trees come to the end of their lives, carpenter ants and other organisms go to work. They build nests in the decaying tree trunks. After some years, these trunks fall to the ground. Soon they decay and become part of the soil.

This example shows the life cycle of two trees. Their life cycles are connected. In fact, the life cycles of many living things are connected.

These mushrooms are decomposers. They find this dead log a good food source.

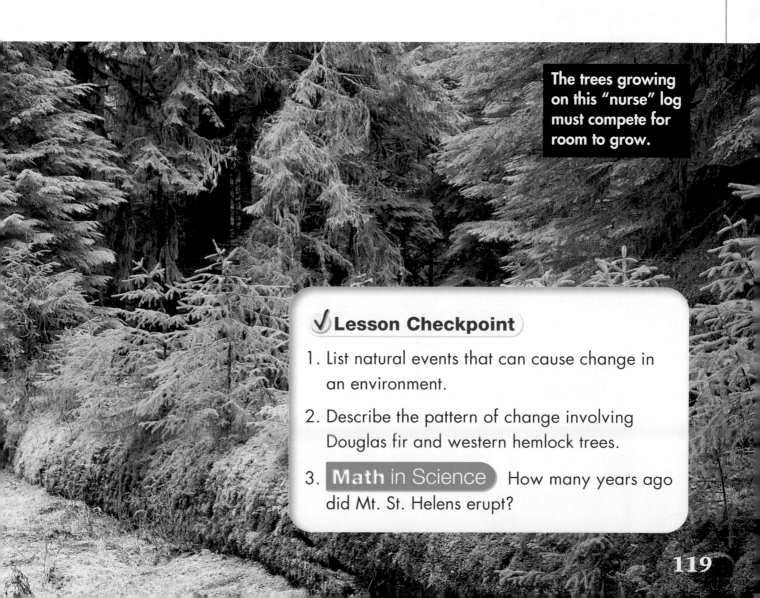

The trees growing on this "nurse" log must compete for room to grow.

**✓ Lesson Checkpoint**

1. List natural events that can cause change in an environment.

2. Describe the pattern of change involving Douglas fir and western hemlock trees.

3. **Math in Science** How many years ago did Mt. St. Helens erupt?

119

# What is a healthy environment for people?

*People find what they need for life in their environment. The environment affects how people live.*

## What People Need

Like all living things, people need food to live. Most people buy food at a store. That food comes from farms and ranches. Some people have the job of making sure the food we eat is safe.

People need water that is safe to drink and air that is safe to breathe. People also need shelter to protect them from the weather. Shelter helps keep people at a comfortable temperature.

People need a clean environment. Wastes must be removed. Garbage may be taken to places such as landfills.

**The water from this fountain was purified, or made clean, at a water treatment plant.**

### ✓ Checkpoint

1. Name three things people need to survive.

2. **Writing** in Science **Persuasive**
   Write a paragraph in your **science journal** explaining why we should protect the environment.

# Basic Needs of People

## Food

The food you eat may come from close by. It may be grown thousands of miles away. Fresh food is shipped on airplanes, boats, and trucks. Other foods may be canned or frozen before being shipped.

## Water

In some countries, people get their water from streams. In the United States, most water comes from wells or from special lakes. These special lakes are called reservoirs.

## Shelter

Shelter changes according to where someone lives. In hot places, people need cool living spaces. In cold places, they need warm ones. In cities, people often live in large buildings.

## Air

Fewer people live outside the cities. In these open spaces there are fewer cars and factories. As a result, the air is often cleaner.

## Clean Environment

Everyone should help protect the environment. The environment affects the health of the people living in it.

## Healthful Foods

To be sure you are getting all the vitamins, minerals, and other nutrients your body needs, you must eat a variety of healthful foods. This variety includes whole grains, fruits, and vegetables, as well as nuts, fish, eggs, dairy foods, and meats. Your body also needs a good amount of water each day.

To be kept healthful, food should be stored carefully. Fresh fruits and vegetables should be washed and kept in a cool place. Fish, eggs, dairy foods, and meats must be wrapped and kept cold. Using food while it is still fresh is also important.

Cooks and others who handle food must have clean hands and clean tools. Their tools include knives and cutting boards as well as mixers, bowls, spoons, and forks.

Drinking juice is a healthful choice.

Dairy products help bones grow strong.

Vegetables such as carrots and broccoli make good snacks.

Eat fruit, such as grapes, every day.

Fish contain materials your body needs to grow.

## From Food to Energy

What happens to food after you eat it? The body's digestive system goes to work. It breaks foods down into a form that our bodies can use to live and grow. These are the main parts of the digestive system.

**Food goes down a long tube to reach your stomach. Your intestines also are tubes, all curled up. The small intestine is longer, but narrower, than the large intestine.**

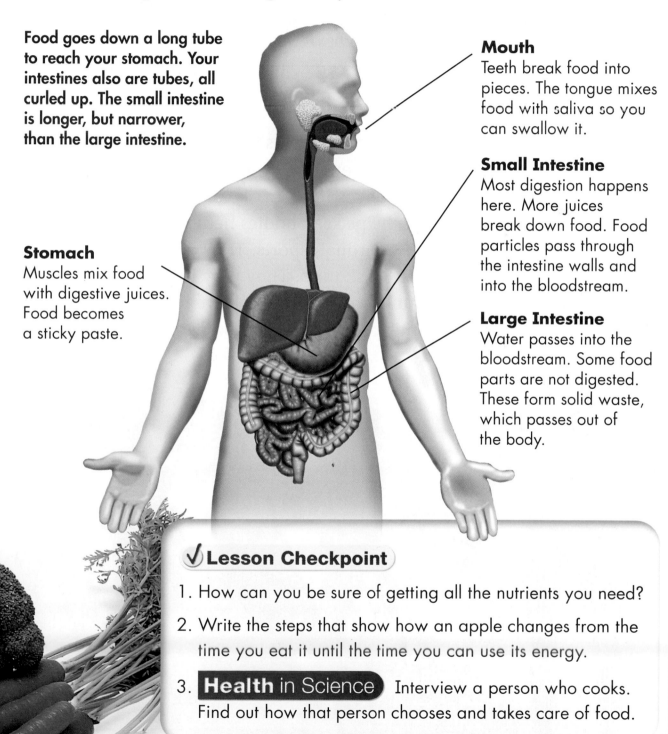

**Mouth**
Teeth break food into pieces. The tongue mixes food with saliva so you can swallow it.

**Small Intestine**
Most digestion happens here. More juices break down food. Food particles pass through the intestine walls and into the bloodstream.

**Stomach**
Muscles mix food with digestive juices. Food becomes a sticky paste.

**Large Intestine**
Water passes into the bloodstream. Some food parts are not digested. These form solid waste, which passes out of the body.

### ✓ Lesson Checkpoint

1. How can you be sure of getting all the nutrients you need?

2. Write the steps that show how an apple changes from the time you eat it until the time you can use its energy.

3. **Health** in Science  Interview a person who cooks. Find out how that person chooses and takes care of food.

# How can people stay healthy?

*People want to be as healthy as possible. There are many things they can do to help keep their bodies healthy.*

## Exercise

Safe, regular exercise is important. People in good shape have the energy to work, play, and feel good about themselves.

Exercise helps keep bodies healthy. Some people get exercise through sports. They go biking, swimming, or skating. They play basketball or soccer. But exercise does not have to be a sport. House and yardwork can be exercise too.

**When you rest, your heart beats about ninety times per minute. It beats faster when you exercise.**

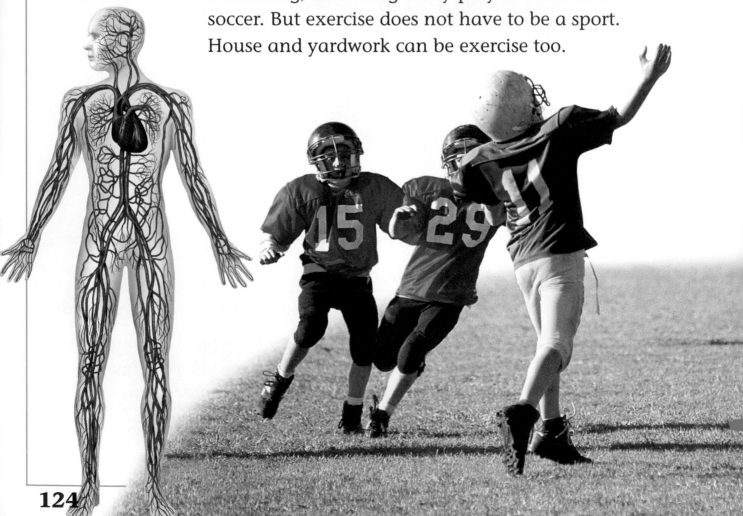

Exercise keeps a person's lungs, heart, and muscles strong. These are parts of your body systems. For example, your lungs are part of your respiratory system. They put oxygen from the air you breathe into your blood. Your heart and blood vessels are part of your circulatory system. The heart pumps blood through blood vessels. Blood carries oxygen and other materials to your muscles. Blood also carries wastes away from your muscles. Exercise helps your systems work together well so you stay in good shape.

People who feel good about themselves take care of their bodies. They eat a variety of good foods. They get enough exercise and rest. They avoid things that are unhealthy.

**When you breathe in, air goes down a long tube called the windpipe. The windpipe divides into two tubes. Each tube leads to a spongy lung.**

**The proper equipment keeps these young football players safe.**

**✓ Checkpoint**

1. Why is exercise important for your body?

2. **Writing in Science**  **Persuasive**
   Write a speech persuading your class to eat healthy foods and exercise more.

## Avoiding Germs

Lin is sneezing. Shauna is coughing. Aidan has a runny nose and teary eyes. Several of their classmates are at home, sick with the flu. What are causing these illnesses? Germs.

**Germs** are very small living things or particles. Examples include bacteria and viruses. Many germs can make people ill. The pictures show germs that can cause disease. A **disease** is a condition in which the body or a part of the body does not work properly. You may have had one or more diseases such as the flu, chicken pox, or strep throat.

There are many other diseases that you have probably not had. These include measles, mumps, and whooping cough. Years ago, many people caught these illnesses. They were very dangerous. Today, children are protected from these diseases. They get this protection before they start school.

Most illnesses that people get are not dangerous. Still, no one likes to be sick. Everyone can help to stop the spread of germs.

This picture shows the virus that causes the flu. This picture was taken through a special, very powerful microscope.

Microscopes are used to observe things that are very small.

**The germs shown below cause whooping cough.**

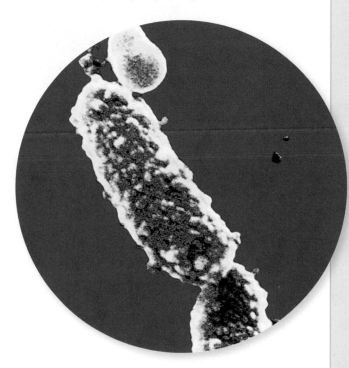

# Stopping the Spread of Germs

People can help stop the spread of germs by remembering some simple rules.

- Stay home from school and work when you are ill.
- Wash your hands often, especially after using the restroom and before and after working with food.
- Cover your nose and mouth when you sneeze or cough. Wash your hands if you sneeze or cough into them.
- Clean and cover cuts and scrapes.

Wash your hands often with soap and warm water so that you don't spread germs.

**The germs that cause strep throat look like tiny beads.**

## ✓ Lesson Checkpoint

1. How do your respiratory and circulatory systems work together?

2. Make a list of things you can do to stop the spread of germs.

3. **Technology** in Science
   Choose an illness to research. Find out its causes and possible cure. Use the Internet or other technology to help in your research.

127

# Lab zone Guided Inquiry

## Investigate What can happen in a place without predators?

Without predators, a population of prey can starve. In this activity, your teacher will pick some students to be deer. All live in a place without predators. The deer pretend to eat the same kind of food (unpopped popcorn).

### Materials

unpopped popcorn

### What to Do

**1** If you are picked to be a deer, line up on the side of the marked area. This is where you find food.

**2** **Round A** When told, cross the area one deer at a time. Collect 5 pieces of food (unpopped popcorn) to "stay alive." Do not take more than 5 pieces.

| Round | Number of Deer Alive at End of Round |
|---|---|
| Round A | |
| Round B | |
| Round C | |
| Round D | |
| Round E | |

The number of rounds will depend on the number of deer and the amount of food supplied.

Record how many deer are alive at the end of each round. After each round your teacher will add food.

**3** If you survive, you reproduce. Pick another student to join for the next round.

**4** **Round B** Cross again and collect 5 more pieces of food.

### Process Skills

You can use the **data** you **collect** during an investigation to help make an **inference**.

Deer line up here.

area where deer find food

5 Repeat until "starvation" begins. Make a bar graph to show the **data** you **collected**.

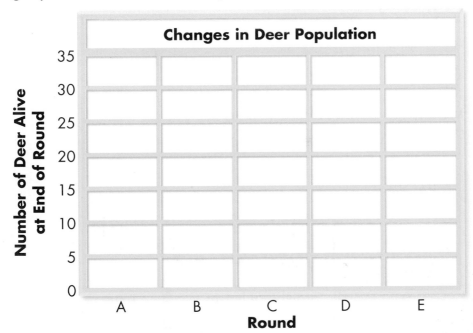

**Changes in Deer Population**

Number of Deer Alive at End of Round

35
30
25
20
15
10
5
0

A    B    C    D    E

**Round**

## Explain Your Results

1. While there was plenty of food, how did the number of deer change? What finally happened?

2. **Infer** What can happen in a place without predators?

## Go Further

What might happen if predators were added? Make a plan to answer this or a question of your own.

# Health
## By the Numbers

You have learned how important it is to choose the right foods for good health. It is also important to know how many calories you need and how many are in the foods you eat.

**Smiley Flakes**
Serving Size 1 cup (30 grams)
Calories: 110
Total Fat: 2 grams
Cholesterol: 0 grams
Sodium: 210 milligrams
Carbohydrates: 23 grams
Fiber: 1 gram
Sugar: 1 gram

**Mega Grain**
Serving Size 1 cup (30 grams)
Calories: 165
Total Fat: 1 gram
Cholesterol: 0 grams
Sodium: 0 milligrams
Carbohydrates: 39 grams
Fiber: 3 grams
Sugar: 0 grams

| Fresh Fruit or Fruit Juice | Serving Size | Calories |
|---|---|---|
| Banana slices | 1 cup | 133 |
| Strawberry halves | 1 cup | 49 |
| Peach slices | 1 cup | 66 |
| Orange juice | 1 cup | 112 |

| Milk Products | Serving Size | Calories |
|---|---|---|
| Whole milk | 1 cup | 146 |
| Reduced-fat milk (2%) | 1 cup | 122 |
| Low-fat milk (1%) | 1 cup | 102 |
| Fat-free milk (Skim) | 1 cup | 83 |

eTools Take It to the Net
sfsuccessnet.com

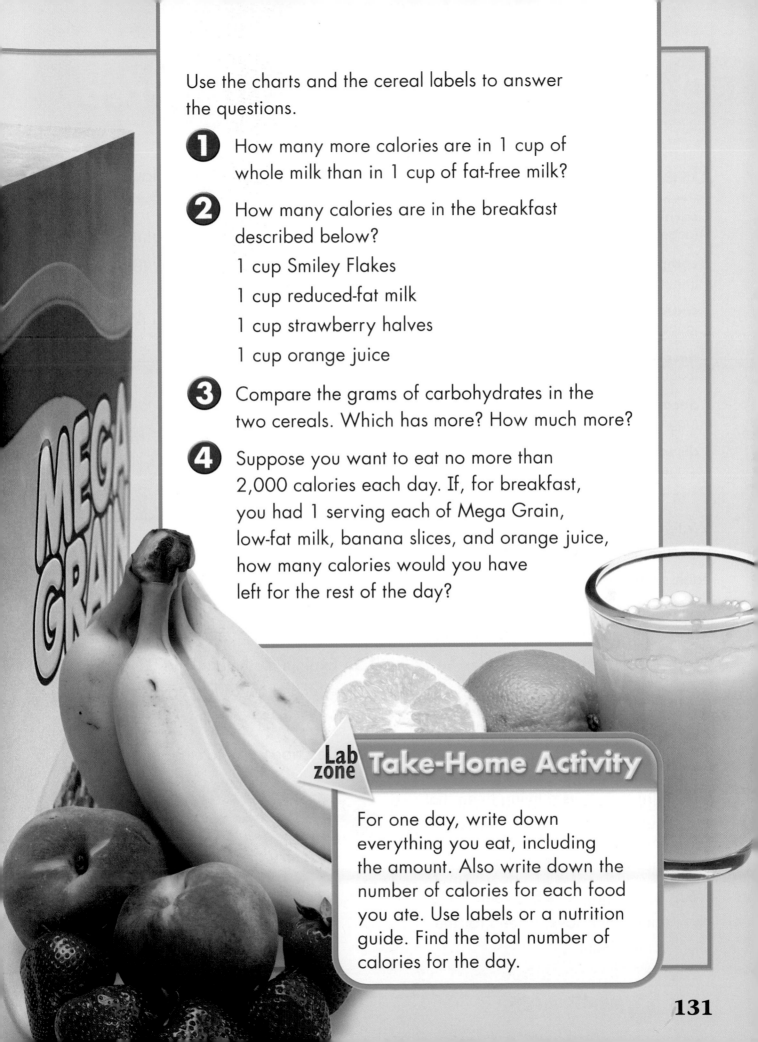

Use the charts and the cereal labels to answer the questions.

**1** How many more calories are in 1 cup of whole milk than in 1 cup of fat-free milk?

**2** How many calories are in the breakfast described below?
1 cup Smiley Flakes
1 cup reduced-fat milk
1 cup strawberry halves
1 cup orange juice

**3** Compare the grams of carbohydrates in the two cereals. Which has more? How much more?

**4** Suppose you want to eat no more than 2,000 calories each day. If, for breakfast, you had 1 serving each of Mega Grain, low-fat milk, banana slices, and orange juice, how many calories would you have left for the rest of the day?

**Lab zone** Take-Home Activity

For one day, write down everything you eat, including the amount. Also write down the number of calories for each food you ate. Use labels or a nutrition guide. Find the total number of calories for the day.

131

# Chapter 4 Review and Test Prep

## Use Vocabulary

| | |
|---|---|
| **carnivore** (page 106) | **germs** (page 126) |
| **competition** (page 110) | **herbivore** (page 106) |
| **consumer** (page 106) | **omnivore** (page 106) |
| **decomposer** (page 118) | **predator** (page 107) |
| **decay** (page 118) | **prey** (page 107) |
| **disease** (page 126) | **producer** (page 106) |

Write the vocabulary word or words from the list above that best completes each sentence.

1. A(n) _____ eats only animals while a(n) _____ eats only plants.

2. Bacteria and viruses are _____, which can cause _____.

3. A(n) _____ is a consumer that hunts another for food.

4. A(n) _____ is a living thing that must eat food to get energy,

5. A(n) _____ makes its own food.

6. _____ happens between living things that have a need for the same resources.

7. A(n) _____ eats both plants and animals.

8. _____ happens when a(n) _____ breaks down a living thing that has died.

9. _____ is an animal that is hunted by others.

## Explain Concepts

10. Trace the flow of energy from beginning to end in the following food chain: a ferret eats prairie dogs which eat grasses and other plants.

11. Explain why some plants that are put into a new area can become dangerous weeds.

12. Explain the helpful and harmful effects ground fires have on plants in a forest community.

13. Describe ways to stay healthy.

### Process Skills

14. **Classify** the following living things as producers or consumers: prairie dog, whale, purple loosestrife, barnacle, Douglas fir.

MindPoint Quiz Show

**15. Predict** The lemming population keeps growing. There are just enough resources. Predict what might happen to the lemmings if their population grows more.

**16. Interpret Data** You collect data in a field next to a stream. You trap and count 16 field mice and 10 rabbits. A beaver dam floods the field. You trap and count 7 field mice and 4 rabbits. Interpret this data.

 **Draw Conclusions**

**17.** Make a graphic organizer like this one. Fill it in with three facts about whales and whale barnacles from the chapter. Then write a conclusion based on those facts.

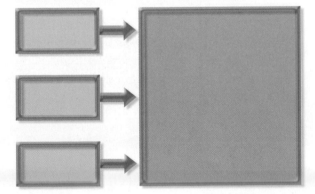

**Facts**          **Conclusion**

## Test Prep

Choose the letter that best answers the question.

**18.** Which living thing helps the second living thing in the pair to survive?

   Ⓐ barnacle–crayfish
   Ⓑ yucca moth–whale
   Ⓒ Douglas fir tree–western hemlock tree
   Ⓓ raccoon–cattail

**19.** Which of the following is true?

   Ⓐ Your lungs are a part of your circulatory system.
   Ⓑ Exercise maintains health.
   Ⓒ Washing your hands after coughing into them spreads germs.
   Ⓓ Nutrients pass through the walls of the intestine into the stomach.

**20.** **Writing** in Science

**Expository** Write a short paragraph describing how yucca moths and the yucca plant interact.

# Moon Trees

Astronaut Stuart Roosa took seeds with him into space.

Did you know there might be Moon trees growing where you live? You may be asking yourself, "What do Moon trees look like? Did they come from the Moon? Where are they growing on Earth?"

Well, Moon trees did not come from the Moon. They are trees grown from seeds that traveled to the Moon and back on the Apollo 14 mission in 1971.

Astronaut Stuart Roosa took the seeds into space. Astronaut Roosa worked for the U.S. Forest Service fighting forest fires before he joined NASA. He loved forests and wanted to protect them. He took seeds of pine, sycamore, redwood, Douglas fir, and sweet gum into space to honor the U.S. Forest Service.

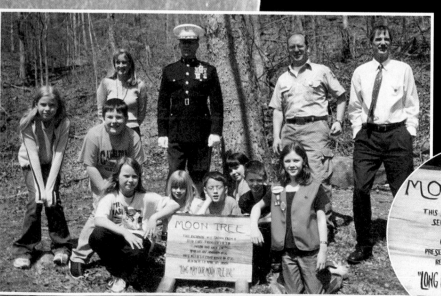

A third-grade class in Indiana made this sign for their Moon tree. Astronaut Roosa's son, Col. Christopher Roosa, visited the tree with the students and their teacher.

MOON TREE
THIS SYCAMORE WAS GROWN FROM A SEED THAT TRAVELED TO THE MOON AND BACK ON APOLLO XIV JANUARY 1971. PRESENTED TO CAMP KOCH IN 1975 REDEDICATED APRIL 10, 2003
"LONG MAY OUR MOON TREE LIVE"

The Moon trees grew until they were big enough to plant outside. People all over the world began to learn about the Moon trees. They wanted one of their own. In 1975 and 1976, the little trees were sent to places around the world. Most Moon trees were sent to schools, parks, and public buildings.

Today you can find a Moon tree growing near the Liberty Bell in Philadelphia. Another grows at the White House. Let NASA know if you find that a Moon tree is growing where you live.

You can see this Moon tree at the NASA Goddard Space Flight Center in Maryland.

## Lab zone Take-Home Activity

Space travel might have had what effect on the Moon tree seeds and the way they would grow? Write a paragraph.

# Park Ranger

**Do you like being outdoors? Would you like to work outside with plants and animals? If so, then this career might be for you.**

If you visit a national park, you will probably see park rangers. Park rangers have many tasks. They help visitors decide what to see and do during a visit. They plan programs, give talks, and lead hikes. They know about the plants, animals, and history of the park.

Park rangers also help take care of visitors. Rangers keep these visitors safe. They show them where to go in the park. They help visitors who are lost or hurt. They make sure that park rules are followed.

Sometimes fires start in parks. These might be caused by visitors or by lightning. Rangers help put out fires.

Most park rangers go to college. They may start working as rangers during the summer. They later take full-time jobs.

## Lab zone Take-Home Activity

Locate the National Park Service site nearest to where you live. Find out and describe what the rangers there do.

# Unit A Test Talk

## Find Important Words

Finding important words and their meanings in a passage can help you answer test questions.
You can underline the important words as you read the passage. Some important words are underlined in the passage below.

> All animals grow and change as they go through their life cycle. The first stage of an animal's life cycle is an egg. In mammals, eggs grow and develop inside the mother and the young are born. In other kinds of animals, such as birds and insects, the mother lays eggs outside of her body. The young develop in the eggs and then they hatch.
>
> Some animals that hatch look like their parents. Baby chicks look like chickens. When a butterfly egg hatches, it is a caterpillar or <u>larva</u>. Larvae don't look like their parents. The larva develops and becomes a <u>pupa</u>. The pupa spins a covering over itself. Inside the covering, the pupa grows into a butterfly, just like its parent.

## Use What You Know

To help you answer the questions, find the important words in the passage. As you read each question, decide which word choice is being described.

1. What is the first stage of an animal's life cycle?
   - Ⓐ pupa
   - Ⓑ larva
   - Ⓒ adult
   - Ⓓ egg

2. In which kind of animal do eggs grow and develop inside the mother until the young are born?
   - Ⓕ insects
   - Ⓖ mammals
   - Ⓗ birds
   - Ⓘ fish

3. What is the stage of a butterfly between a caterpillar and an adult?
   - Ⓐ larva
   - Ⓑ pupa
   - Ⓒ egg
   - Ⓓ seed

# Unit A Wrap-Up

## Chapter 1

### How do the different parts of a plant help it live and grow?

- Most plants have roots, stems, leaves, and flowers. Each kind of part helps the plant grow, make food, or make seeds.

- Some kinds of plants have flowers. Other kinds have cones.

## Chapter 2

### How do different animals live, grow, and change?

- All animals begin as eggs. The eggs of some animals develop inside the mother while other animals lay eggs that hatch outside the mother.

- Some young animals look like their parents. Other young animals must go through different stages of development before they look like their parents.

## Chapter 3

### How are ecosystems different from each other?

- Environmental conditions determine the major types of ecosystems.

- Grasslands, deserts, tundras, and forests are land ecosystems. Water ecosystems include fresh water, salt water, or both.

# Chapter 4

## How do plants and animals interact?

- Animals interact by living in groups and sharing jobs. Some animals benefit by living with other kinds of animals. Animals often compete for the things they need to survive.

- Plants and animals belong to food chains. In a food chain plants produce their own food, some animals eat the plants for food, and other animals get food by eating animals.

# Performance Assessment

## Group Materials for Making Food

Plant leaves make food for the plant. The cards show the materials that are used to make food and the materials that are made. Place all the materials that a leaf uses to make food to the left of the leaf card. Place all the materials that the leaf makes to the right of the leaf card. What do plant leaves use to make food? What do plant leaves make?

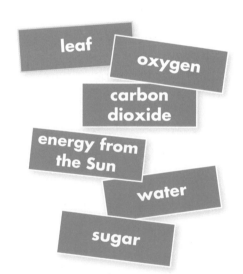

# Read More About Life Science!

Look for books like these in the library.

# Full Inquiry

## Experiment How can a garden spider move across its web?

A garden spider weaves a web with some threads that are sticky. Prey stick to these threads. Other threads are not sticky. The spider can walk on both types and not get stuck. In this **experiment**, you make a model to find out how a garden spider reaches its prey without getting stuck in its own web.

### Materials

Spider Web Pattern

regular tape

double-stick tape

eraser

toothbrush

Process Skills

Every experiment must have a **hypothesis**, a testable statement.

### Ask a question.

A garden spider has stiff hairs on the ends of its legs. Do these hairs help the spider move across its web?

### State a hypothesis.

If a spider has stiff hairs on its legs, then will getting stuck in its web be more likely or less likely than if it did not have these hairs, or do these hairs have no effect? Write your **hypothesis**. You will use a **model** to help test your hypothesis.

### Identify and control variables.

In the model used in this experiment, the **variable** that you change is the structure of a spider's "leg" (hairs or no hairs). The variable you **observe** is whether or not the "spider" gets stuck. The structure of the "web" is a variable you keep the same.

## Test your hypothesis.

**1** Make a model of $\frac{1}{4}$ of the web of a garden spider. Use the Spider Web Pattern.

**2** First put down double-stick tape where shown. The double-stick tape is a model of the sticky threads of a spider's web.

**3** Next put down regular tape. The regular tape is a model of the non-sticky threads of a spider's web.

**4** Put an eraser on one of the sticky outer pieces of tape. The eraser is a model of a spider's prey.

**5** Start your "spider" at the center point of the web. Tap the side of the toothbrush without the brush along one of the non-sticky pieces of tape. Move from the center toward the prey. Record what happens.

**6** When you reach the outer ring, tap across the sticky tape. Record what happens.

The eraser is the spider's "prey."

The toothbrush acts like a spider's leg. The side with the brush is a model of the spider's leg with stiff hairs. The side without the brush is a model of what a spider's leg would be like if the leg did not have stiff hairs.

**7** Repeat steps 4 and 5, but this time use the side of the toothbrush with the brush.

## Collect and record your data.

| Model | Observations | |
|---|---|---|
| | **Moving Across Non-Sticky "Thread"** (regular tape) | **Moving Across Sticky "Thread"** (double-stick tape) |
| **Without stiff hairs** (side of toothbrush without brush) | | |
| **With stiff hairs** (side of toothbrush with brush) | | |

Think of a way to use a diagram or a sketch of your model to show your observations. If your teacher wishes, explain your results orally or in writing.

## Interpret your data.

What on the leg of a garden spider helps it easily reach its prey? How do you know?

## State your conclusion.

Explain why a garden spider does not get stuck in its web. Compare your hypothesis with your results. **Communicate** your conclusion.

Tell how a model can help you make and test predictions. What did you learn from the model in this experiment?

### Go Further

Butterfly wings are powdery. How does the powder help a butterfly escape from the sticky threads in a spider web? Design and carry out a plan for an experiment to answer this or other questions you have.

143

### Using Scientific Methods

1. Ask a question.
2. State a hypothesis.
3. Identify/control variables.
4. Test your hypothesis.
5. Collect and record your data.
6. Interpret your data.
7. State your conclusion.
8. Go further.

## Germinating Seeds

Seeds need the right conditions to germinate and grow.

**Idea:** Use plastic cups, potting soil, and bean seeds to find out how well seeds germinate and grow with different amounts of water.

## Growing Mealworms

When mealworm eggs hatch, they look nothing like their parents.

**Idea:** Use mealworms and a habitat to observe and record the different stages in their life cycle.

## Selecting a Habitat

Different plants and animals need different habitats to survive.

**Idea:** Select a plant or an animal and make a habitat in which it can survive.

## A Food Chain Model

Living things are connected by their need for food.

**Idea:** Choose a food chain and use paper chains with names or pictures to show the connections among the living things.

# Unit B

# Earth Science
## in Indiana

Did you know that a sand dune can move?
Every year, Mount Baldy moves a little more than
1 meter. Mount Baldy is a tall sand dune that is
part of the Indiana Dunes National Lakeshore.
As it moves, it covers the forest in its path.

# Earth Science in Indiana

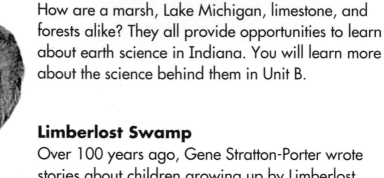

How are a marsh, Lake Michigan, limestone, and forests alike? They all provide opportunities to learn about earth science in Indiana. You will learn more about the science behind them in Unit B.

## Limberlost Swamp

Over 100 years ago, Gene Stratton-Porter wrote stories about children growing up by Limberlost Swamp near Geneva. In 1913, the swamp was drained so it could be used for farming. In 1997, part of the swamp was restored. The restored area is known as Loblolly Marsh. It is now home for many wetland plants and animals. You will learn more about wetlands in Chapter 5.

## The Lake Effect

During winter, cold air moves south over the warmer waters of Lake Michigan and gains moisture. This moist air can produce heavy snowfall over northern Indiana. Areas close to Lake Michigan get more snow than other areas in Indiana. You will learn more about weather in Chapter 6.

| Average Monthly Snowfall (in centimeters) | | | |
|---|---|---|---|
| **Month** | **Gary** | **Indianapolis** | **Evansville** |
| December | 23 cm | 13 cm | 5 cm |
| January | 20 cm | 15 cm | 10 cm |
| February | 15 cm | 15 cm | 10 cm |
| March | 18 cm | 8 cm | 8 cm |

## Limestone

Lawrence County is known as the "Limestone Capital of the World." Limestone is found throughout southern Indiana. It is used as a building material. It is very strong and long-lasting. Limestone formed from seashells and fossils of plants and animals that lived long ago. You will learn more about rocks in Chapter 7.

## Indiana Forests

Trees are a natural resource. Indiana's settlers cleared many forests to make way for farms. The area that is now Morgan-Monroe State Forest was cleared, but the rocky soil was not good for farming. The Division of Forestry has worked to reforest land in Indiana. Morgan-Monroe State Forest now covers a large area. You will learn more about natural resources in Chapter 9.

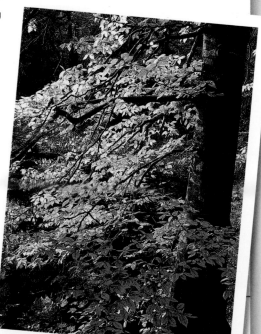

Answer the questions below. Write your answers on a separate sheet of paper.

**Multiple-Choice Questions**

1. What is the name of the restored wetlands area near Geneva?
   Ⓐ Lake Michigan
   Ⓑ Limberlost Swamp
   Ⓒ Loblolly Marsh
   Ⓓ Morgan-Monroe State Forest

2. What is limestone NOT made from?
   Ⓐ seashells
   Ⓑ rocky soil
   Ⓒ animal fossils
   Ⓓ plant fossils

3. On average, how much more snow falls in Gary than in Evansville during December?
   Ⓐ 28 centimeters
   Ⓑ 23 centimeters
   Ⓒ 18 centimeters
   Ⓓ 10 centimeters

**Constructed-Response Questions**

4. What is one reason that people in Indiana drained swamps and cut down trees?

5. Which body of water causes more snow to fall in northern Indiana than in many other areas in Indiana?

# Field Trip
## Indiana Dunes National Lakeshore

Visit Indiana Dunes National Lakeshore along Lake Michigan. Lake Michigan formed thousands of years ago when a large glacier began melting. Over time, the water level in the lake rose and fell. Different shorelines formed at different times. Forested dunes and prairies are part of older shorelines. Beaches and sand dunes are part of newer shorelines. The shoreline at Indiana Dunes National Lakeshore is still changing today.

## Find out more:

Research to find out more about Indiana Dunes National Lakeshore. Draw a diagram or make a model of the different landforms in the national lakeshore. Then answer these questions:

- What is the name of an animal that lives in the national lakeshore? Tell why the habitat there is a good home for this animal.
- What can harm the dunes? Make a poster to tell about something people can do to take care of the dunes.

EC IN 109876543

# Chapter 5
# Water

online
**Student Edition**
sfsuccessnet.com

# How does water change form?

wetland

water cycle

water vapor

groundwater

evaporation

146

## Chapter 5 Vocabulary

precipitation

condensation

## Explore Where is Earth's water?

What if all of Earth's water would fit in a bottle?

### Materials

2 L plastic bottle filled with water

4 cups

dropper
and masking tape

funnel and
graduated cylinder
(or measuring cup)

### What to Do

**1** Label the 4 cups.

| Earth's Water | Amount of Water (total = 2200 mL) |
|---|---|
| Atmosphere (fresh water) | about $\frac{1}{2}$ drop |
| Lakes, rivers, streams (fresh water) | about 4 drops |
| Groundwater (fresh water) | 13 mL |
| Icecaps and glaciers (fresh water) | 47 mL |
| Oceans and seas (salt water) | 2139 mL |

**2** Look at the chart. Find the amount of water shown for the atmosphere. Take out that amount of water from the bottle. Put it in the atmosphere cup.

Hold the bottle with both hands.

**3** Repeat for the other places water is found. Use the graduated cylinder when needed.

**4** Label the bottle *oceans and seas*.

### Explain Your Results

**Infer** Why should people use fresh water wisely?

# How to Read Science

 **Cause and Effect**

A **cause** makes something happen. An **effect** is what happens. Science writers often use clue words and phrases such as *because, so, since,* and *as a result* to signal cause and effect. The following example will help you **infer** why people should use fresh water wisely.

**Science Article**

### Clean Streams

Factories make things for people. They often use water that gets dirty. Dumping this water into streams can harm wildlife and our water supply. As a result, the government makes laws to reduce the harm done. These laws help keep our environment clean.

## Apply It!

Make a graphic organizer like the one shown. Then use it to list three causes and an effect from the science article.

149

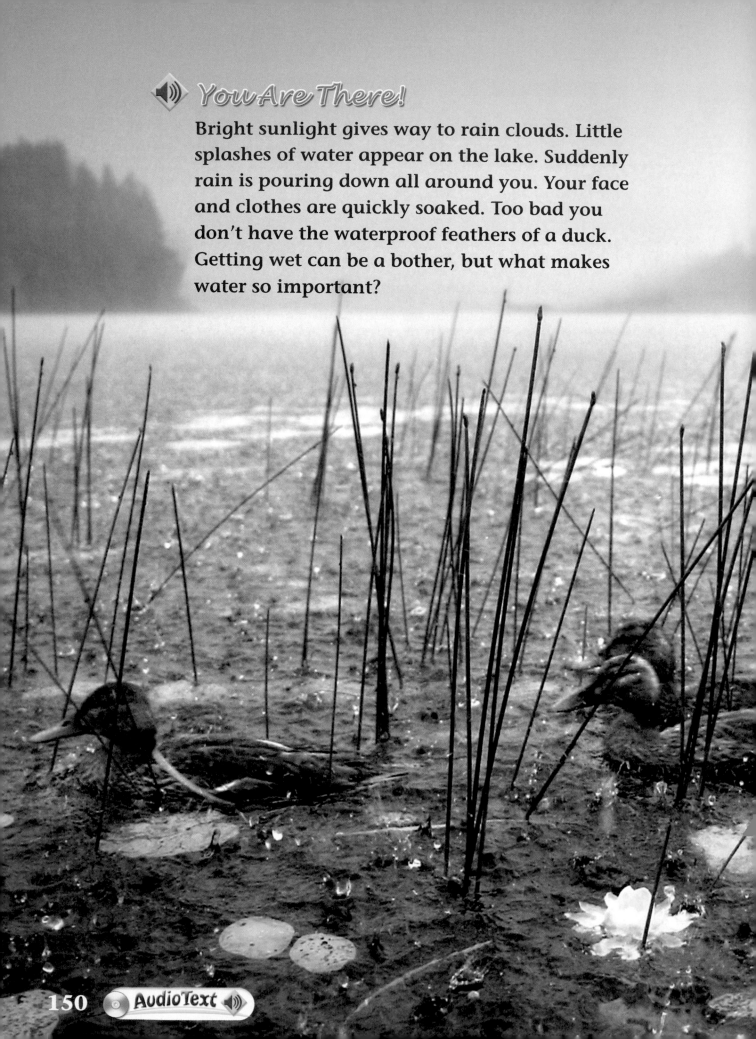

Bright sunlight gives way to rain clouds. Little splashes of water appear on the lake. Suddenly rain is pouring down all around you. Your face and clothes are quickly soaked. Too bad you don't have the waterproof feathers of a duck. Getting wet can be a bother, but what makes water so important?

## Lesson 1

# Why is water important?

*You could go without sweets or TV if you had to. But you can't give up water. You could not live more than a few days without it.*

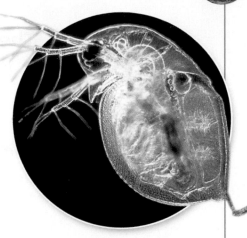

Daphnia are very tiny. This picture was taken through a microscope.

## Living Things and Water

Living things from big trees to small snails need water to survive and grow. Green plants need water to make food. Fish and other animals need oxygen in water to breathe.

Water makes up about two-thirds of your body. Water is busy helping every part of your body. For example, water helps digest food into small particles. Water in your blood carries materials to every part of your body. Water also carries wastes away from every part.

Water helps keep your body at the correct temperature. What if the air temperature turns cold? Water in your body tends to hold onto its heat, keeping you warm. If your body heats up, you might sweat. The water in sweat carries heat away from your body.

Some organisms must spend their whole lives in water. Many of these creatures are very small. Daphnia, for example, are less than 1.5 mm long. Daphnia live mostly in ponds and lakes.

1. **✓Checkpoint** How does water help you live?
2. **Health in Science** Why is it important to drink water, especially after you exercise?

## The Uses of Water

People use water in many ways. Lakes, rivers, and oceans supply us with fish and shellfish. Farmers use water to help make crops grow. Some of this water falls from the sky. But some flows through pipes to fields.

People use the power of moving water to make electricity. They build dams and power stations across rivers. Rushing water turns giant wheels inside turbines. Turbines help make electricity. This electricity can travel long distances through wires.

We also use water for transportation and enjoyment. Large ships carry goods from one place to another. Some people row on ponds or sail across oceans. Others go tubing, or swimming, or canoeing. People can have fun in the water.

Most plants take in water through their roots to grow.

1. ✓ **Checkpoint** List three ways that people use water.

2. **Cause and Effect** What would happen if we did not protect our supply of fresh water?

152

## Use of Water

### Drinking

People need to drink water. All animals need water too. This impala slurps up a drink. The tiny bird on its horn will have some too.

### Food

Water provides food. People get animals from the sea. Some fish live near the bottom of the sea. Others can be seen from boats. Boats bring back seaweed as well as fish. Seaweed is food for people and animals.

### Crops and Farms

In many parts of the world, farmers irrigate land. They bring water to it. The water lets farmers grow crops in many places where no crops grew before. One third of water used in the U.S. is for irrigation.

### Industry

Factories use water in many different ways. Water is used to clean foods and the insides of buildings. It is used to make paper and steel. Most of the water used in manufacturing is later put back into rivers and streams.

### Electricity

Water is used to make electricity. Moving water or steam can turn large turbines. Turbines are special engines that help make power. Electric power can be used for light, heat, and to run machines.

153

## The Planet of Water

You could call Earth "the blue planet." That's because three fourths, or 75 percent, of Earth's surface is covered with water.

Most of Earth's water is salty ocean water. Some of the salt in ocean water comes from rock on the ocean floor. Other salt is washed off the land into the oceans. The salt mixes with the water. You can't drink, wash clothes, or water plants with ocean water. Nor can you use this water to make products in factories.

Water is found in many different places. Some water moves downward into the ground. Some is frozen into ice. A small amount of water is found in the air as an invisible gas called **water vapor.** The water vapor rises from oceans and lakes and becomes part of the air. Some water vapor changes and becomes visible clouds.

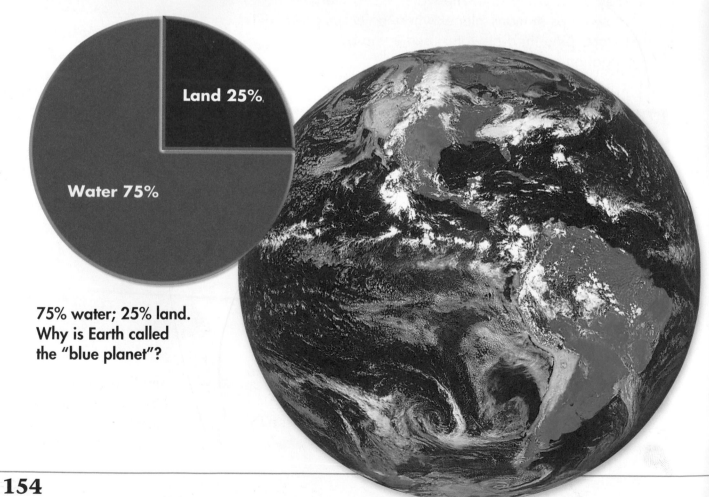

Land 25%

Water 75%

75% water; 25% land. Why is Earth called the "blue planet"?

## Fresh Water

Fresh water has little salt in it. We need to drink fresh water. Only a very small amount of the water on Earth is fresh water. And most of the fresh water is frozen as ice. This ice is near the North and South Poles.

So where do we get the fresh water that we need? Some of it comes from underground. Water seeps down slowly through the soil. It collects in spaces between underground rocks. This water is called **groundwater.** People dig wells to bring groundwater to the surface.

Many lakes, rivers, and streams also supply fresh water. These water sources move. Streams run together to form rivers. Rivers can flow into and out of lakes. In places where ground is low, water can move very slowly. Water makes the ground very wet at least part of the year. A place with wet or water-covered ground is called a **wetland.**

Wetlands are important resources. They are homes for many animals. They also help prevent floods by soaking up extra water. The water in wetlands seeps down and helps refill the groundwater supply.

A spring is a stream of groundwater that flows out of the ground.

Fresh water is "locked up" in huge chunks of ice. This iceberg is near Antarctica.

Small rocky streams like this one can come together to form larger streams and rivers.

### ✓ Lesson Checkpoint

1. Why is fresh water important?
2. What are four sources of fresh water?
3. **Writing** in Science **Descriptive** In your **science journal**, write a paragraph about a time you spent near water. What did you see? What did you hear? What did you feel?

# How do forms of water change?

*Follow a particle of water for a year. One day the particle is rushing down a mountain stream. Later, it is locked in frozen pond ice. Later still, it is drifting high in the air. On its journey, water goes through many changes.*

## Forms Water Can Have

Cold weather can freeze water from a liquid to a solid. In some places, the weather is below 0 degrees Celsius all year long. In other places, the weather is cold just part of the year. In these places, water may freeze only when the weather is very cold.

Warm temperatures in the spring and summer keep the water in this marsh in its liquid form. What is the temperature in this marsh in degrees Fahrenheit? in degrees Celsius?

When water freezes, it takes up more space. The water in the bottle on the right has frozen. It pushes out the sides of the bottle and out of its top because it takes up more space.

156

Water can also become a gas called water vapor. The process of a liquid becoming a gas is called **evaporation.** The Sun's energy evaporates surface water. Then the water becomes water vapor in the air. You cannot see water vapor, but sometimes you can feel its effects on hot summer days. On these days water leaves your skin as sweat. But sweat cannot easily evaporate if there is a lot of water vapor in the air. So you feel "sticky" from the sweat.

Water vapor in the air can turn back into a liquid. This process is called **condensation.** When the air cools, condensation turns invisible water vapor back into drops of water. Small droplets form clouds and fog. Large drops that form on plants are dew.

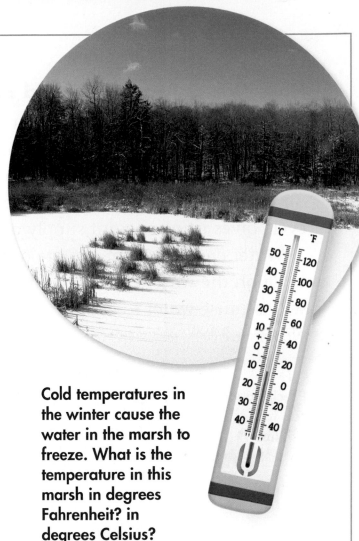

Cold temperatures in the winter cause the water in the marsh to freeze. What is the temperature in this marsh in degrees Fahrenheit? in degrees Celsius?

Water vapor in air condenses as dew-drops on plants.

1. ✔**Checkpoint** What are the three forms of water?

2. **Math** in Science What is the difference between the temperature of the marsh in spring and in winter? Give your answer in °F and °C.

## How Water Moves Around Earth

There is only a certain amount of water on Earth. It must be used again and again. The movement of water from Earth's surface into the air and back again is the **water cycle.** The water cycle gives us a constant supply of fresh water.

Water changes form or state as it moves through the water cycle. The Sun's energy and winds cause water to evaporate and become water vapor.

Rain is just one form of precipitation.

Precipitation can fall as snow.

*Precipitation*

*Stream water flow*

*Groundwater flow*

The arrows show some of the main paths water takes as it cycles through the environment.

Water vapor rises into cooler air, cools, and turns into water droplets or ice crystals. This process is called condensation. These water particles collect and form clouds.

When water particles in clouds grow in size and weight, they fall faster. Water that falls to Earth is called **precipitation.** Precipitation might be rain, snow, sleet, or hail. The form of precipitation depends on the temperature at the Earth's surface.

Some precipitation seeps into the ground. There it becomes groundwater. Other precipitation falls onto streams, rivers, lakes, and oceans. Water that flows across Earth's surface is constantly moving downstream toward the ocean. A lot of ground water reaches the surface in lower areas where there are streams and rivers. This surface water evaporates. In this way, the water cycle continues all the time—everywhere.

Condensation

Water vapor

Evaporation

The water in these snowflakes was once water vapor. Condensation turned the vapor into water droplets. These fell to Earth as frozen precipitation.

1. ✔ **Checkpoint** Name the main steps in the water cycle.

2. 🎯 **Cause and Effect** What kind of precipitation would occur if the temperature was above freezing?

159

## Ways to Clean Water

The water that people use must be clean. Water may contain germs. It may contain dirt, salt, or things that make it taste and smell bad. These things are usually removed from the water that people use.

Germs in water can make people sick. Dirt or salt in water can harm machines. Most people want to drink water that tastes good.

In some places, families clean their own water. These families often get water from their own wells. Then they filter the water to remove dirt and chemicals.

In cities, people do not need to clean their own water. The water for most cities is cleaned in one place. This process has several steps. First, the water is sent through pipes to a water-treatment area. There, several things may happen.

This filter cleans only the water that comes out of this faucet.

This kind of filter cleans all the water that comes into this building.

Sometimes, chemicals are added to the water. Some chemicals kill germs. Others, such as fluoride, help make teeth strong. In some treatment plants, the water is sprayed into the air. This makes the water taste and smell better. Often, the water is stored in big tanks for a while. Sitting in tanks lets tiny pieces of dirt sink to the bottom of the tank. This cleans the water even more.

Finally, the water is pumped through a filter. As the water moves through a filter, even more dirt is removed.

By now, the water is clean. It is ready to be pumped all over the city. Homes and businesses will have clean, fresh water to use.

**Map Fact**

The city of Chicago has two of the largest water-cleaning plants in the world. These clean between one and two billion gallons of water a day. People who live in and around Chicago use this water.

**A water-cleaning plant in Chicago**

✔ **Lesson Checkpoint**

1. What properties of water allow the water cycle to take place?

2. Why must water be cleaned?

3. **Writing in Science**  **Expository** Explain in your **science journal** what happens to the water in a puddle on a hot day. Include at least two steps of the water cycle.

**Investigate** How can you make a model of the water cycle?

## Materials

ice cube

cup

resealable plastic bag

tape

## What to Do

**1** Put an ice cube in the cup.

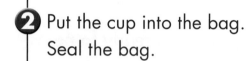

**2** Put the cup into the bag. Seal the bag.

**3** Tape the bag to a sunny window. **Predict** what will happen over the next 3 days.

### Process Skills

An **inference** about a future event is called a **prediction**.

**④ Observe** the bag. Record what happens.
Compare your results with your predictions.

| Time | Predictions | Observations |
|---|---|---|
| After 2 hours | | |
| Day 2 | | |
| Day 3 | | |

## Explain Your Results

1. Make a drawing. Show how the water from the ice cube moved to the bottom of the bag. Use arrows. Use these words as labels: *melting, evaporation,* and *condensation.*

2. **Infer** What do you think would happen if the entire bag was put in a freezer?

3. Identify the different forms in which water exists in the air. How does water change from one form to another?

### Go Further

How do you think you could make the water cycle happen faster or slower in the bag? Design and conduct a scientific investigation to test your prediction. Keep a record in a journal.

# Math in Science

# Snowflake Geometry

If water droplets in the clouds freeze, they form snow crystals. Snow crystals join with others and fall as snowflakes.

All snowflakes have six sides. Remember, a six-sided shape is called a **hexagon.** Many snowflakes are **symmetrical.** A symmetrical shape is exactly the same on both sides of a line, called the **line of symmetry.** There can be one or more lines of symmetry in a symmetrical shape. The snowflake below shows (with dotted lines) 3 of the possible lines of symmetry. If you were to cut out the snowflake and fold it on any one of these lines, the two sides would match.

@ Tools Take It to the Net
sfsuccessnet.com

**Use the shapes below to answer the questions.**

A    B    C    D

**1** Which shape is NOT symmetrical?

A. shape A          B. shape B

C. shape C          D. shape D

**2** Shape A is a snowflake. Two lines of symmetry are shown. How many total lines of symmetry does the snowflake have?

F. 1    G. 3    H. 5    I. 6

**3** Trace the hexagon at left and cut it out. Fold the hexagon along one of the lines of symmetry shown. What is the name of the new shape? How many sides does it have?

**Lab zone Take-Home Activity**

Make paper snowflakes by folding and cutting. You may use the library or the Internet to find detailed instructions. See how intricate you can make snowflakes, starting with a paper square or circle!

# Chapter 5 Review and Test Prep

## Use Vocabulary

| | |
|---|---|
| **condensation** (page 157) | **water cycle** (page 158) |
| **evaporation** (page 157) | **water vapor** (page 154) |
| **groundwater** (page 155) | **wetland** (page 155) |
| **precipitation** (page 159) | |

Use the vocabulary word from the list above that best completes each sentence.

1. _____ happens when water changes into water vapor and rises into the air.

2. A soggy area that collects water is called a(n) _____.

3. The _____ moves water from Earth's surface into the air and back again.

4. When water evaporates, it turns into an invisible gas called _____.

5. Water that falls from clouds in the form of rain, snow, sleet, or ice is called _____.

6. _____ occurs when water vapor changes back into water droplets.

7. Fresh water found under the ground is _____.

## Explain Concepts

8. Explain why all living things need water.

9. Describe where water is found on the Earth.

10. Why is most of Earth's water salt water?

11. Describe the changes that water goes through in the water cycle.

### Process Skills

12. **Infer** Why is it important that poisonous materials do not leak into the ground?

13. **Predict** What might happen to a glass bottle if it is filled with water, capped tightly, and put in the freezer?

## Cause and Effect

**14.** Make a graphic organizer like the one shown below. Fill in the correct effect.

**Causes**   **Effect**

Water is spilled on the outside door steps. →

The outside temperature is −5°C. →

Water freezes at 0°C. →

## Test Prep

Choose the letter that best completes the statement or answers the question.

**15.** About 75 percent of Earth's surface is covered by
   (A) air.     (B) water.
   (C) plants.  (D) animals.

**16.** The step in the water cycle in which water forms water vapor in the air is called
   (F) evaporation.
   (G) condensation.
   (H) precipitation.
   (I) groundwater.

**17.** When the temperature of water falls below 0 degrees Celsius, the water will
   (A) evaporate.
   (B) shrink.
   (C) freeze.
   (D) condense.

**18.** Wetlands help refill the groundwater supply when
   (F) water evaporates.
   (G) water seeps down into the ground.
   (H) the winds blow.
   (I) water freezes.

**19.** Explain why the answer you chose for Question 17 is best. For each of the answers you did not choose, give a reason why it is not the best choice.

**20.** Writing in Science

**Persuasive** Practice writing a letter to the editor of your town newspaper. Explain why you think it is important for everyone in your town to conserve water, rather than waste it.

# Oceanographer

Oceanographers learn skills to study the ocean using many special tools.

Oceanographers study the water of the ocean, the area beneath it, and the living things in it. Would you like to sail the deep blue sea? Then think about being an oceanographer. Oceanographers are scientists. They use tools to keep track of ocean temperatures, ocean currents, and life in the ocean. These scientists study the ocean as a whole, but there are many specific jobs in the field of oceanography. For example, you might want to study whales and other living things in the ocean. Then you can become a marine biologist. Do you like to tinker with tools and gadgets? Maybe you could be an engineer who designs the special equipment needed to study the underwater world.

Becoming an oceanographer requires four years of college.

## Lab zone Take-Home Activity

Choose one specific job you might like to do as an oceanographer. Use resources at home to find out more about the job.

EC NTL 10 9 8 7 6 5 4 3

# Chapter 6

# Weather

## You Will Discover

- patterns of weather.
- how people measure and predict weather.
- ways people stay safe during storms.

online
**Student Edition**
sfsuccessnet.com

# How does weather follow patterns?

weather

hurricane

tornado

170

# Chapter 6 Vocabulary

atmosphere

blizzard

171

# You Are There!

You are playing outside on a sunny day. Suddenly you hear a loud rumble in the sky. You look up. Huge black clouds are moving toward you. You see a flash of lightning in the distance. Uh-oh! Here comes a big change in the weather. What caused it? Time to get to safety.

AudioText

## Lesson 1

# What makes up weather?

*Weather changes all the time. Measuring weather helps people predict weather accurately.*

## Parts of Weather

What will the weather be like this weekend? Will it be sunny or rainy? **Weather** is what the air is like outside. It includes the kinds of clouds in the sky and the kind and amount of water in the air. It also includes the temperature of the air and how the wind is blowing.

Clouds are made of water droplets in the air. Different kinds of clouds form in different weather. Because of this, clouds can help predict what will happen to the weather. Some kinds of clouds form in sunny weather. Others form in rainy or stormy weather.

Look at clouds on a warm, bright day. The clouds are white and fluffy. On a stormy day, clouds are dark.

These cumulus clouds look a little like balls of cotton. You see these on sunny days.

These are very high, thin cirrus clouds. They are made of tiny ice crystals. You see these clouds on sunny days too.

1. **✓Checkpoint** How do clouds look on stormy days?

2. **Writing in Science** **Narrative** Write a paragraph in your **science journal** that tells what the weather would be like on a perfect day for you. Explain why you like this weather.

**175**

# Layers of the Atmosphere

The space shuttle circles the Earth here.

This is where our atmosphere meets outer space.

Have you ever seen a shooting star? This is where pieces of rock from outer space burn up.

Many jet airplanes fly here above the weather.

Weather happens in this part of the atmosphere.

## Measuring Weather

How do you describe the weather? You might say it's too hot, but someone else might not agree. That person might like this weather. Words like *hot* mean different things to different people. The word *hot* is an opinion. But 34° Celsius (93° Fahrenheit) means just one thing. It is a fact that describes the temperature.

Many tools help scientists measure and describe weather. They also help describe the atmosphere. The **atmosphere** is the blanket of air that surrounds Earth. This air is made up of gases that have no color, taste, or odor. The atmosphere has different parts, or layers. Each layer is a different temperature. Each has different amounts of gases.

The atmosphere has weight, so it presses down with a certain force. This force is called air pressure. Weather reports often describe air pressure. When the air presses down a lot, the air pressure is high. When it presses less, the air pressure is low.

## Clues Help Predict Changes

Changes in air pressure are useful clues. They suggest that other weather changes are on the way. Low air pressure often means that weather will be cloudy or rainy. High air pressure often means skies will be clear. Scientists can measure air pressure with a tool called a barometer.

Wind speed and direction are useful clues. A tool called an anemometer measures wind speed. A wind vane records the direction of the wind.

Scientists use tools such as hygrometers to measure how much water vapor is in the air. The amount of water vapor in the air is called humidity. The humidity is low when air is dry. The humidity is high when air has more water in it. Rain gauges also measure water. They show how much rain has fallen.

Weather tools or instruments help scientists learn more about weather. They also help scientists predict what the weather will be like.

1. ✓**Checkpoint** How do tools help scientists describe the weather?

2. **Make Inferences** High pressure is moving into an area. Use this observation and what you know about air pressure to predict the weather change.

## Tools for Measuring Weather

**Barometer**
This tool measures air pressure.

**Anemometer**
This tool measures wind speed.

**Wind Vane**
This tool measures the direction of the wind.

**Hygrometer**
This tool measures how much water is in the air.

**Rain Gauge**
This tool measures how much rain has fallen.

## Weather Map

Weather tools gather weather data. Scientists show this data on weather maps. Weather maps show data for a large area. They show temperatures and storms. Some maps give information about areas of high and low air pressure.

Look at the weather map below. It shows the United States. The numbers show the temperatures in different cities. The small pictures show what the weather is like. You can probably guess what some pictures mean. The key shows the meaning of all the pictures.

Weather satellites gather weather data from all over the world. These satellites move high above the Earth. They can take pictures of large areas of the planet. They send these pictures and data back to scientists on Earth.

Information from satellites is very useful to scientists. For example, they can see storm clouds form and can tell the direction that the storms are moving.

**This weather map uses pictures to interpret data that weather tools have gathered. What can you learn from this weather map?**

Weather satellites like this one gather weather data.

Maps made from satellite data can show the direction storm clouds are moving.

## Pollution Alerts

Weather news may include smog and ozone pollution alerts. In many cities, cars and trucks help cause these alerts. The gases that leave their engines are called exhaust. On some days, a lot of exhaust stays in the air. The Sun's rays can turn that air into smog and ozone. On days with little wind, the smog and ozone do not move away.

Smog and ground-level ozone can be harmful to health. They can make people cough. Some people might not be able to breathe easily. During air pollution alerts, some people must stay inside.

The Sun's rays strike the exhaust from gasoline burned in cars and trucks. This causes smog.

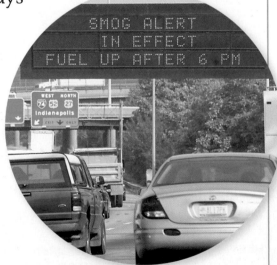

### ✓ Lesson Checkpoint

1. What can weather maps show?

2. What is one effect that humans can have on weather?

3. **Make Inferences** If there is a smog alert, what can you infer about the weather?

## Lesson 2

# How are weather patterns different?

*Patterns of weather vary from place to place. People must protect themselves during severe weather.*

## Weather Patterns

Changes in weather follow patterns. Weather patterns depend on the Sun and water and where you live. Places near oceans have different weather patterns than places far from oceans.

For example, the western part of Washington State touches the Pacific Ocean. Air moves in from this ocean. In winter, warm air from over the ocean has lots of condensed water vapor in the form of clouds. Precipitation falls from the clouds as rain over the western valleys.

As they move east, the clouds get pushed up the side of the Cascade Mountains. The clouds get colder as they rise. The condensed water vapor in them falls as snow. The western part of the state thus has a pattern of wet and snowy weather in winter.

The eastern part of the state has another weather pattern in winter. After the air has crossed the mountains, much of the water vapor is gone. As a result, the eastern part of the state has a pattern of cold, dry weather.

Western Washington State has a pattern of cool, wet winters.

Eastern Washington State has a pattern of cold, dry winters.

| Winter in Washington State | | |
|---|---|---|
| Locations | Average Temperature | Average Rainfall (cm) |
| West | 5°C (41°F) | 30 |
| East | –2°C (28°F) | 6 |

All deserts are dry. But deserts are not all the same. Some deserts are cold, while others are hot. Each has its own weather pattern. North America has four large desert regions. One desert with a rainy summer season is the Sonoran Desert. It is in the southern part of Arizona and California.

The Sonoran Desert receives some winter rain from storms that reach it from the Pacific Ocean. But most rain occurs as short, heavy downpours during the hot summer. The average rainfall during the summer is 5 centimeters (2 inches). The moist air for this rain comes up from the Gulf of California. The wide, shallow roots of the saguaro cactus soak up the rain. The tall spires of the cactus then fill up like sponges. The cactus stores the water for later use.

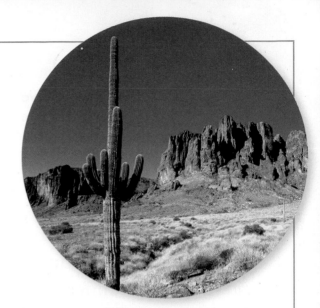

In the hot summer the saguaro cactus stores water from storms.

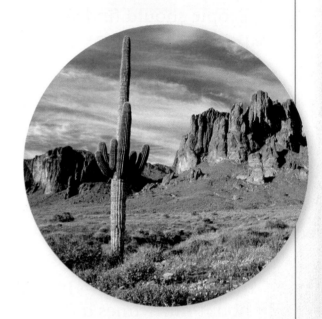

Winter rain causes spring wildflowers in the Sonoran Desert.

1. ✔Checkpoint What do weather patterns depend on?

2. 🎯 Make Inferences Moist air from the Gulf of California causes storms in the Sonoran Desert in summer. What weather does moist air from the Gulf of Mexico cause in the Midwest in summer?

| Seasons in the Sonoran Desert | | |
| --- | --- | --- |
| Season | Average Temperature | Average Rainfall (cm) |
| Fall | 16°C (61°F) | 2 |
| Winter | 12°C (54°F) | 2 |
| Spring | 24°C (75°F) | 1 |
| Summer | 29°C (84°F) | 5 |

A satellite high above Earth took this picture of the swirling winds of a hurricane.

## Dangerous Storms

Some storms bring only rain. Other storms can be dangerous. Thunderstorms can be dangerous because lightning can strike people or objects. People should find shelter during thunderstorms. Other storms are even more dangerous.

A **hurricane** is a huge storm. Hurricanes form over oceans. They have winds of at least 119 kilometers (74 miles) per hour. Heavy rains, strong winds, and huge waves cause damage. These waves can lift boats right out of the water and flip them over. In most cases, people know about hurricanes a day or two before they strike.

A **tornado** is a spinning, funnel-shaped, column of air that touches the ground. Tornadoes are much smaller than hurricanes. However, their winds are stronger. Tornadoes form beneath thunderstorm clouds. They can form suddenly and without warning. When a tornado starts, people must go to safe places. They must stay away from windows.

Sudden heavy rains can cause floods. Very high waves can cause floods too. Water from flooding can block roads and damage homes. People usually have some warning that an area may flood. Then they must move to higher ground.

A **blizzard** is a winter storm. Blizzards have low temperatures and lots of blowing snow. People can get lost or stuck in the snow. They can also get too cold to move to warm shelter.

Radio and television stations send out storm safety information. The National Weather Service puts out watches and warnings. These warn people about dangerous storms. A *watch* means that a storm could happen where you live. A *warning* means that a storm is already in or near your area. Everyone should listen to storm safety reports. Anyone who hears a warning should take action to stay safe.

Hurricanes do the most damage when they move over land.

Students head for home when a winter storm watch warns of a blizzard.

Most tornadoes do damage along a narrow path.

### ✓ Lesson Checkpoint

1. What part of the State of Washington has a wet and snowy weather pattern in winter?

2. What does a severe thunderstorm warning mean? What should people do in response?

3. **Writing** in Science   **Descriptive**
   In your **science journal** write about a storm that happened near your home. Tell how people prepared themselves or didn't before the storm came.

Heavy rains caused a flood that blocks this road.

183

## Investigate Can different amounts of carbon dioxide have different effects?

Carbon dioxide gas in the air helps keep Earth warm. An increase can cause a planet to get warmer. On Earth carbon dioxide has been increasing for hundreds of years. Some changes have been observed. Many scientists think if it keeps increasing, bigger changes will be observed.

### Materials

safety goggles

2 cups and masking tape

funnel and graduated cylinder (or measuring cup)

BTB

2 pieces of plastic wrap and straws

### Process Skills

You **interpret data** when you look closely at your data and see how it can help you to answer your questions.

### What to Do

**1** Prepare 2 cups of BTB.

Put 30 mL of BTB into each cup. Cover the cups with plastic wrap.

Label the cups.

Safety Procedure
Be careful!
• Wear safety goggles.
• Do not share straws.
• Use the straws to breathe out only!

**2** Push a straw through the plastic wrap. Breathe out once through the straw into Cup A.

**3** Repeat with Cup B but breathe out 10 times.

④ Look at the color of BTB in each cup.

⑤ **Collect data** and make a chart like the one below to show your results.

| Cup | Color of BTB | |
|---|---|---|
| | **Before Breathing into Cup** | **After Breathing into Cup** |
| **Cup A** 1 breath | | |
| **Cup B** 10 breaths | | |

## Explain Your Results

1. What happened to the BTB in each cup?

2. **Interpret Data** When you breathed out, you added carbon dioxide to the BTB. Can a small amount of carbon dioxide show a different effect than a larger amount? Explain.

## Go Further

How many breaths can you breathe out without observing a change? Make a plan to answer this or another question.

185

# Math in Science

# Comparing Temperatures

Places near oceans have different weather patterns than places far from oceans. The tables on page 187 compare the average high and low temperatures in two cities for January and for July. Notice that Seattle is warmer than Indianapolis in January.

July

January

Seattle

Indianapolis

July

January

🖥 ⚙ **Tools** Take It to the Net
sfsuccessnet.com

## Average Temperatures in January

| | Seattle, Washington | Indianapolis, Indiana |
|---|---|---|
| Average High | 8°C (46°F) | 1°C (34°F) |
| Average Low | 2°C (36°F) | −8°C (18°F) |

## Average Temperatures in July

| | Seattle, Washington | Indianapolis, Indiana |
|---|---|---|
| Average High | 24°C (75°F) | 30°C (86°F) |
| Average Low | 13°C (55°F) | 18°C (65°F) |

Use the tables and the map to answer the following questions.

1. Use the map to explain why Seattle is usually warmer than Indianapolis in January.

2. What is the average high temperature in July in Seattle? in Indianapolis?

3. What are the average low temperatures in the two cities in July?

4. Which city is usually warmer in July? Use the map to help explain why this is true.

**Lab zone Take-Home Activity**

Find information about the average high and low temperatures in January and July where you live. Compare these temperatures to the temperatures in Seattle and Indianapolis.

# Chapter 6 Review and Test Prep

## Use Vocabulary

| | |
|---|---|
| **atmosphere** (page 176) | **tornado** (page 182) |
| **blizzard** (page 183) | **weather** (page 175) |
| **hurricane** (page 182) | |

Use the vocabulary word from the list above that best completes each sentence.

1. A(n) _____ is a spinning column of air that touches the ground and happens quickly.

2. Temperature, wind speed, and clouds are parts of the _____.

3. A(n) _____ is a huge, strong storm that forms over the warm ocean.

4. A winter storm with low temperatures, strong winds, and lots of blowing snow is a(n) _____.

5. The _____ is made up of gases that surround Earth.

## Explain Concepts

6. Why is weather important?

7. If you had tools for measuring parts of the weather, what information could you collect?

8. List some clues that indicate a change in the weather.

9. Give an example of a weather pattern and describe it in detail.

10. How does the National Weather Service help people stay safe?

11. Use the chart below to tell which city has warmer average temperatures in July. Which city has the biggest difference between the average high and average low?

| | Birmingham, Alabama | Santa Fe, New Mexico |
|---|---|---|
| Average High in July | 33°C (91°F) | 29°C (85°F) |
| Average Low in July | 21°C (70°F) | 12°C (53°F) |

### Process Skills

12. **Predict** It is a rainy day, but the air pressure is getting higher. How might the weather change?

13. **Infer** How might weather be different if water never evaporated? Explain your answer.

MindPoint Quiz Show

##  Make Inferences

**14.** Copy the table below. Fill in the missing inference.

| Facts | Inference |
|---|---|
| Earth has become slightly warmer over the past 100 years. | |
| Many places get more or less rain than before. | |

 ## Test Prep

Choose the letter that best completes the statement or answers the question.

**15.** What kind of winter weather would a city near the ocean in the western U.S. most likely have?

&#9398; warm and rainy
&#9399; warm and snowy
&#9400; cold and snowy
&#9401; cool and rainy

**16.** A severe thunderstorm watch means

&#9403; a severe thunderstorm is in the area.
&#9404; a tornado is in the area.
&#9405; flooding could happen soon.
&#9406; a thunderstorm might happen.

**17.** If a tornado forms, people should

&#9398; go to safe places.
&#9399; move to higher ground.
&#9400; close windows.
&#9401; drive to another city.

**18.** Most smog and ozone in cities are caused by

&#9403; acid rain.
&#9404; forest fires.
&#9405; carbon dioxide.
&#9406; burning gasoline.

**19.** Explain why the answer you chose for Question 15 is best. For each of the answers you did not choose, give a reason why it is not the best choice.

**20.** Writing in Science

**Expository** Write a paragraph that describes both helpful and harmful effects that the weather can have on people.

# Studying Clouds From
# SPACE

You know that NASA studies space. NASA also studies Earth's clouds from space. NASA satellites orbit Earth and use different tools or instruments to collect information about clouds and other parts of the Earth system, including weather. Some of the tools measure the amount of sunlight that bounces off clouds. Other tools measure how much heat is trapped by clouds and how much escapes into space.

**Cumulus**

**Cirrus**

**Cumulonimbus**

**Stratus**

Clouds are an important part of weather patterns. They are part of the water cycle. They interact with the gases that trap heat and warm Earth. NASA scientists are studying how clouds affect Earth's climate.

Many schools are helping NASA study clouds. Students and teachers at these schools observe and measure clouds and other weather conditions. They are given special times to take their measurements. These are the same times when NASA satellites are recording information for their area.

**Cirrostratus**

**Altocumulus**

## Lab zone Take-Home Activity

Record your own observations of clouds and the temperature at the time of day you observed them. Collect this data for a week. Organize data into a chart. Decide if the kinds and amounts of clouds affected the temperature.

# Air Traffic Controller

You are in the control tower at an airport. You can see all the planes and runways. Computers tell you the height, speed, and course of all aircraft.

As an air traffic controller, you make sure planes take off and land safely. You give pilots directions so they can keep their planes a safe distance from other planes. You also give them information about weather patterns. Pilots need to know about any storms. They also must know about sudden changes in the speed or direction of the wind. They need to know what the weather is like near the airport. Is it foggy, snowing, or rainy? Is it clear? The information you give pilots helps keep them and their passengers safe.

People who become air traffic controllers usually have four years of college. Then they must take tests to make sure they would make good air traffic controllers.

## Lab zone Take-Home Activity

Suppose you are watching planes as they approach an airport. Describe the information that you need to give the pilots.

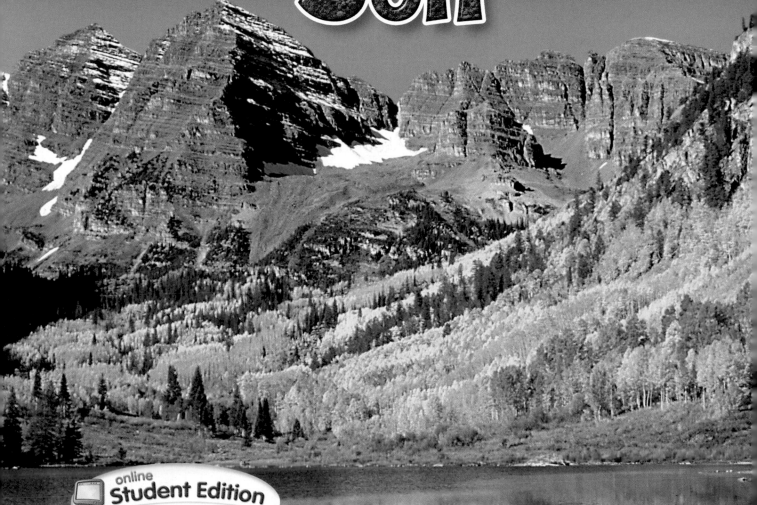

# Chapter 7
# Rocks and Soil

## You Will Discover

- how to tell one kind of rock from another.
- how rocks are formed.
- what soil is made of.
- why soil is important.

# What are some kinds of rocks and soils?

rock

igneous rock

sedimentary rock

metamorphic rock

194

loam

soil

mineral

decay

The slow breaking down of the remains of living things in soil

nutrient

Material in soil that plants need to grow

## **Explore** What can you learn from rock layers?

Wind, water, or ice can carry away sand and other materials. Often these materials are dropped in places in layers. Over time, the materials can join together to form rock. This is one reason rocks are often found in layers. In this model the layers of rock are shown by the sand, salt, coffee, sugar, and clay soil.

### Materials

small measuring cup and large cup

sand, salt, coffee

sugar and clay soil

small paper clip
rubber band
piece of crayon

### What to Do

**1** **Make a model** of rock layers. Fill the small cup with sand. Pour it into a large cup. Put a paper clip in the sand. Place it touching the side of the cup. The paper clip stands for a fossil animal.

**2** Add layers of the other materials to the cup. Place a "fossil animal" (a rubber band or a piece of crayon) in 2 of the layers.

crayon
clay soil
sugar
coffee
rubber band
salt
paper clip
sand

### **Process Skills**

A **model** of something is different from the real thing but can be used to learn something about the real thing.

### Explain Your Results

1. Which layer was added first? Which layer in your **model** is the "oldest"? How do you know?

2. **Infer** Where would you expect to find an older fossil—in an upper layer of rock or in a lower layer? Explain.

# How to Read Science

## Compare and Contrast

When you **compare** things, you tell how they are alike. When you **contrast** things, you tell how they are different.

- Words and phrases such as *similar*, *like*, *all*, *both*, or *in the same way* are clues that things are being compared.

- Words and phrases such as *different*, *unlike*, or *in a different way* are clues that things are being contrasted.

**Magazine Article**

### Rock Collectors

Ben and Misha both collect rocks. Ben prefers brightly colored rocks. He is a member of a rock hunters club that goes on collecting trips. Misha has a different way of collecting his favorite kinds of rocks—fossil rocks. His uncle sends Misha fossil rocks from all around the world. Unlike Ben, Misha just has to make a trip to his mailbox to add to his collection.

## Apply It!

You can use a graphic organizer as a **model** to show how things compare and contrast.

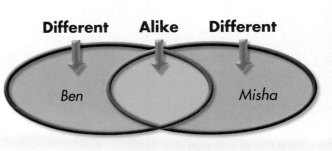

Use a graphic organizer to show ways that Ben and Misha are alike and different in the way they collect rocks.

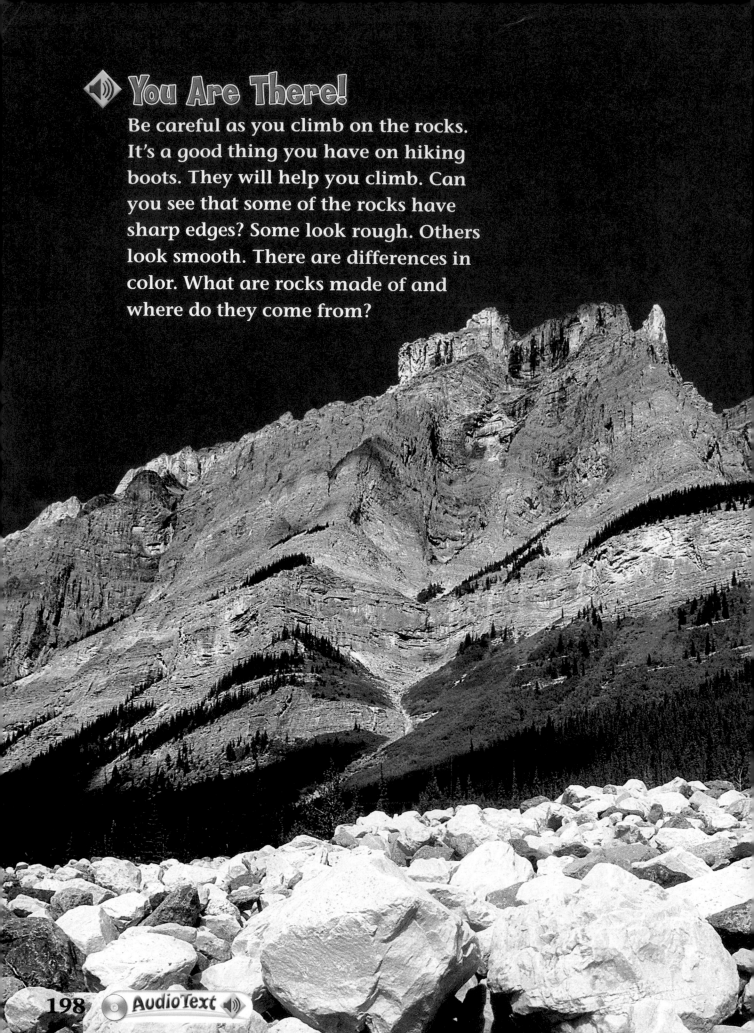

# You Are There!

Be careful as you climb on the rocks. It's a good thing you have on hiking boots. They will help you climb. Can you see that some of the rocks have sharp edges? Some look rough. Others look smooth. There are differences in color. What are rocks made of and where do they come from?

AudioText

## Lesson 1

# How do rocks form?

*Rocks are everywhere. Some are as large as a mountain. Others are smaller than a grain of sand. Minerals make up rock. Rock forms in different ways.*

## Rocks

Earth consists of mostly different kinds of rocks. **Rock** is natural, solid, nonliving material made of one or more minerals. A **mineral** is a natural material that forms from nonliving matter.

You can tell rocks apart by looking at their physical properties. The physical properties of rocks include color, what minerals they are made of, and texture.

The rocks you see here range in color from gray to brown. Sometimes the minerals are so small that they aren't easy to see. Texture is the size of the bits of minerals, or grains, that make up the rock. Some rocks may have grains that are big enough to see. These different sizes of minerals make rocks feel smooth, rough, or bumpy.

1. ✓**Checkpoint** What are some physical properties of rocks?

2. **Compare and Contrast** How are the rocks shown in the pictures alike? How are they different?

## Rock Groups

Rocks can be placed into three main groups. Rocks in each group formed in a certain way. Each group contains many kinds of rocks.

*Igneous* means "from fire." That tells you something about this kind of rock. **Igneous rock** forms from a red-hot mixture of melted minerals and gases. If this mixture cools slowly below ground until it hardens, its mineral grains may be large. If the rock cools quickly above ground or on the ocean floor, the grains may be too small to see.

Your clue to a second group of rocks is *sediment*. Sediment is made up of bits of rocky matter that settle to the bottom of rivers, lakes, and oceans. Over thousands of years, pressure and special processes press together and cement the bits into **sedimentary rock.** Sedimentary rock forms in layers—one layer at a time.

Fossil remains of extinct plants and animals are often found in sedimentary rocks. Their bodies were buried in sand and mud that hardened into rock. Layers of rocks containing fossils record the history of life over time.

### Fossils in Sedimentary Rock

Crinoids were ancient animals that looked like plants.

Trilobites were like modern crabs.

Ammonites looked similar to today's snails.

Igneous rock can come from volcanoes.

200

*Metamorphic* means "that changes form." **Metamorphic rock** is rock that has been changed by heat, pressure, or both. Slate, for example, used to be a sedimentary rock called shale. As rock formed on top of it, the shale became buried deep underground. Heat and pressure changed the minerals in the shale. The shale has become slate, a metamorphic rock. Igneous and sedimentary rocks can be changed into metamorphic rock.

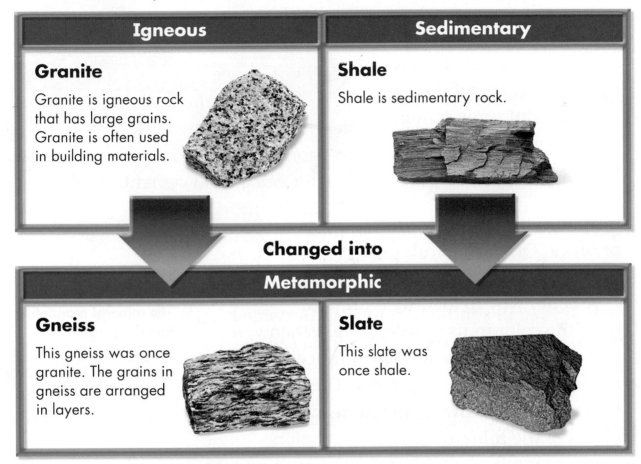

| **Igneous** | **Sedimentary** |
|---|---|
| **Granite** Granite is igneous rock that has large grains. Granite is often used in building materials. | **Shale** Shale is sedimentary rock. |

**Changed into**

| **Metamorphic** | |
|---|---|
| **Gneiss** This gneiss was once granite. The grains in gneiss are arranged in layers. | **Slate** This slate was once shale. |

## ✓ Lesson Checkpoint

1. How is igneous rock that forms above ground different from igneous rock that forms below ground?

2. Describe clues, found in sedimentary rock, which show that living things have changed over time.

3. **Writing in Science** **Expository** List facts in your **science journal** about the three kinds of rocks. Then write a paragraph describing each of the three kinds.

# Lesson 2

# What are minerals?

*Minerals are the most common solid material found on Earth. Gold and silver are rare minerals. Rock salt and quartz are common minerals.*

## Identifying Minerals

Color is a property you notice easily about a mineral. But some minerals can be found in different colors. For example, the mineral quartz can be pink, purple, yellow, brown, white, or black. Other minerals always have the same color.

A better way to identify a mineral is by the color in its powder form. When you rub a mineral across a rough surface, it may leave a streak mark or powder. The color of these effects are always the same even if two pieces of the mineral are different colors.

Luster is a property that shows how a mineral reflects light. Minerals can be metallic, pearly, silky, greasy, glassy, or dull.

The mineral magnetite has the property of magnetism. Objects that contain iron are pulled to the magnetite.

Vinegar fizzes on limestone that contains the mineral calcite. The fizzing happens because the vinegar reacts with the calcite. The reaction gives off carbon dioxide.

# Properties of Minerals

| Mineral | | Color | Luster | Streak | Hardness |
|---------|---|-------|--------|--------|----------|
| **Mica** Mica breaks into flaky pieces when struck. | | black, gray, green, violet | pearly on surfaces | white | can be scratched with a knife |
| **Molybdenite** This mineral is one of the strongest and most commonly used heat-resistant metals. | | silvery | metallic | bluish gray | can be scratched with a fingernail |
| **Crocoite** Much of this mineral comes from Australia. | | reddish-orange | very shiny | orange-yellow | can be scratched with a coin |

Another way to identify a mineral is to test its hardness. Some minerals, such as talc, are so soft you can scratch them with your fingernail. The hardest mineral is diamond. It can be scratched only by another diamond.

Some minerals can be identified by their appearance. Gold, for example, appears sometimes in nugget form. Other minerals can be identified by taste, smell, or touch.

1. ✓**Checkpoint** What are ways to identify minerals?

2. 🎯 **Compare and Contrast** How are rocks and minerals alike? How are they different? Use a graphic organizer to show your answer.

## How the Body Uses Minerals

These are some ways that the body uses minerals.

| Mineral | How Used |
| --- | --- |
| Calcium | Helps form bones and teeth and helps cause muscles to contract |
| Chromium | Helps change digested food into energy |
| Copper | Helps form skin and other tissues |
| Iron | Carries oxygen in blood to all parts of the body |
| Potassium | Helps nerves and muscles work |
| Phosphorus | Helps release energy and form bones and teeth |
| Sodium | Helps control water levels and carry messages through nerves |

## How We Use Minerals

It is almost impossible to go through a day without using minerals. The cavity-fighting fluoride in your toothpaste came from the mineral fluorite. The glass you look through in your window came from the minerals quartz, soda ash, and limestone. The salt in your food is the mineral halite. The metal in your spoon is a mineral. Even the graphite that you write with in your pencil is a mineral. Almost everything we use is made from minerals or contains minerals.

## Minerals Keep Us Healthy

People also need minerals to keep their bodies healthy and full of energy. Many of these minerals are found in plants. Green leafy vegetables, such as spinach, contain calcium. Iron is found in fruit and green vegetables. Sodium in vegetables such as celery, and potassium in fruits work together to help transmit nerve impulses and control muscles. Almost everything we eat has some minerals in it.

### ✓ Lesson Checkpoint

1. What is a mineral?
2. Why are minerals important to your health?
3. **Writing** in Science **Expository** In your **science journal** list five things you did today that used minerals. Use a chart with two columns. Head the first column, *Activity*. Head the second, *Mineral*.

# Other Ways We Use Minerals

## Halite

The mineral halite is crushed and then ground up. We use it to flavor and preserve food. (We know this mineral as table salt.)

## Copper

The mineral copper is found in igneous rock. The rocks are mined from the ground. When the rocks are crushed and heated, the copper becomes separated from the rock. Then, the copper can be made into objects such as pots and pans.

## Fluorite

The mineral fluorite is found in many rocks, such as granite. The rocks are crushed and the fluorite is separated out. Then, it is used to make many products such as toothpaste.

## Lead

Lead is found in a mineral known as galena. The rocks are crushed and heated to produce lead. Lead is put into aprons such as the ones shown to protect people while X-ray pictures are taken.

## Iron

Iron is a mineral found in the rock called hematite. The rocks are crushed and heated. Then, iron in the melted material is separated out. Iron is mixed with other materials to make steel. Steel is used for many tools and machines.

Earthworms mix up the topsoil as they dig through it. That improves the soil.

We depend on topsoil to grow our food.

Soil must pack down hard and stay firm so that houses built on it don't shift.

# Why is soil important?

*Soil is an important part of the system that supports all life on land. Soil and parts of soil have different properties.*

## Parts of Soil

**Soil** is the thin layer of loose material that covers most of Earth's land. Soil is not simply dirt. Natural processes develop soil over a long period of time. It takes hundreds of years for nature to rebuild lost topsoil. Soil has the material plants need to grow.

Squeeze a handful of soil and see that it's more than bits of rock. Soil might clump together because it holds water and material that was once living.

Living things in soil break down the remains of plants and animals. This process is called **decay.** Decay releases things plants need in order to grow. Each of these things is a **nutrient.** Some minerals also release nutrients. Water and nutrients support most plants on land, including crops. When you think about it, soil is more valuable than gold!

## Soil Layers

Soil is organized into layers. Different places have layers of different thicknesses and color.

## Topsoil

Topsoil is the top layer. Topsoil includes rock particles mixed with the dark products of decay. The decayed parts of plant and animal remains are called humus. Humus contains much of what plants need to grow.

## Subsoil

Subsoil is under topsoil. It is often lighter in color than topsoil. It doesn't have as much humus as topsoil. Subsoil includes pieces of broken rocks. Tree roots grow into the subsoil. Water from precipitation may be in this layer.

## Bedrock

As this rock breaks down, it provides raw material for making new soil.

1. ✓**Checkpoint** What is soil made of?

2. **Math** in Science Suppose it takes 1,500 years for 1 centimeter of soil to form in a certain place. How long would it take for 2 centimeters of soil to form? Show your work.

207

## Comparing Soils

Soil is not the same everywhere. Soil near your home may be different than soil at your school. The kind of soil depends in part on the types of rock particles that help make up the soil. Sand, silt, and clay are the three main types of particles found in soil. They differ in size. Sand particles are the largest. Clay particles are the smallest.

### Sand
Large spaces in sand allow water to easily pass through. Roots of many plants in sandy soil may not have time to soak up the water. Sandy soil feels rough and gritty.

### Silt
The medium-sized particles in silt are more closely packed together. Although water passes through silt, silty soil also holds water well.

### About Loam
Loam is good soil for growing plants. The graph shows the amount of each ingredient in loam.
- Sand, Silt, Clay
- Air
- Water
- Humus

sand, silt, clay
**45%**

air
**25%**

water
**25%**

humus
**5%**

All soil has the same four ingredients. Weathered rocks containing minerals make up most of the soil. Humus makes up another part. Humus is made up of decaying plants and animals. Humus is a very important part of soil. Air and water fill in the spaces between particles of rock and humus.

Most soils are a mixture of sand, silt, and clay. Soils with this mixture are called **loam.** Loam also contains humus, which has many minerals and other nutrients. Loam soil with its minerals, humus, air, and water is a very good mixture for growing most plants. Loam soils hold onto water loosely enough for plant roots to soak it up.

**Clay**
Clay particles are the smallest. Water passes slowly into clay. Once clay absorbs water, the particles hold tightly together. Very wet clay feels smooth and sticky.

✓ **Lesson Checkpoint**

1. Explain the importance of soil.

2. Compare the ability of sand, silt, and clay to hold water.

3. **Social Studies** in Science  Find information about states that have many large farms. Find out which fruits, vegetables, and grains grow in each area.

# Guided Inquiry

## Investigate How much water can soil hold?

### Materials

small measuring cup

3 clear plastic cups and
3 foam cups

sandy, clay, and loam soils

hand lens and pencil

paper towel and scissors

spoon and masking tape

graduated cylinder
(or measuring cup)

water

### Process Skills

By **measuring** carefully, you can find out which type of soil can hold the most water.

### What to Do

**1** Get 60 mL of each type of soil.

Label the cups.

sandy soil

clay soil

loam soil

**2** **Observe** the soil samples with a hand lens. Describe their properties (color, texture).

sandy soil

loam soil

clay soil

**3** Punch 10 holes in the bottom of each foam cup.

**4** Set each cup on the paper towel and trace around the bottom. Cut out the 3 circles you traced and put one inside each cup, over the holes.

**5** Put each of your soil samples into a different foam cup. Pack down the soil using a spoon.

inside view

clay soil

paper towel

foam cup

plastic cup

outside view

clay soil

**6** Put each foam cup inside a clear plastic cup. Pour 50 mL of water on each soil sample. Wait 10 minutes. Use a graduated cylinder to **measure** the amount of water in the clear plastic cups. Record your **data**.

| Type of Soil | Amount of Soil (mL) | Amount of Water Added (mL) | Amount of Water Collected in 10 Minutes (mL) |
|---|---|---|---|
| Sandy soil | | | |
| Clay soil | | | |
| Loam soil | | | |

## Explain Your Results

1. Describe the color, texture, and other properties of each soil you **observed**. What do you think each is made of?

2. Based on your **measurements**, which type of soil holds the most water? the least?

### Go Further

In which soil would desert plants grow best? Make a plan to answer this or another question you may have.

# Living Soil

Soil is made mostly of bits of rock. But it contains a lot of other things, too. Students at different schools wanted to explore the living things in soil. You might be surprised by what they found and how "alive" the ground is under your feet.

Students at Maple Creek School dug 10 samples of soil. They looked at each sample carefully. They counted the numbers of different animals in the soil samples. Their table on page 213 shows the totals. They found more ants than any other kind of animal. Students at Forest Grove School also dug 10 soil samples and counted animals. Their table is also on page 213.

eTools Take It to the Net
sfsuccessnet.com

## Soil Animals at Maple Creek School

| Beetles | Ants | Spiders | Earthworms |
|---------|------|---------|------------|
| 55 | 430 | 32 | 189 |

## Soil Animals at Forest Grove School

| Beetles | Ants | Spiders | Earthworms |
|---------|------|---------|------------|
| 24 | 235 | 48 | 95 |

Use the tables above to answer the questions.

**1** How many animals were found in the samples at Forest Grove School?

A. 299  B. 402

C. 706  D. 1,020

**2** How many more ants were found at Maple Creek School than at Forest Grove School?

F. 205  G. 665

H. 195  I. 470

**3** How many earthworms were found all together?

A. 284  B. 174

C. 274  D. 94

**Lab zone** **Take-Home Activity**

With an adult, get a small shovel full of soil. Spread it out on a driveway, outdoor table, or sidewalk. Be sure to wear gloves. Keep a record of the animals you find. Don't harm the animals. Remember to return them and the soil to the place you found them.

# Chapter 7 Review and Test Prep

## Use Vocabulary

| | |
|---|---|
| **decay** (page 206) | **mineral** (page 199) |
| **igneous rock** (page 200) | **nutrient** (page 206) |
| **loam** (page 209) | **rock** (page 199) |
| **metamorphic rock** (page 201) | **sedimentary rock** (page 200) |
| | **soil** (page 206) |

Use the vocabulary word from the list above that best completes each sentence.

1. Rock made up of layers of sediment that have hardened is _____.

2. Most of the land is covered with a thin layer of loose material called _____.

3. A(n) _____ is a natural material that makes up rock.

4. When living things _____, they break down, or rot.

5. Soil that is a mixture of sand, silt, clay, minerals, and decayed matter is called _____.

6. Any kind of solid, nonliving material found on Earth and made of minerals is a(n) _____.

7. Each type of small particle that plants take into their roots is a(n) _____, found in good growing soil.

8. Rock that has changed to another type of rock by heat and pressure is _____.

9. Rock that forms when melted Earth materials cool and harden is _____.

## Explain Concepts

10. What is one way that sedimentary rock forms?

11. Explain why a bone is not considered a mineral.

12. Describe the layers of soil from top to bottom.

MindPoint Quiz Show

## Process Skills

**13. Predict** Which would dry faster after it rains: a sandy beach or a grassy field? Give a reason for your answer.

**14. Model** Make a model or a drawing that shows the different layers of soil.

**15. Infer** You observe that a mineral sample can be scratched with a coin. What do you infer about the hardness of the mineral?

## Compare and Contrast

**16.** Make a graphic organizer like the one below. Fill it in to compare and contrast sandy soil and clay soil.

| Sandy soil | Both types of soil | Clay soil |

## Test Prep

Choose the letter that best completes the statement or answers the question.

**17.** All rocks contain
- (A) loam.
- (B) minerals.
- (C) water.
- (D) sediments.

**18.** In what rocks are fossils most often found?
- (F) sedimentary
- (G) igneous
- (H) metamorphic
- (I) all of the above

**19.** The layer of soil just below the topsoil is
- (A) loam.
- (B) decayed matter.
- (C) rock.
- (D) subsoil.

**20.** **Writing in Science**
**Persuasive** Write a letter to a member of a city council that discusses why rich farmland is valuable to everyone in the community.

**215**

# Dr. Elissa R. Levine

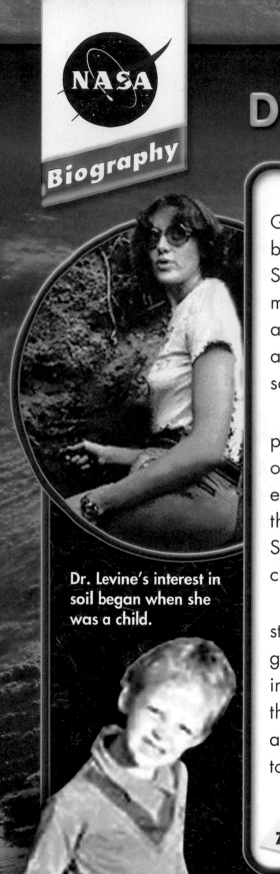

Dr. Levine's interest in soil began when she was a child.

Dr. Levine is a Soil Scientist for NASA's Goddard Space Flight Center. She has been interested in soil for a long time. She once said, "When I was little my mother sat me in the soil and showed me all kinds of interesting things to look at and play with. I've been interested in the soil ever since."

Dr. Levine gathers information from pictures taken by satellites that travel high over Earth. The pictures tell about our environment. She also studies the ways that soil changes all around the world. She is trying to find the causes of these changes.

Dr. Levine also teaches about soil to students all over the world. The students gather data about soil. Dr. Levine uses the information to make computer models of the soils. She has found that soil connects all the other parts of our environment together.

## Lab zone Take-Home Activity

Make a list of all the things that Dr. Levine might have found in soil when she was a child. How would each thing help the soil?

216

You Will Discover

- layers of the Earth
- how some forces change Earth's surface quickly.
- how other forces change Earth's surface slowly.

# Chapter 8

# Changes on Earth

online
Student Edition
sfsuccessnet.com

Discovery Channel School
Student DVD

# How do forces cause changes on Earth's surface?

magma

lava

landform

mantle

crust

core

218

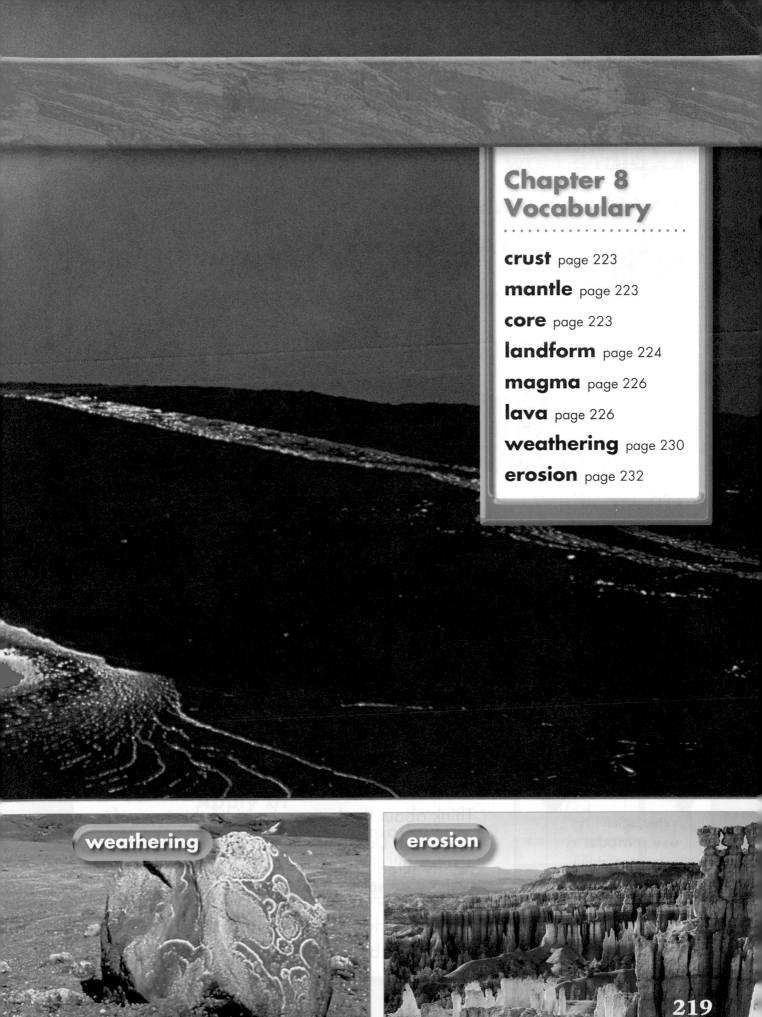

## Chapter 8
## Vocabulary

weathering

erosion

219

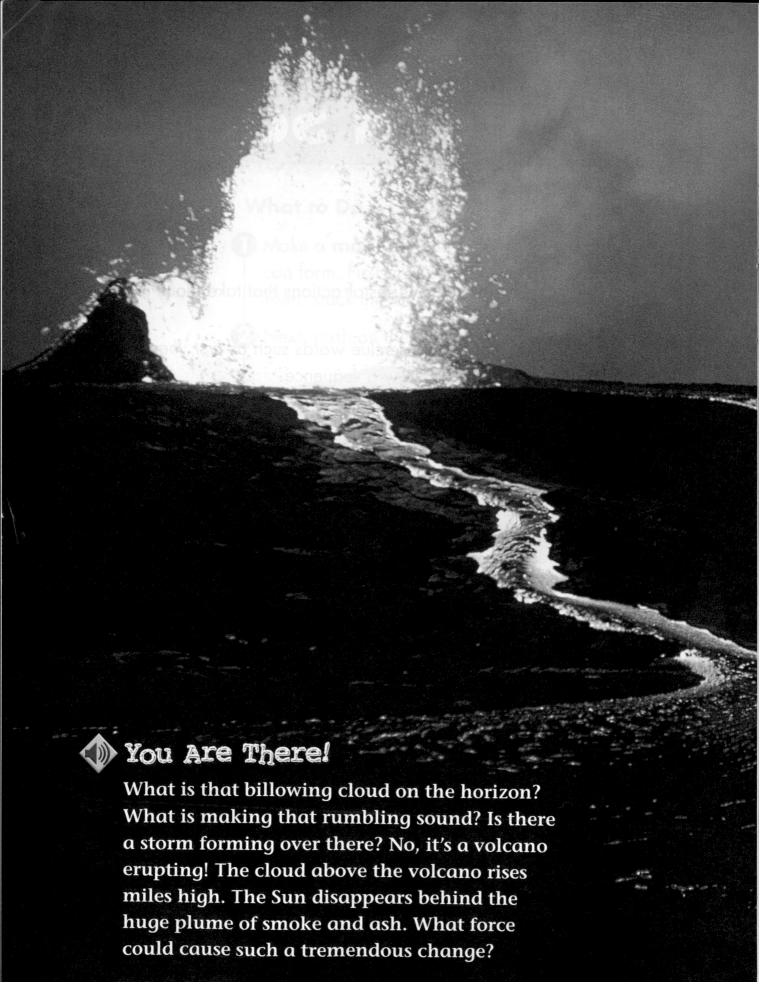

### 🔊 You Are There!

What is that billowing cloud on the horizon? What is making that rumbling sound? Is there a storm forming over there? No, it's a volcano erupting! The cloud above the volcano rises miles high. The Sun disappears behind the huge plume of smoke and ash. What force could cause such a tremendous change?

AudioText 🔊

## Lesson 1

# What are Earth's layers?

*If you could remove a big chunk of Earth, you would see that it is made up of layers.*

Mantle

Crust

Core

### Earth's Layers

Earth can be divided into three main layers. You live on the outer layer of Earth—the **crust.** Earth's crust is made of different kinds of rock. The thickness of the crust varies from place to place. Its thickness under the continents is about 37 kilometers (23 miles). That may seem pretty thick. If you compare all the Earth to a peach, however, the Earth's crust would be just the skin.

Beneath the crust lies the **mantle.** Earth's mantle is made of very hot igneous and metamorphic rock. It may flow like oozing toothpaste.

The **core** is the innermost layer of Earth. It is made of metal. The core is hot enough to melt. The center of the core is packed together so tightly, however, that it remains mostly solid. The much larger outer part of the core is a very hot, dense liquid.

1. **✔ Checkpoint** What is Earth's core like?

2. **Writing in Science** **Expository** Compare Earth's layers to the parts of a peach. Make a labeled drawing in your **science journal**. Then, write a paragraph that compares the two.

## Shapes on Earth's Surface

Does the land near you have mountains, hills, and valleys? Each is an example of a **landform.** Landforms are the solid features formed on Earth's crust. Other features include bodies of water.

Many forces shape landforms. These forces come from above and below Earth's crust. Moving water, though, is the main force. For example, rivers can act like saws. Pebbles and sand in the moving water slowly cut through rock. Flooding rivers deposit pebbles, sand, and silt on their banks. These processes help shape valleys. Notice how many of the landforms below were shaped by water.

**Glacier**
A glacier is a large, moving body of ice. It forms in cold places where snow and ice pile up year after year. It slowly moves downhill.

**Valley**
A valley is a low, narrow area on the crust. Some valleys are formed by rivers, while others are formed by glaciers.

**Plateau**
A plateau is a plain that is higher than the land around it.

**Ocean**
The ocean is the salt water that covers almost three-fourths of Earth's surface.

**Coast**
The coast is land next to the ocean, which helps to shape the coastline.

**Volcano**
A volcano is an opening in Earth's crust through which hot, melted rock is forced up by pressure inside the Earth.

**Mountain**
A mountain is a landform high above the land around it. Some mountains form when blocks of rock are pushed up or drop down along cracks in the Earth's crust.

**River**
A river is a natural stream of water that helps to shape the valley or plain it passes through.

**Hill**
A hill is a high place on the Earth's surface, but not as high as a mountain. Hills often have rounded tops.

**Plain**
A plain is a large, mostly flat area.

**Lake**
A lake forms when the flow of water slows enough to fill an area.

## ✔ Lesson Checkpoint

1. Contrast Earth's crust, mantle, and core.

2. 🎯 **Sequence** List the events that occur as rivers move through rock.

3. **Art** in Science  Draw a picture that has mountains and valleys. Write how they might have formed on your picture.

225

# What are volcanoes and earthquakes?

*Volcanoes and earthquakes cause rapid and sometimes dangerous changes in the landscape.*

## How Do Volcanoes Form?

Volcanoes begin deep within the mantle where **magma** forms. Magma is hot, pasty rock that moves within the mantle. Magma close to the suface melts and flows easily because the pressure is less. Magma can gush out of weak spots in the crust, aided by the pressure of gases it contains. A volcano is an opening out of which this hot material erupts.

An eruption is like opening a can of shaken soda. Bubbles of gas separate from the liquid and force the liquid out. Material that erupts from a volcano contains ash, cinders, and hot, molten rock called **lava.** As lava cools and hardens, it becomes igneous rock. That's brand-new crust! If the rock builds to great heights, a mountain or island forms.

The red hot lava from this volcano hisses as it meets the cool water.

## Volcanoes

Magma collects in large pockets called magma chambers. As magma leaves the chamber, it moves up a tunnel or central vent. Sometimes, magma escapes from the central vent and erupts from side vents. Most magma, however, erupts at the top of the volcano through a bowl-shaped crater.

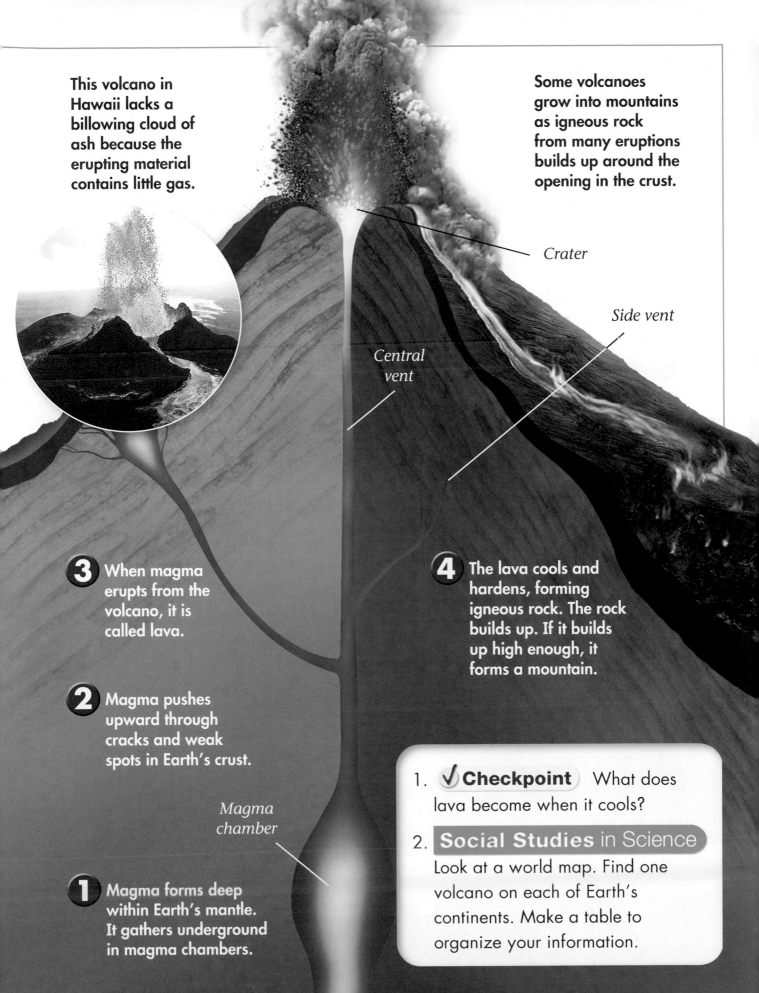

This volcano in Hawaii lacks a billowing cloud of ash because the erupting material contains little gas.

Some volcanoes grow into mountains as igneous rock from many eruptions builds up around the opening in the crust.

*Crater*

*Side vent*

*Central vent*

**3** When magma erupts from the volcano, it is called lava.

**4** The lava cools and hardens, forming igneous rock. The rock builds up. If it builds up high enough, it forms a mountain.

**2** Magma pushes upward through cracks and weak spots in Earth's crust.

*Magma chamber*

**1** Magma forms deep within Earth's mantle. It gathers underground in magma chambers.

1. ✔**Checkpoint** What does lava become when it cools?

2. **Social Studies** in Science
Look at a world map. Find one volcano on each of Earth's continents. Make a table to organize your information.

## Earthquakes

Have you ever built a play house out of flimsy cardboard? A sudden bump sends vibrations through the house and it can fall over. In a similar way, sudden shifts in direction between parts of Earth's crust cause the ground to vibrate in all directions. This shaking is an earthquake. Most earthquakes happen along faults. A fault is a large crack in the Earth's crust.

The vibrations of an earthquake move as waves that travel through the Earth. Waves that travel along Earth's surface move back and forth and up and down. These waves can cause cracks and can pile up rubble in areas around the parts of the crust that moved.

The 7-second Loma Prieta earthquake in 1989 destroyed this road in Oakland, California.

## Earthquake Damage

The damage an earthquake causes depends on how close the earthquake is to the surface and how long the crust shakes. Also, the closer an earthquake is to a city or town, the more damage it can cause to buildings, bridges, and underground pipes.

An earthquake can cause landslides. Landslides are just what you might think they are. They are downhill movements of rocks and earth. The loose surface of the land slides down a slope.

Landslides can happen on the ocean floor or on land. Undersea landslides can form giant waves. Landslides on hills and mountains can ruin homes and destroy roads. They can bury large areas.

Vibrations from an earthquake cause cracks such as this one.

Parts of this parking garage snapped during a 1994 earthquake.

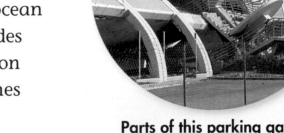

Loose soil and rock slid down this hillside during a landslide.

### ✓ Lesson Checkpoint

1. Compare and contrast magma and lava.

2. Where do most earthquakes happen? Why?

3. **Sequence** Use a graphic organizer to show the steps in the eruption of a volcano.

229

The growing roots of this tree in Arizona are helping to break the rock apart.

# What are weathering and erosion?

*Weathering and erosion are forces that change the surface of the Earth.*

## Weathering

You might not see this happen but landforms change constantly. For this to happen, rocks in landforms must first break apart. **Weathering** is any action that breaks rocks into smaller pieces.

Weathering changes can be very slow. Some may take less than a year. Others might take centuries. Still, weathering goes on all the time.

Plants sometimes cause weathering. Their roots grow into soil and rocks. As the roots grow, they split and break up the soil and rocks.

When water mixes with the products of decay in soil, the water can change. This water weathers rock in a special way. Water changes the minerals in rock upon which the soil rests. The change in minerals weakens the rock and it begins to break apart.

While in a glacier, this rock became smaller and smoother as forces acted upon it.

Freezing and thawing of water are powerful agents of weathering. Water first seeps into cracks in a rock. Next, it freezes during cold weather. Freezing makes water expand. The ice then pushes against the sides of the crack. Over the years the rock finally breaks apart.

Ice wears rocks in another way. Glaciers are huge bodies of ice that move slowly over Earth's crust. As the glacier moves, rocks and ice scrape against the ground. The tremendous force of this action grinds valleys wide and smooth. When the glacier melts, weathered rocks of all sizes drop to the ground. Ridges of ground-up rocks line the edges where the glaciers once stood.

1. **✓ Checkpoint** Describe weathering, giving three examples.

2. **Math in Science** Look at the pictures of rocks on this page. How much bigger is a boulder than a cobble? How much smaller is a sand grain than a pebble? How many sand grains could you line up along a meter stick?

## Sizes of Rocks

Weathering breaks rocks into smaller and smaller pieces. Water wears many rocks to a smooth and rounded shape. The following lists the order of size from largest to smallest.

**Boulder** 300 mm

**Cobble** 100 mm

**Pebble** 30 mm

**Sand** 1 mm

**Silt** Each is a tiny speck!

**Clay** You need a microscope to see clay particles!

**231**

It took millions of years for waves carrying sand and pebbles to carve a hole in this cliff.

This island formed as sand dropped from moving water. Waves will continue to shape it.

Do you ever slump down in your chair? The whole side of this hill slumped down.

## Erosion

Sometimes weathered material stays in place. Sometimes it is picked up and slowly or quickly carried to other places. The movement of weathered material is **erosion.** Water, wind, gravity, and glaciers can cause erosion.

## Erosion by Water and Wind

Erosion by water changes many landforms. Rivers carry bits of rock from place to place. Sand and mud flow over a river's banks during a flood. New islands can form as a result of erosion. This happens when rivers carry rock and bits of soil to the ocean. These particles build up over time. Some form islands just off the coast. Wind and waves continue to shape these islands.

Rainwater causes erosion when it carries away soil from hilly farm fields. Waves cause erosion along shorelines.

Erosion by wind is common in dry regions, such as deserts. Wind can pick up the dry sand and soil and blow them to other places. Few tall plants grow in deserts, so there is little to stop the particles from blowing around. The particles bump into rocks and break off tiny grains. Over time, more grains are broken off. At some point, you notice the rocks are changing.

## Erosion by Gravity and Living Things

Gravity can cause erosion. Gravity pulls rocks and soil downhill. This material moves slowly if the slope is gentle. However, weathered material can move quickly on steep slopes. A mudflow is the quick movement of very wet soil. A rockslide is the quick movement of rocks down a slope.

Living things can cause erosion. For example, ground squirrels tunnel through soil. Worms mix and move soil. Ants move soil to make underground nests. All this tunneling allows water and air to move into the ground. These non-living agents of erosion continue the process.

**Rain and melting snow carved out these rock columns.**

### ✓ Lesson Checkpoint

1. How are weathering and erosion different? How are they alike?

2. How does most erosion happen in dry regions?

3. **Writing in Science** **Expository**
Use the photos on page 232 and this page to explain in your **science journal** how water is causing erosion.

233

# Lab zone Guided Inquiry

## Investigate How can you observe erosion?

### Materials

safety goggles

small paper cups and pencil

tub and spoon

sand, mud, rocks

eraser and ruler

water

### Process Skills

Recording your careful **observations** in a chart is one way of **collecting data**.

### What to Do

**1** Poke 4 holes in the bottom of a paper cup. This is your Rain Cup.

Poke from the inside!

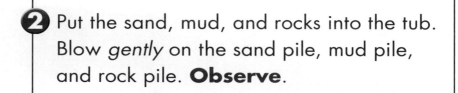
Rain Cup

**Be careful!** Wear safety goggles!

**2** Put the sand, mud, and rocks into the tub. Blow *gently* on the sand pile, mud pile, and rock pile. **Observe**.

**3** Use an eraser to prop up the back edge of the tub. Fill a small paper cup $\frac{1}{2}$ full with water. Hold the Rain Cup 4 cm above the sand. Quickly pour water into the Rain Cup. Observe. **Collect data**. Record your observations in a chart.

| | Amount of Erosion by Wind and Water | |
| --- | --- | --- |
| | Effect of Blowing | Effect of Moving Water |
| Sand | | |
| Mud | | |
| Rocks | | |

**4** Repeat step 3 for the mud pile and the rock pile.

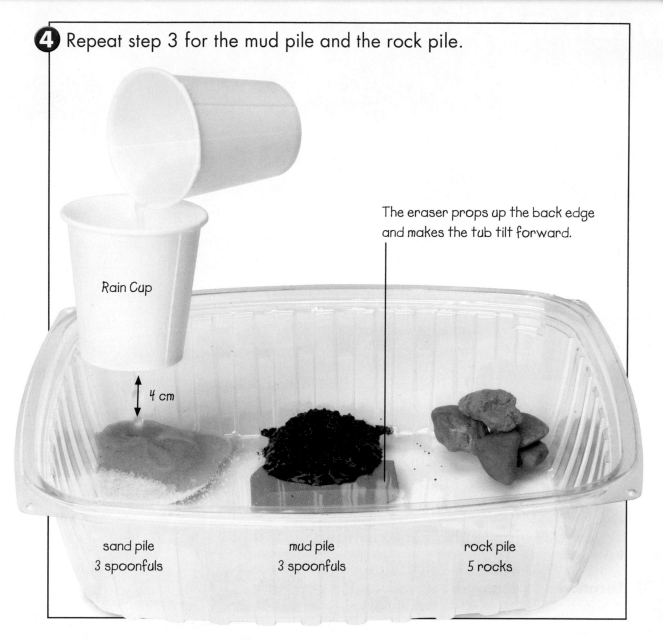

The eraser props up the back edge and makes the tub tilt forward.

Rain Cup

4 cm

sand pile
3 spoonfuls

mud pile
3 spoonfuls

rock pile
5 rocks

## Explain Your Results

1. **Interpret Data** Which caused more erosion, blowing air or moving water? Which was eroded the most, the sand pile, the mud pile, or the rock pile? Which was eroded the least?

2. How is your **model** like what happens in the real world? How is it different? How can your model be used to learn about erosion?

### Go Further

How could you change your model to prevent water or wind erosion? Think of a way to solve the problem. Then use your model to test your solution.

235

# Math in Science

## Measuring an Earthquake

"The earthquake measured 6.7 on the Richter scale." Did you ever hear a news reporter talk about an earthquake this way? The number tells how strong the earthquake was. The strength of an earthquake depends on how much the rocks along the fault moved and how long the earthquake lasts.

In the table below, 9 earthquakes are listed in order of their strength, from least to greatest.

| Some Major California Earthquakes | | | |
|---|---|---|---|
| **Location** | **Strength** | **Length of Fault (kilometers)** | **Time (seconds)** |
| Whittier Narrows | 5.9 | 6 | 3 |
| North Palm Springs | 5.9 | 20 | 4 |
| Borrego Mountain | 6.5 | 25 | 6 |
| Northridge | 6.7 | 14 | 7 |
| Loma Prieta | 7.0 | 40 | 7 |
| Landers | 7.3 | 70 | 24 |
| Kern County | 7.5 | 75 | 27 |
| San Francisco | 7.7 | 400 | 110 |
| Fort Tejon | 7.8 | 360 | 130 |

Tools Take It to the Net
sfsuccessnet.com

Use the table on page 236 to answer these questions.

**1** Which earthquake was the strongest?

A. San Francisco      B. Kern County

C. Loma Prieta      D. Fort Tejon

**2** Which earthquake lasted the least amount of time?

F. Whittier Narrows      G. Fort Tejon

H. Landers      I. North Ridge

**3** Which earthquake happened along the longest fault?

A. North Palm Springs      B. Borrego Mountain

C. Fort Tejon      D. San Francisco

**4** Which of these statements is true?

F. Shorter faults produce stronger earthquakes.

G. Longer faults produce weaker quakes.

H. Stronger quakes last longer than weaker quakes.

I. Weaker quakes last longer than stronger quakes.

**Lab zone Take-Home Activity**

Use the library to find data about these earthquakes: Chile, 1960; Alaska, 1964; Kuril Islands, 1963; Indonesia, 1938; and Kamchatka, 1952. Arrange the earthquakes in a table like the one shown. How do these quakes compare with those that struck California?

# Chapter 8 Review and Test Prep

## Use Vocabulary

| | |
|---|---|
| **core** (page 223) | **lava** (page 226) |
| **crust** (page 223) | **magma** (page 226) |
| **erosion** (page 232) | |
| | **mantle** (page 223) |
| **landform** (page 224) | **weathering** (page 230) |

Use the vocabulary word from the box above that best completes each sentence.

1. Hot, molten rock on Earth's surface is _____.

2. Earth's _____ is the innermost layer of the planet.

3. A hill, a mountain, and a valley are each a(n) _____.

4. The thinnest layer of Earth is the _____.

5. Hot, molten rock that forms deep underground is _____.

6. Magma forms in Earth's thickest layer, which is called the _____.

7. The breaking of rocks into smaller pieces is _____.

8. The moving of weathered materials is _____.

## Explain Concepts

9. Which is a better model of Earth's layers, a raw egg or a hard-boiled egg? Explain your choice.

10. Explain how weathering and erosion change Earth's landforms.

11. How do volcanoes change Earth's surface?

12. Compare and contrast erosion that wind causes and erosion that water causes.

### Process Skills

13. **Classify** Classify each of the following as either weathering or erosion.
    - Ⓐ a river carrying silt flooding its banks
    - Ⓑ water freezing in the crack of a cliff
    - Ⓒ mud sliding down a hill

14. **Model** Make a series of four drawings to show how a volcano builds up over time.

MindPoint Quiz Show

**15. Infer** A fault lies between a town with a few buildings and a city with many skyscrapers. The town is 10 miles from the fault. The city is 5 miles from the fault. Infer which area might have the most damage in an earthquake.

## Sequence

**16.** Make a graphic organizer like the one below. Fill in the spaces to show the steps that water may take to weather rocks.

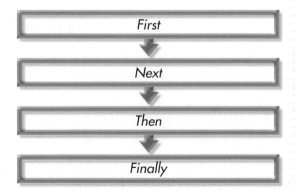

First

↓

Next

↓

Then

↓

Finally

 **Test Prep**

Choose the letter that best completes the statement or answers the question.

**17.** Why is Earth's core solid when it is hot enough to melt?

Ⓐ It is in the middle of the planet.

Ⓑ It is smaller than the mantle.

Ⓒ It is made of igneous rocks.

Ⓓ It is under great pressure.

**18.** What makes water a powerful cause of weathering?

Ⓕ It is a liquid.

Ⓖ It takes up more space when it freezes.

Ⓗ It evaporates.

Ⓘ It rains all the time.

**19.** Why is erosion by wind so effective in deserts?

Ⓐ Deserts are very moist.

Ⓑ Deserts are very dry.

Ⓒ Deserts are landforms.

Ⓓ Deserts do not have living things.

**20.** Writing in Science

**Narrative** Think of being in San Francisco in 1906. That year, a violent earthquake shook the city. Write a paragraph about your experience in this earthquake. Tell what happened during the earthquake and in the week following it.

# Dr. Jean Dickey

**Dr. Jean Dickey uses views of Earth from space to measure Earth's movements.**

As a child growing up in Pennsylvania, Jean Dickey, like her mother, had a strong interest in math and science. While she was still in college, she worked at the Argonne National Laboratory. This laboratory does work in many areas of math and science.

Today, Dr. Dickey is a physicist at NASA's Jet Propulsion Laboratory. One of Dr. Dickey's recent projects was to investigate why Earth appears to be bulging around its middle. That's right! Earth is getting about 1 millimeter "fatter" near the equator each year. After much study, Dr. Dickey and others found two causes for Earth's "weight gain." One is the rapid melting of glaciers. Another is a change in the size and shape of Earth's oceans.

Dr. Dickey's group is also responsible for keeping an eye on Earth's movements in space. They measure and record even the smallest shifts in Earth's place in space. This information is used to help navigate spacecraft.

## Lab zone Take-Home Activity

Draw and color a cartoon that shows what is happening to Earth around the equator. Include sentences that explain why it is getting larger.

# Chapter 9
# Natural Resources

## You Will Discover

- ways we use natural resources.
- the difference between renewable and nonrenewable resources.
- ways you can help conserve natural resources.

online
**Student Edition**
sfsuccessnet.com

# How can people use natural resources responsibly?

natural resource

renewable resource

nonrenewable resource

## Chapter 9 Vocabulary

conservation

recycle

243

# Explore How can you classify resources?

A resource is something people use. All the materials on this page come from or are made from resources.

## Materials

grape

paper

wool cloth

aluminum foil

cup with water

plastic bottle

solar energy

solar energy

## What to Do

**1** **Classify** each resource in the List of Resources. Does it belong in group A, B, or C?

**2** Look at each material in the Materials list. Match each with the resource it comes from.

| List of Resources |
|---|
| grapevine |
| river |
| trees |
| bauxite (mined from the ground, contains aluminum) |
| sheep |
| sunlight |
| petroleum (oil, pumped out of the ground, used to make plastic) |

**Group A**
Cannot be replaced

**Group B**
Can be replaced within a fairly short time

**Group C**
Cannot be used up

**3** Now classify each material into a group based on the resource it comes from.

plastic bottle
wool cloth
aluminum foil
paper
water
solar energy
grape

## Process Skills

When you sorted the materials into the groups, you **classified** them based on the type of resource they came from.

## Explain Your Results

Explain how you **classified** the resources and materials.

# How to Read Science

## Compare and Contrast

When you **compare** things, you tell how they are alike. When you **contrast** things, you tell how they are different.

- Words such as *similar, like, all, both,* or *in the same way* are clues that things are being compared.

- Words such as *different, unlike,* or *in a different way* are clues that things are being contrasted.

**Science Article**

### Worm Tunnels

Soil in which earthworms live is not like other soil. Earthworms dig tunnels in soil. As a result, plants grow in a different way.

Plant roots grow more quickly down tunnels. Rainwater and air that roots need move easily through them too. Also, earthworms leave body wastes in tunnels. These have a lot of nutrients that plants need to grow.

Unlike soil with worms, soil without earthworms cannot support plants as well.

## Apply It!

Study the graphic organizer below.

Contrast     Compare     Contrast

Soil with earthworms    Both soils    Soil without earthworms

Make a graphic organizer like the one shown. Use it to **classify** ways that these two soils are alike and different.

You are walking through a lush, green forest. A soft cushion of needles keeps your footsteps silent. You smell the trees. You hear chipmunks twittering in the branches. Birds dart back and forth. This is a beautiful place. But the trees may soon be cut down for lumber and paper. Can we keep our forests and still have the products we need?

## Lesson 1

# What are resources?

*Everything we use comes from in and above the Earth. Some of these materials can be replaced, but others cannot. A few resources are never used up.*

## Resources That Can Be Replaced

The things we need come from natural resources. A **natural resource** is an important material from the Earth that living things need.

Some natural resources can be replaced. For example, trees and crops grow in soil on Earth's surface. Both need water and air. Water comes from rain, rivers, lakes, and groundwater. Air is everywhere above ground.

People cut down trees for their wood. They use wood to build new houses and turn wood chips into pulp. Pulp is made into paper. Paper products include boxes, newspapers, and this book.

People can plant new trees to replace those cut down. In time, the trees will grow big enough to be cut down again. A resource that can be replaced in a fairly short time is called a **renewable resource.** Trees are a renewable resource.

These logs at a lumber or paper mill came from trees.

Lumber mills saw tree trunks into boards that are used to build new houses.

1. ✔**Checkpoint**  What makes some resources renewable?

2. **Writing** in Science  **Expository** In your **science journal** make a table with two columns. Title one column *Wood.* Title the other *Paper.* Use the table to list things found in your home made from each. Then, write two paragraphs about how your family uses wood and paper products.

## Resources That Cannot Be Replaced

Many natural resources come from below the ground. Miners dig into the ground to get rocks called ores. Ores are important natural resources because they contain metals or other minerals that people use. Examples of useful metals are copper, iron, and aluminum. Hematite, for instance, is an ore that contains the metal iron.

Steel is made from iron. What will you use today that has steel in it? How about a bus or a fork? Lots of things are made of steel. But there is only so much iron ore in the ground. Once we use it up, it cannot be replaced. A resource that cannot be replaced is a **nonrenewable resource.**

Coal is another nonrenewable resource. Like oil and natural gas, coal is a fuel. When it is burned it releases useful energy. Energy from these fuels provides heat in buildings and power for cars, trucks, and planes. The energy from these fuels can be used only once. We can get more fuel by digging more of these materials from the ground. But supplies of these fuels are limited.

| Using Resources | |
| --- | --- |
| **Resource** | **Uses** |
| **Oil** | Gasoline, paint, plastic, shampoo |
| **Coal** | Electricity, heat, paint thinner, insecticides |
| **Iron ore** | Machines, bicycles, autos, buildings |

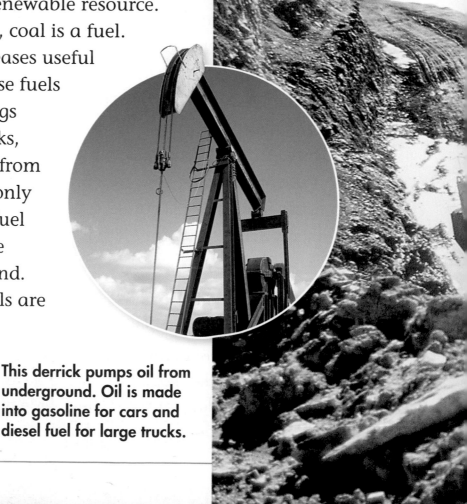

This derrick pumps oil from underground. Oil is made into gasoline for cars and diesel fuel for large trucks.

When we use up an ore, mineral, or fuel resource in one place, we must find new places to look. Mining and drilling can leave permanent marks, such as the open pit mine in the picture. Getting important natural resources from Earth can change its surface.

Hematite is an ore that contains iron.

## An Endless Supply of Resources

Some natural resources are not used up. Plants, for instance, receive an ongoing supply of sunlight. The Earth can cleanse and return the air we breathe and water we need. Sunlight, air, and water are examples of resources that are always available on Earth.

This coal formed in the Earth from plant life that lived millions of years ago.

A huge crane loads coal into a dump truck at a mine.

✓ **Lesson Checkpoint**

1. List two nonrenewable resources.

2. Why is coal a nonrenewable resource?

3. **Compare and Contrast**
   How are renewable and nonrenewable resources alike? How are they different?

Dirty water is piped into a wetland in Florida. It will become clean enough to be piped back into a river.

Water from homes is filtered through sand in ponds like these. Farmers use the recycled water for their orange trees.

# How can we protect our resources?

*We must protect natural resources by not using them up or damaging them.*

## Using Resources Responsibly

When people walk or ride a bicycle or a bus instead of riding in a car, they are saving fuel. When they choose products that have less packaging, they are saving paper and plastic and making less garbage. Saving in these ways is called conservation. **Conservation** is the wise use of natural resources so that people do not waste them or use them up.

Clean water is an important resource. We can conserve water by using less of it. You can, for instance, turn off the water while brushing your teeth and take shorter showers.

One way that communities conserve water is to clean the water that is used. A wetland, for instance, cleans dirty water. First, the dirty water is piped into wetlands. Soil filters out harmful particles. Then, plants and tiny living things break down the particles. Afterward, the water is clean enough to flow back into a river and be used again.

Soil is another resource that must be used wisely. Soil needs protection from water and wind erosion. Some farmers help conserve soil when they plant their crops around hills instead of up and down the hills. The curved rows of plants act like dams to hold back rainwater. Soil soaks up water instead of being washed away. Farmers also plant trees alongside fields to keep soil from blowing away.

As people in cities need more room, they often build new houses on nearby farmland. Buildings and roads cover the soil. The soil is then lost to farming. What can we do to protect land that has good soil for growing crops?

We can start by protecting soil in our own backyard. We can put yard clippings and leaves where they decay instead of sending them to the landfill. This natural process turns them into compost. You can add compost to garden soil for fertilizer.

We could allow these leaves to decay into compost. Then they would add nutrients to soil.

Contour plowing keeps soil from washing away.

1. **✓ Checkpoint** Describe ways people can conserve water.

2. **Writing** in Science **Expository** Research ways to make a compost pile that will become fertilizer. In your **science journal** write a paragraph to explain it.

251

## Using Up Land Space for Trash

Everything we use is made from natural resources. For example, plastic milk jugs are made from oil. Food cans are made from metals such as steel and tin. When we no longer need these products, we throw them away. They become trash. The trouble with our trash is that it never really goes away. A truck often hauls trash to a landfill. A landfill is a large area in which trash is buried. Trash rests on top of a liner so that pollution does not leak into groundwater. Once in place, we no longer have to see, smell, or worry about our garbage making us sick. But it still exists and the landfills continue to grow.

**We put more than two hundred million tons of trash each year into landfills like this one.**

| What is in a Year's Worth of My Trash? | |
| --- | --- |
| **Materials** | **Mass (in kilograms)** |
| Paper | 250 |
| Plastic | 80 |
| Metal (steel cans) | 40 |
| Metal (aluminum cans) | 10 |
| Glass | 40 |
| Food scraps | 80 |

Landfills are filling up and closing down. The number of landfills has fallen from 8,000 in 1988 to less than 2,000 today. Our need for land in which to bury our trash continues to grow. Most people, however, would rather see land used for other purposes.

One way we are reducing the need for landfill space is by burning garbage in special furnaces. Burning garbage also gives off energy that can heat buildings and generate electricity. However, the smoke from the burning must be cleaned. If the smoke is not cleaned, it can harm the air we breathe. Special smoke cleaners are expensive.

Another way we are lessening the need for landfill space is by reducing the amount of trash we make. If we were not doing this, we would have needed 100 new landfill areas. What are ways we are reducing the amount of trash we make?

These are objects we use every day. Can some of these materials be used again?

**✓ Lesson Checkpoint**

1. Where does most garbage go after it is taken from your home?

2. What are some ways to save landfill space?

3. **Math in Science** If you throw away 2 kilograms of trash each day, how much trash would you throw away in a year?

# What are ways to use resources again?

*Many things can be used more than once. Old materials can be used to make new things. Reusing and recycling conserves land, keeping it from becoming landfill space.*

## Using Resources Again

When you reuse things, you conserve resources. For example, you can reuse cloth napkins, but not paper ones. You can reuse empty jars to store leftover food. Or you can give toys and clothes you have outgrown to others to use.

Another way to conserve resources is to recycle things that contain useful material. You **recycle** when you change something so that it can be used again. The useful resources that went into making objects can then be made into new products. Many of these new products are made from recycled metal, glass, plastic, or paper.

**1 Sort Glass**
Recycled glass bottles and jars are separated by color. They are broken into small pieces.

**2 Ship to Glass Company**
Pieces of glass are put into boxes. The boxes are shipped to a glass reprocessing company.

Let's follow the process used to recycle things that contain glass. Workers at the recycling plant sort glass by color. Common colors are clear, brown, and green. The bottles and jars are then broken into pieces called shards. Shards are shipped to glass companies. Glass shards must be passed under a magnet to remove metal caps and rings. Shards are then crushed into grain-sized particles called cullet. The cullet is cleaned and dried. Now the cullet is ready to be turned into new glass things. It is melted in furnaces and blown by machines into glass bottles and jars. Some is flattened into windowpanes. If glass is recycled, it can be used over and over again.

1. ✔**Checkpoint** What are the four main types of materials that are recycled?

2. **Compare and Contrast** How is recycling glass the same as recycling water? How does recycling glass differ from recycling water?

**Process Crushed Glass**
Glass bits are crushed into grain-sized particles. They are cleaned and dried.

**Make New Glass Bottles**
The bits are melted and reformed into glass bottles or jars.

**Saving Energy**

*100-watt light bulb*

*Food can*

*Glass bottle*

It takes more energy to make new steel cans and glass bottles than to recycle them. Recycling one soup can may save enough energy to light a 100-watt bulb for about half an hour. Recycling one glass bottle saves enough energy for four hours of light.

## Using Recycled Materials

Reusing and recycling are not new ideas. Your great-grandparents might have bought flour in cloth sacks. They cleaned the empty sacks, cut them, and sewed them into rags, towels, and even clothing!

Today, recycling is easier than ever. Many communities collect items to be recycled when they collect the regular garbage. Places such as movie theaters and office buildings have special containers for bottles and cans. Grocery stores collect used plastic shopping bags that can be recycled.

Conserving recycled material requires buying or using products that include it. For example, you can shop for products made out of recycled material. Your next sleeping bag might include stuffing made out of shredded plastic bottles. Your next sweater might be knit out of yarn recycled from old garments. Or you can play on playgrounds that have a surface made out of shredded car tires.

This park bench was made from recycled plastic. It will last for about 50 years.

This wall is made of old tires and aluminum cans held together with mud and straw.

A reused plastic barrel makes a terrific flower pot.

This playhouse was made from recycled plastic milk bottles.

## The Three *R's*

What's a good way to remember what you've learned to protect natural resources? Just think about the three *R's*—reduce, reuse, and recycle. *Reduce* the amount of resources you use and the trash you make. *Reuse* old things in new ways. *Recycle* everything you can. Every time you practice one of the three *R's*, you are helping to care for Earth.

Stuffing in this sleeping bag and yarn in this sweater are from recycled materials.

### ✓ Lesson Checkpoint

1. Why is it important to recycle?

2. What are the three *R's*?

3. **Art** in Science Draw or make a model showing how you might reuse something in an unusual way.

## Investigate Where are some freshwater resources?

When it rains, some water soaks into the ground. This water collects in aquifers, layers of underground rock, gravel, and sand. People drill wells to get this water. People also get water from lakes and rivers.

### Materials

safety goggles

container and gravel

paper cups and water

metric ruler

pencil and tape

spray nozzle and piece of nylon

plastic bag

### Process Skills

When you **collect data**, you can make and use a table or a chart to help record your **observations**.

## What to Do

❶ Make the **model** of an aquifer shown below.

❷ Slowly add water until the lake is 1.5 cm deep.

Use a pencil to poke 5 small holes in the bottom of a cup.

❸ Make it rain. Hold the cup with holes over the land. Move the cup as your partner pours a cup of water into your cup. **Observe** the water level.

5 cm

Water above ground forms lakes and rivers.

land

lake

water level   1.5 cm

gravel

You are modeling the effect on an aquifer of a year of heavy rains.

④ Cover the bottom end of a spray nozzle with nylon. Tape on the nylon. Put the end deep into the aquifer. Pump the nozzle. Spray water into a plastic bag held by your partner. **Observe**.

water between rocks

 Be careful!

Wear safety goggles!

You are modeling the effect of very heavy pumping.

⑤ Record your observations in a chart. Make and label a sketch or diagram of your model.

| | Observations | | |
|---|---|---|---|
| | **Changes in Height of Water Table** (increased, decreased, no change) | **Changes in Depth of Lake** (increased, decreased, no change) | **Explanation of Your Observations** (How do you know? Why do you think so?) |
| **Rain** | | | |
| **Pumping** | | | |

## Explain Your Results

1. **Infer** Think about a real aquifer. How might rain and pumping from wells affect the water level?

2. What problems might be caused by too much pumping? How might the problems be solved?

## Go Further

Change your model. Show how pollution from rain could enter the aquifer.

# Recycling

Almost everything we throw away can be recycled. But we do a better job recycling some things than other things.

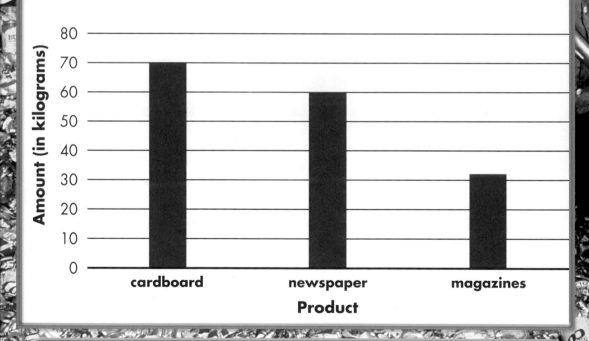

**Amount of Paper Products Recycled for Every 100 Kilograms**

The bar graph shows how much of three different paper products we recycle. We recycle 70 kilograms of cardboard boxes from every 100 kilograms we make. We recycle 60 kilograms of newspapers from every 100 kilograms we make. But we recycle only 32 kilograms of magazines from every 100 kilograms we make.

**Cans and Bottles Recycled for Every 100 Kilograms Made**

Amount (in kilograms)

80
60
40
20
0

steel cans | aluminum cans | plastic soft-drink bottles | plastic milk bottles | glass containers

Product

This bar graph shows how many kilograms of cans and bottles we recycle from every 100 kilograms we make.

Use the graph to answer the questions.

**1** About how many kilograms of glass containers do we recycle from every 100 kilograms made?

A. about 58 kilograms
B. about 32 kilograms
C. about 28 kilograms
D. about 22 kilograms

**2** Which container is recycled most?

F. steel cans
G. aluminum cans
H. plastic soft drink bottles
I. plastic milk bottles

**3** From every 100 kilograms of aluminum cans we make, about how many kilograms do we **not** recycle?

A. about 50 kilograms
B. about 20 kilograms
C. about 80 kilograms
D. about 100 kilograms

**Lab zone Take-Home Activity**

Recycling 1 glass jar saves enough energy to run a TV for 3 hours. Find how many glass jars you have in your kitchen. How many hours of TV-watching in your home would recycling the jars pay for in energy savings?

# Chapter 9 Review and Test Prep

## Use Vocabulary

| | |
|---|---|
| **conservation** (page 250) | **recycle** (page 254) |
| **natural resource** (page 247) | **renewable resource** (page 247) |
| **nonrenewable resource** (page 248) | |

Use the term from the list above that best completes each sentence.

1. Trees, iron ore, water, and air are each a _____.

2. A natural resource that can be replaced in a fairly short period of time is a _____.

3. When we change something so it can be used again, we _____ it.

4. A resource that cannot be replaced once it is used up is a _____.

5. The saving and wise use of Earth's resources is called _____.

## Explain Concepts

6. Explain the difference between a renewable resource like trees and a nonrenewable resource like iron ore.

7. What is the difference between a limited resource like iron ore and a limitless resource like air?

8. What are ways to conserve soil?

9. How is making compost out of yard wastes and food scraps one solution to the garbage problem?

10. Why is conserving natural resources important to everyone?

11. Why should people try to buy products made from recycled materials?

## Process Skills

12. We get milk from cows and wool to make clothing from sheep. **Infer** whether milk and wool are renewable or nonrenewable resources. Explain your answer.

13. Copy the table below on a sheet of paper. Then **classify** each kind of trash as paper, plastic, or metal.

| Trash | Classification |
|---|---|
| Milk carton | |
| Soft-drink can | |
| Magazine | |
| Laundry detergent bottle | |

## Compare and Constrast

**14.** Make a graphic organizer like the one below. Write in each part ways to show how reusing and recycling are similar and different.

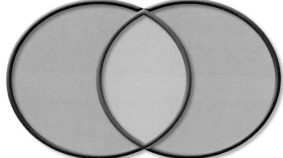

**Both**
Reusing    Reusing/    Recycling
            Recycling

## Test Prep

Choose the letter that best completes the statement or answers the question.

**15.** Which of the following is a renewable resource?

Ⓐ coal        Ⓑ oil
Ⓒ aluminum    Ⓓ sunlight

**16.** Which of the following does NOT conserve soil?

Ⓕ planting different crops
Ⓖ planting trees along the edges of fields
Ⓗ plowing up and down hillsides
Ⓘ adding compost to soil

**17.** Which of the following is a nonrenewable resource?

Ⓐ soil
Ⓑ iron ore
Ⓒ water
Ⓓ trees

**18.** Many power plants use coal to make electricity. Which of the following is a way you could help conserve coal?

Ⓕ Ride a bicycle instead of riding in a car.
Ⓖ Leave the television on when going outside.
Ⓗ Turn off lights when leaving a room.
Ⓘ Plant a flower garden using compost.

**19.** Explain why the answer you selected for Question 18 is best. For each of the answers you do not select, give a reason why it is not the best choice.

**20.** Writing in Science

**Narrative** Write a story about a person who saw how natural resources were not being protected and did something about it.

# Recycling Plant Worker

Workers sort paper to be recycled.

Recycled paper has become a roll of paper to be used again.

Many people work to conserve our natural resources. They have many different kinds of jobs. This is just one of them. But remember, conserving resources is a job you can do every day by using resources wisely.

Workers at recycling plants do their part to battle the garbage problem. Some work at plants that recycle aluminum or steel. Some workers drive trucks that pick up metals and take them to the plant. At the plant, other workers operate machines that shred the metal into small pieces. Still other workers melt and reshape the metal into new products.

Most recycling plant workers need at least a high school education.

## Lab zone Take-Home Activity

Paper, aluminum and steel cans, and plastic are recyclable. List the steps you take or would take to recycle these materials in your home.

# Unit B Test Talk

## Choose the Right Answer

To answer a multiple-choice test question, you need to choose an answer from several choices. Read the passage and then answer the questions.

> **Evaporation** changes water to an invisible gas called water vapor. **Condensation** changes water vapor into tiny drops of liquid water. These processes are parts of the water cycle.
>
> Water also causes **weathering** by breaking rocks into smaller pieces. Water then carries the weathered rock to different places.
>
> There is always the same amount of water on Earth. However, it is important to conserve fresh water and not waste it.

## Use What You Know

To choose the right answer, eliminate answer choices that you are sure are incorrect.

1. In the passage, the word "condensation" means
   - (A) liquid water changes into water vapor.
   - (B) water vapor changes into liquid water.
   - (C) liquid water changes into solid ice.
   - (D) solid ice changes into liquid water.

2. In the passage, the word "weathering" means
   - (F) causing weather patterns.
   - (G) changing water vapor into clouds.
   - (H) carrying pieces of rock to different places.
   - (I) breaking rocks into smaller pieces.

3. Which of the following statements about water is true?
   - (A) The amount of Earth's water always changes.
   - (B) Water can change Earth's surface.
   - (C) Condensation changes liquid water to water vapor.
   - (D) Evaporation changes water vapor to liquid water.

# Unit B Wrap-Up

## Chapter 5

### How does water change form?

- Living things need water to survive. People use water in many ways.
- Heating and cooling changes water between the forms of liquid, solid, and gas.

## Chapter 6

### How does weather follow patterns?

- Ways in which the sun heats the Earth and influences the water cycle cause weather patterns.
- Knowing about weather patterns helps people predict the weather and be safe.

## Chapter 7

### What are some kinds of rocks and soils?

- Rocks differ on the basis of how they form and what minerals they are made of.
- Soil covers most of Earth's land and is made of bits of rock, water, and humus.

## Chapter 8

### How do forces cause changes on Earth's surface?

- Forces within the Earth cause volcanoes and earthquakes to change Earth's surface quickly.
- Earth's surface can be changed slowly or sometimes quickly by weathering and erosion.

# Chapter 9

## How can people use natural resources responsibly?

- People can plant trees to replace ones they cut down and do things to make soil healthy and useful again.

- People can conserve natural resources by reducing the amount of resources they use and trash they make. They can also reuse and recycle materials.

## Performance Assessment

### Identify Changing Forms of Water

Water can be a solid, a liquid, or a gas. What changing forms of water can you identify? Place ice cubes and water in a plastic cup. Put the cup in a warm place and observe it over time. What forms of water were in the cup when you started? How did the forms change?

## Read More About Earth Science!

Look for books like these in the library.

# Lab zone Full Inquiry

## Experiment What settles first?

As a river flows to an ocean, it can carry particles of soil. The soil particles may be small, large, or in between. Some of them may settle out of the water quickly and are not carried far. Some may settle out of the water very slowly. These may be carried a long distance.

### Materials

3 small measuring cups

small gravel, sand, clay soil

hand lens

plastic bottles with caps

funnel and water

### Process Skills

**Experiments** have a **variable** you change, a variable you **observe**, and variables you **control**.

### Ask a question.

How do particles in water settle out?

### State a hypothesis.

If particles are larger, then do those particles settle faster, slower, or at about the same speed as smaller particles? Write your **hypothesis**.

### Identify and control variables.

The **variable** you change is the size of the particles. The variable you **observe** is how fast the particles settle. Every other part of the experiment must be **controlled**, or kept the same.

Control the amount of each type of particle. Use equal amounts of gravel, sand, and clay soil. Control how long the bottles are shaken. Shake all bottles the same length of time. Control when the particles start to settle. Stop shaking all the bottles at the same time.

## Test your hypothesis.

**1** **Measure** 30 mL of gravel, 30 mL of sand, and 30 mL of clay soil. Observe the particles. Use a hand lens. Observe their size, shape, and color. In a chart, record their sizes (smallest, medium-sized, largest).

**2** Put each kind of particle into a different bottle. Use a funnel. Fill each bottle $\frac{3}{4}$ full with water.

**3** Screw the caps on tightly. **Predict** which particles will settle out fastest. Along with 2 others in your group, begin shaking the bottles.

Hint: If the funnel jams, tap it or shake it.

gravel

sand

clay soil

$\frac{3}{4}$ full with water

269

**4** At the same time, stop shaking the bottles. Put them on a table. Observe what happens.

**5** Record the order in which the contents settle.

**6** Repeat twice. Do a total of 3 trials. Compare your results with your prediction and with those of other groups.

## Collect and record your data.

| Type of Particles | Size of Particles (smallest, medium-sized, largest) |
|---|---|
| Small gravel | |
| Sand | |
| Clay soil | |

## Interpret your data.

Complete the charts. Analyze the information. Compare the sizes of the particles and how fast they settle.

| Type of Particles | Speed of Settling (fastest, medium, slowest) | | | | |
|---|---|---|---|---|---|
| | Predicted | Trial A | Trial B | Trial C | Overall |
| Small gravel | | | | | |
| Sand | | | | | |
| Clay soil | | | | | |

Why do you think scientists repeat experiments?

| Type of Particles | Size of Particles (smallest, medium-sized, largest) | Speed of Settling (fastest, medium, slowest) |
|---|---|---|
| Small gravel | | |
| Sand | | |
| Clay soil | | |

## State your conclusion.

Cooperate with others in your group. Discuss your results. Consider the explanations of others. Respect their ideas. Draw a conclusion from your data. Does it agree with your hypothesis? **Communicate** your conclusion.

## Go Further

What would happen if soil particles of different sizes were mixed together? Make a prediction based on the results of this activity. Design and carry out a plan to investigate.

## Full Inquiry

### Using Scientific Methods

1. Ask a question.
2. State your hypothesis.
3. Identify/control variables.
4. Test your hypothesis.
5. Collect and record your data.
6. Interpret your data.
7. State your conclusion
8. Go further.

## Predicting Weather

Weather patterns help people predict the weather, but predictions can be wrong.

**Idea:** Compare your observations of the weather with weather forecasts from TV and radio stations, and newspapers to see how accurate they are.

## Comparing Soils

Soils have different amounts of sand, silt, clay, and humus.

**Idea:** Use a hand lens to compare soil samples in your area.

## An Earthquake Model

Most earthquakes happen along breaks in Earth's crust.

**Idea:** Use clay, heavy cardboard, and objects to model what happens to Earth's crust, roads, and other objects during an earthquake.

## Recycling

Recycling conserves landfill space and resources.

**Idea:** Use information about your community's recycling program to make a display with examples of what can be recycled and ways to sort it.

# Unit C
# Physical Science
## in Indiana

Did you know that some tires used by race cars have a mass of as little as 15 kilograms? Many of the parts of race cars are built specially to keep mass low. Less mass can mean greater speed!

# Field Trip

## Indianapolis Motor Speedway Hall of Fame Museum

When you visit the Indianapolis Motor Speedway Hall of Fame Museum, you may be able to ride around the racetrack. The Indianapolis Motor Speedway's nickname is "The Brickyard" because the track was covered at one time by over 3 million bricks. Today, the only part of "The Brickyard" that is still brick is about one meter, or "yard," at the start-finish line.

Race cars can travel faster on a smooth track because there is less friction. The chart shows how the surface of the Indianapolis Motor Speedway has changed.

| Date | Track Surface |
|------|---------------|
| Summer, 1909 | Crushed rock and tar |
| Fall, 1909 | Brick |
| 1936 | Rough spots covered with asphalt |
| 1941 | Most of track covered with asphalt |
| 1961 | All but start-finish line covered with asphalt |

## Find out more:

Research to find out more about the Indianapolis Motor Speedway Hall of Fame Museum. Find out about the winning speeds of several Indianapolis 500 races.

- Make a chart to compare speeds on a racetrack, a highway, and a street in your community.
- Suppose you are a race car making one lap around the track. Write a story that describes your trip.

EC IN 10 9 8 7 6 5 4 3

# Chapter 10
# Matter and Its Properties

## You Will Discover

- how to observe and describe matter.
- the different states of matter.
- ways to measure different properties of matter.

online
**Student Edition**
sfsuccessnet.com

Discovery Channel School
**Student DVD**

DISCOVERY CHANNEL SCHOOL

Build Background

# What are the properties of matter?

matter

property

pressure

element

atom

274

# Chapter 10 Vocabulary

## periodic table

Periodic Table of Elements

| State at Room Temperature |
| --- |
| = Solid   = Liquid   = Gas |

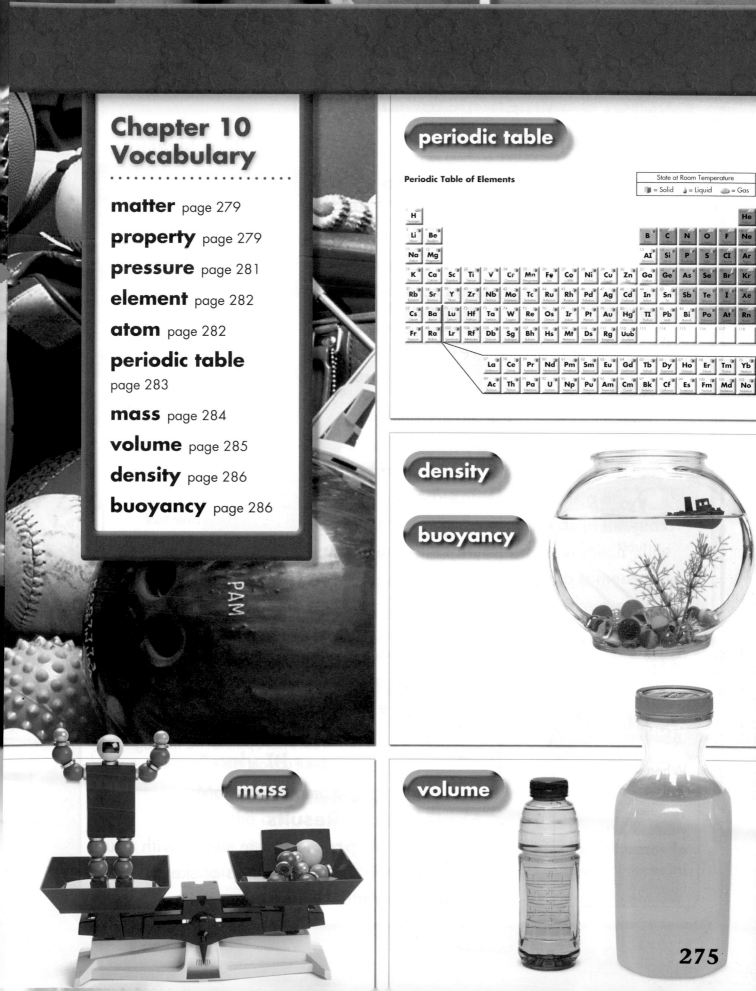

## density

## buoyancy

## mass

## volume

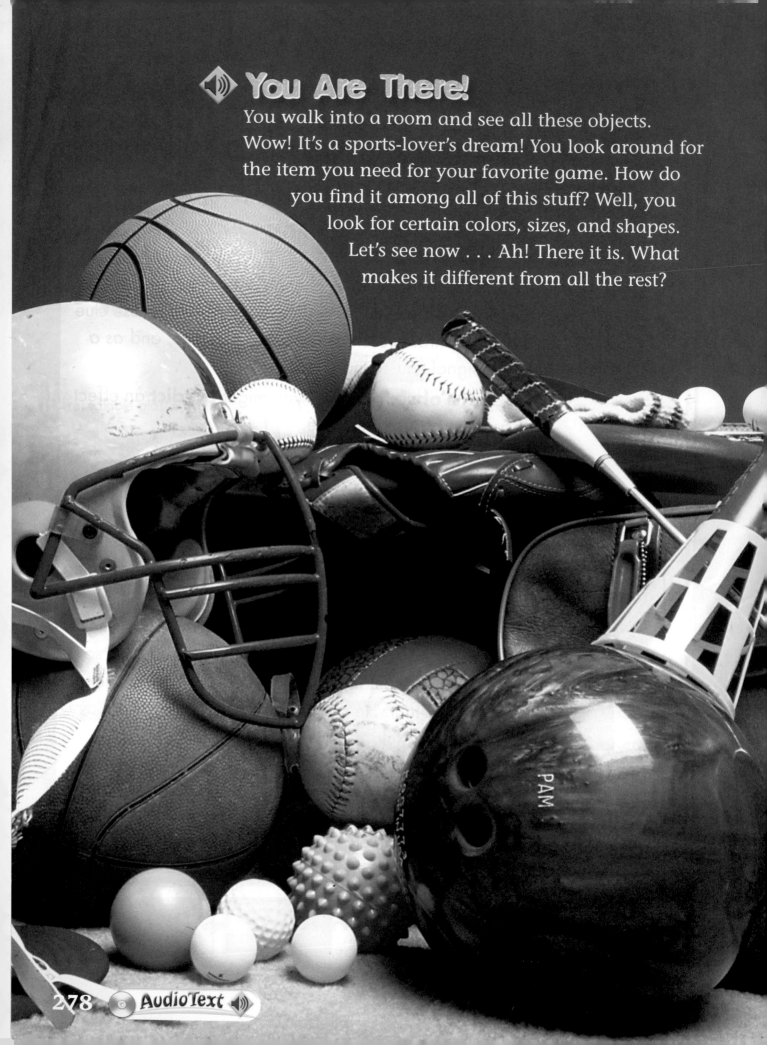

## 🔊 You Are There!

You walk into a room and see all these objects. Wow! It's a sports-lover's dream! You look around for the item you need for your favorite game. How do you find it among all of this stuff? Well, you look for certain colors, sizes, and shapes. Let's see now . . . Ah! There it is. What makes it different from all the rest?

🔊 AudioText 🔊

## Lesson 1

# How can we describe matter?

*Everything you can see, smell, or touch is matter. Many things that you cannot see, smell, or touch are matter too.*

### A World of Matter

All of the objects you see around you are made of matter. **Matter** is anything that takes up space and has mass. You can feel the mass of objects as weight when you pick them up. When you blow up a balloon, you see that even air takes up space.

A **property** is something about matter that you can observe with one or more of your senses. A ball looks round and feels smooth or bumpy. It could be hard or soft. The sound of it bouncing off the floor tells you more about the ball's properties. For other kinds of matter, such as a flower, your sense of smell tells you about other properties.

**These balls, the hockey puck, the baseball mitt, and the air inside the tennis ball are matter.**

1. **✓Checkpoint** What is *matter*?

2. **Writing in Science** **Expository** Draw two columns titled *Object* and *Properties*. Fill in the box with the properties of some things you see. Choose one object and write a paragraph using the information in the Properties column. Exchange your paragraph with a classmate. Try to guess each other's object.

## States of Matter

All the matter around you is a solid, a liquid, or a gas. Each kind of matter is made of very small pieces that we will call particles. The particles are so small that you cannot see them, even under a magnifying lens. The particles always move. In some kinds of matter they just jiggle. In other kinds they bounce around.

## Solids

The bowling ball is a solid. You can put it over a small opening to a large container. But the ball won't change shape and fall through the opening. Like other solids, the ball keeps its shape. The particles of a bowling ball, or any other solid, are packed tightly together and are firmly connected. They jiggle very fast, but they stay in place.

## Liquids

Look at the orange juice being poured into a glass. The juice is a liquid. It will take the shape of the glass into which it is being poured. The particles of orange juice, or any other liquid, are loosely connected. The particles can flow past one another. If you pour the orange juice from the glass into another container, the juice will change shape again. However, the juice will take up the same amount of space in the new container.

Orange juice is a liquid. Its particles are loosely connected.

A bowling ball is a solid. Its particles are firmly connected.

## Gases

The air being pumped into the basketball is a gas. When you pump air into a ball, the air fills the space. Like other gases, air has no shape. The tiniest gas particles are not connected to one another. They bounce off one another as they move freely. Unlike solids and liquids, the amount of space that air takes up changes. The air spreads out, or expands, to fill whatever space is available.

As air is pumped into a ball, the air at first expands. It starts to push against the inside of the ball. This pushing is called **pressure**. As the ball is filled, the air becomes more compact. It presses together. You can feel the pressure by pushing on the ball before and after air is added.

1. ✓**Checkpoint** What are three states of matter?

2. **Cause and Effect** How does melting ice into water, and then letting the water evaporate, change the state of the ice?

Air being pumped into a ball is a gas. Its tiniest particles are not connected.

# Math in Science

# Measuring Properties

**Different tools and different units are used to measure volume, length, and mass.**

The volume of liquid in the measuring cup is 90 milliliters. The graduated cylinder has the same amount of liquid in it.

The small marks on the ruler mark off millimeters. There are 10 mm in 1 cm, so you can count by tens to find the length in millimeters. The paper clip is 30 mm long.

Eraser

The paper clip is 3 centimeters long.

ⓔ **Tools** Take It to the Net sfsuccessnet.com

Use the pictures to answer the questions.

**1** The eraser is more than 6 cm but less than 7 cm long. What is its length in millimeters?

A. 6 mm
B. 65 mm
C. 650 mm
D. 6000 mm

**2** Which tool would you use to find the mass of a marble?

F. graduated cylinder
G. metric ruler
H. pan balance
I. measuring cup

**3** Which has the greatest volume?

A. 1 liter of milk
B. 500 milliliters of milk
C. 50 milliliters of milk
D. 5 milliliters of milk

**Lab zone Take-Home Activity**

Use a metric measuring cup and a metric ruler to measure properties of liquids and objects around your home. Compare the volumes of liquids and the lengths of objects.

293

# Chapter 10 Review and Test Prep

## Use Vocabulary

| | |
|---|---|
| **atom** (page 282) | **periodic table** (page 283) |
| **buoyancy** (page 286) | **pressure** (page 281) |
| **density** (page 286) | **property** (page 279) |
| **element** (page 282) | **volume** (page 285) |
| **mass** (page 284) | |
| **matter** (page 279) | |

Use the vocabulary word from the list above that best completes each sentence.

1. An object's _____ is the amount of matter it has.

2. When you see that a ball is red, you are observing a(n) _____ of the ball.

3. Each of the tiny particles that make up an element is called a(n) _____ .

4. A measuring cup is used to find a liquid's _____ .

5. A balloon gets larger when air is blown into it because of air _____ .

6. An object that floats in water has _____ in water.

7. Anything that takes up space and has weight is _____ .

8. Elements are arranged in a(n) _____ based on their properties.

9. An object's _____ is a measure of the amount of matter the object has in a certain amount of space.

10. Matter that has only one kind of atom is a(n) _____ .

## Explain Concepts

11. List the two properties of matter that are needed to measure density and explain why you need to measure both.

12. List the following metric units from the smallest to the largest: meter, millimeter, kilometer, centimeter.

### Process Skills

13. **Predict** You pour juice from a tall, narrow glass into a short, wide glass. What happens to the volume of the juice?

14. **Infer** An object falls into a pond and sinks. What do you know about the density of the object?

## Cause and Effect

**15.** Carrie and her friends wanted to play soccer. Their ball was too soft, so they needed to use a pump. Explain how the pump changed the ball so they could play with it. Use a graphic organizer to show all the causes and their effects.

| Causes | | Effects |
|--------|--|---------|
|        | → |         |
|        | → |         |

 **Test Prep**

Choose the letter that best completes the statement or answers the question.

**16.** How many states of matter can we observe?

(A) 1      (B) 2
(C) 3      (D) 5

**17.** Which tool is used to observe the visible properties of a tiny object?

(F) balance
(G) metric ruler
(H) graduated cylinder
(I) hand lens

**18.** If you weigh an object and then break it into two pieces, the sum of the weights of its pieces will be

(A) less than the weight of the object.
(B) equal to the weight of the object.
(C) greater than the weight of the object.
(D) half the weight of the object.

**19.** About how many different elements are there?

(F) 3      (G) 5
(H) 100      (I) 500

**20.** **Writing in Science**

**Expository** Make a chart that shows what tools and metric units are used for measuring mass, volume, and length.

| Measurement | Tool | Unit |
|-------------|------|------|
| mass |  |  |
| volume |  |  |
| length |  |  |

Write a paragraph that tells what the chart shows.

# Chemist

Do you like to cook? When you cook you use chemistry. Chemistry is the study of substances and how they change. You might not want to eat all the ingredients separately. After they are mixed and baked, however, they change. Then they taste just right.

Chemists also study the properties of substances. Some materials mix together easily. Sugar dissolves in water quickly. Other substances do not mix together well. Dr. John Pojman is a chemist. He directs experiments that are done in space where gravity won't interfere.

Dr. Pojman and other scientists are developing experiments to find out more about the ways that liquids mix together.

Chemists earn a degree in chemistry. Then they work for companies that make food, plastics, and medicine. Many chemists work for NASA.

**Dr. John Pojman does experiments with fluids in low-gravity conditions.**

## Lab zone Take-Home Activity

Plastics are made from different substances. Each type of plastic has different properties. Find objects around your home that are made of plastic and list their properties.

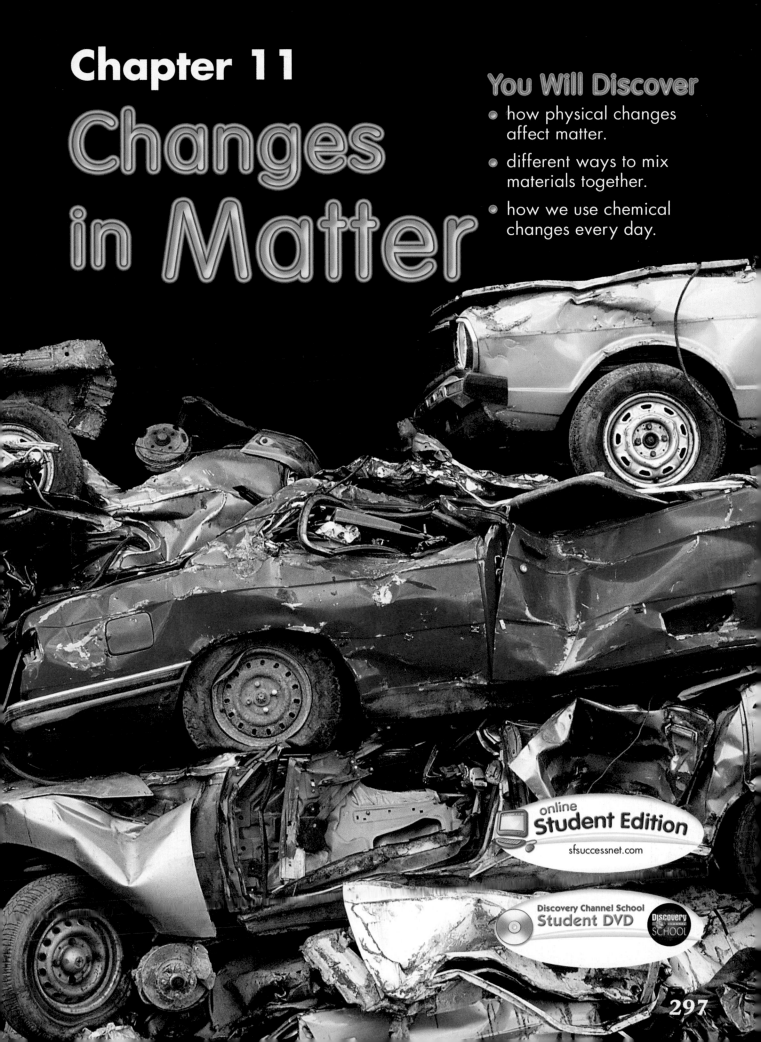

# Chapter 11
# Changes in Matter

## You Will Discover

- how physical changes affect matter.
- different ways to mix materials together.
- how we use chemical changes every day.

online
**Student Edition**
sfsuccessnet.com

Discovery Channel School
**Student DVD**
Discovery SCHOOL

# What are physical and chemical changes in matter?

physical change

solution

mixture

298

chemical change

states of matter

299

# Lab zone Directed Inquiry

## Explore How can matter change?

### Materials

safety goggles

3 cups

ice cube

spoon

water, vinegar, graduated cylinder

salt and baking soda

masking tape

### What to Do

**1** Put 100 mL of water and 1 spoonful of salt in cup A. Stir.

**2** Put an ice cube in cup B.

**Be careful!**
Wear safety goggles!

**3** Pour 50 mL of vinegar in cup C. Add 1 spoonful of baking soda. **Observe** the contents of each cup right away and after 10 minutes.

Label the cups A, B, and C.

100 mL water, 1 spoonful salt

1 ice cube

50 mL vinegar, 1 spoonful baking soda

### Process Skills

Using knowledge obtained by reading the activity and **observations** made during the activity, you were able to make an **inference**.

### Explain Your Results

**Infer** Think about the changes you **observed**. In which cup do you think a different kind of matter formed?

More Lab zone Activities Take It to the Net sfsuccessnet.com

# How to Read Science

 **Cause and Effect**

- A **cause** makes something change. An **effect** is a change you **observe.** Science writers use clue words and phrases such as *because, so, since,* and *as a result* to signal cause and effect.

- A cause may have more than one effect. An effect may have more than one cause.

**Science Article**

## Chemical Properties and Changes

Nothing shines quite like a bright new penny. But over the years, the copper on the outside of the penny changes. It becomes dull brown. Then it becomes dull light green. The copper changes into a new kind of matter. That's a chemical change. The new matter forms because copper reacts with air. The ability to react with air is a chemical property of copper.

## Apply It!

Make a graphic organizer like the one shown below. Fill it in to show the **inferred cause** and each **effect** from the article.

Cause  Effect

| Cause | Effect |
|-------|--------|
| A cause makes something change. | An effect is a change you observe. |

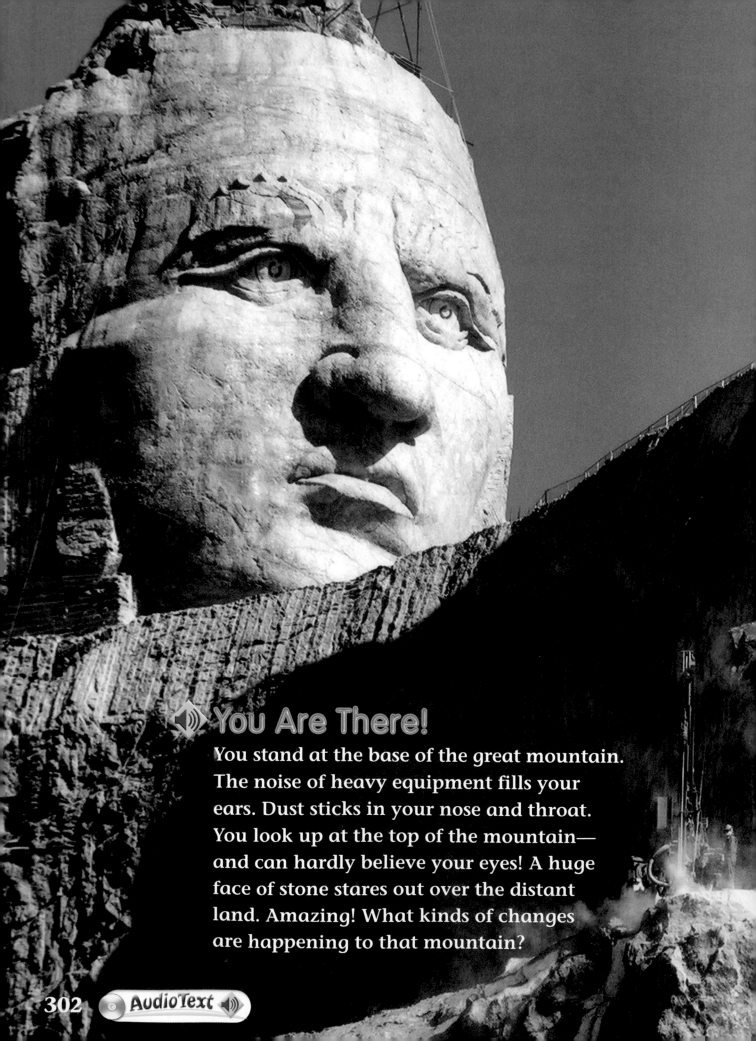

## 🔊 You Are There!

You stand at the base of the great mountain.
The noise of heavy equipment fills your
ears. Dust sticks in your nose and throat.
You look up at the top of the mountain—
and can hardly believe your eyes! A huge
face of stone stares out over the distant
land. Amazing! What kinds of changes
are happening to that mountain?

🔊 AudioText 🔊

## Lesson 1

# What are physical changes in matter?

*Physical properties such as size, weight, color, and position can change. Materials can also change state.*

## Making a Physical Change

The people in the picture are carving a statue of the Native American leader Crazy Horse out of this mountain. They are chiseling, hammering, and even blasting rock to bits. The bits of rock look different than the mountain. But each bit is still the same kind of rock as the whole mountain. The people are making a physical change to the mountain.

Matter goes through a **physical change** when it changes the way it looks without becoming a new kind of matter.

Cutting fruit into pieces causes a physical change. The pieces are made of the same kind of matter as the whole fruit.

1. ✓**Checkpoint** Describe a physical change in matter and explain why it is a physical change.

2. **Technology** in Science Use the Internet to find out more about the Crazy Horse Memorial project. Who started it? When did it begin? How long will it take to finish?

303

## Some Ways to Cause Physical Change

There are lots of ways to change how matter looks. The pictures show some of them.

One special type of physical change is a change in the state of matter. **States of matter** are the forms that matter can take—solid, liquid, and gas. Matter can change from one state of matter to another. Even if the state of one kind of matter changes, it remains the same kind of matter. For example, when liquid water freezes, it becomes ice, which is a solid. However, when ice melts, you can see that it is still water. Ice and water are the same kind of matter.

A change in the temperature of matter can cause it to change its state. For example, when water is heated to 100°C (212°F), it quickly evaporates. That means the water changes from a liquid into a gas. Even though you cannot see the gas, a physical change has happened. The water particles stay the same kind of matter. But the particles are so far apart that you cannot see them in the air. So even though the water has changed state, it has not become a new kind of matter.

As you know, water also changes its state when it is cooled. Above 0°C (32°F), the particles of liquid water slide past one another. At 0°C, water changes from a liquid to solid ice. Each water particle slows down and vibrates very fast in place.

You make a physical change when you fold clothes.

When you cut paper you are making a physical change.

And what happens when you hold an ice cube in your fist? The heat from your hand makes the water particles move faster. They no longer vibrate in place. They move freely, flowing as liquid water, which you feel dripping through your fingers. But no matter how many physical changes you make, the amount and kind of matter remain the same.

You can make a sculpture of water only when it's in a solid state.

## States of Water

In ice, water particles vibrate in place.

In liquid water, the water particles slide past one another.

Some water has evaporated. The water particles in the gas called water vapor are far apart.

### ✓ Lesson Checkpoint

1. List ways that you can make physical changes in matter.

2. What physical changes happen to water as it freezes?

3. **Cause and Effect** Make a graphic organizer like the one on page 301. Fill it with ways to cause physical changes to a piece of paper. Describe the effects each change would have on the paper.

## Lesson 2

# What are some ways to combine matter?

The different coins in this mixture can easily be separated.

*Many kinds of matter can be combined. Sometimes you can separate substances from the combination.*

### Mixtures

Each single coin on this page is made up of matter. So what happens when you put all these different pieces of matter together? You get a mixture. A **mixture** is made of two or more kinds of matter that are placed together. The amounts of each kind of matter do not have to be the same. For example, there may be more quarters than pennies in the coin mixture. But it's still a mixture. In fact, each coin is a mixture. Two or more metals are melted together to form each type of coin.

What parts make up this mixture?

306

What is important about a mixture is that each kind of matter in it does not change into another substance. Each kind of matter can also be separated from every other kind in the mixture.

Some mixtures are very easy to separate. For example, you can separate sand grains and marbles because of their size. You could put the mixture into a strainer with fairly small holes. The marbles are too big to go through the holes of the strainer, but the sand pours right through.

You can also separate sand and iron pieces if you use a magnet. The magnet pulls the iron out of the mixture. The sand remains behind.

How does a magnet help separate the parts of this sand-iron mixture?

1. ✓**Checkpoint** Give three reasons why a bowl of different kinds of beans is a mixture.

2. **Social Studies** in Science
Find out what metals are melted together to make a penny, a nickel, a dime, and a quarter.

A strainer helps separate the parts of this marble-sand mixture.

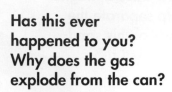

Has this ever happened to you? Why does the gas explode from the can?

## Solutions

Have you ever mixed lemonade powder into water to make lemonade? After you stir the powder into the water, the powder seems to disappear. But it doesn't go away. It dissolves. This means the powder breaks into particles so tiny that you cannot see them. Also, the particles spread evenly throughout the water.

When one or more substances dissolve in another, a **solution** forms. A solution is a kind of mixture. Unlike the mixture of sand and marbles, though, you may not be able to see the particles in a solution. Even though you can't see the powder in the lemonade, you know it's there if you taste it.

You use all kinds of solutions. Soda is a solution of carbon dioxide gas and other substances dissolved in water. Shake a can of soda and the gas separates quickly from the water. In a closed can, the bubbling gas has no place to go. It builds up pressure. When you open the can, the gas escapes.

Straining doesn't separate the salt from salt water. But if you boil away the water, the salt is left behind.

## Separating Parts of Solutions

Just like in other mixtures, you can separate the parts of a solution. Think about a pitcher of salt water. How can you separate the salt from the water after it's been mixed? You can try pouring the salt water through a strainer. That worked pretty well with the marble-sand mixture. But if you taste the water that runs through the strainer, it's still salty. The salt particles are too tiny to be trapped by the strainer.

What if you heat the salt water until it boils? The water evaporates. The salt is left in the container. You've done it! The salt separates from the water when the water evaporates. The same thing happens with lemonade. As the water evaporates, the substances in the powder stay behind.

Remember that all these "disappearing acts" are physical changes. The changes may make the substance look different. But each is still the same substance in the same amount.

Some substances, like lemonade mix, will dissolve in water.

Some substances, like these small stones, will not dissolve in water.

### ✓ Lesson Checkpoint

1. What makes ocean water a mixture?

2. What makes ocean water a solution?

3. **Writing** in Science **Descriptive** In your **science journal,** describe some things for a mixture. What do you think will happen when you mix them? Be sure to name the parts of your mixture.

# What are chemical changes in matter?

*Some changes in matter can produce new kinds of matter. We use these changes all the time.*

## Forming Different Materials

Mmmmm . . . there's nothing like the smell of fresh, warm bread. It tastes so good right out of the oven. But you wouldn't want to eat it before it was baked. A bowl of flour, baking powder, and eggs wouldn't taste very good.

In a **chemical change,** one kind of matter changes into a different kind of matter. A chemical change happens when bread is baked. The batter is a mixture of ingredients. But the heat of the oven causes chemical changes to happen. Then a new substance, bread, is formed.

A chemical change happens when eggs cook. They can never change back into the same form as raw eggs.

Baking bread produces a chemical change. You cannot get the ingredients back because a new substance is formed.

310

Remember that after water freezes into ice, the ice can melt back to water. Each change is a physical change. The water and ice are the same material. But what about the materials that make up the bread? Can you ever separate them from the bread? Probably not. Materials that have gone through a chemical change usually cannot be changed back to the original kind of matter.

Sometimes a chemical change can happen quickly. For example, fire can burn wood in minutes. Other times, a chemical change happens slowly. Think about an iron chain that's left outside. Aided by water, the iron slowly combines with oxygen gas from the air. Then the iron and oxygen change to rust. The rust is now a different kind of matter, and it will not change back into iron and oxygen gas.

Rusting is a slow chemical change.

Burning is a fast chemical change. When the sticks burn, the wood changes to gases and ashes. Some of the gases and ashes make up smoke.

1. ✓ **Checkpoint** How do you know that burning wood is a chemical change?

2. 🎯 **Cause and Effect** Let's say you paint an iron door the color of iron rust. Meanwhile, the bread you are baking turns a rust color on top. Which is a physical change? Which is a chemical change? Explain.

## Using Chemical Changes

We use chemical changes every day. From eating pizza to watching a fireworks show, chemical changes are part of our lives.

Chemical changes start in your mouth the moment you begin to chew a piece of food. Then more changes happen as the food goes through your body. It's a good thing too. Chemical changes give your body the material it needs for energy and growth.

Chemical changes also help move us from place to place. Gasoline burning is a chemical change that releases the energy that the car's engine uses.

Chemical changes make many things in life easier to do. For example, laundry soap often has additives that cause chemical changes which break down stains. Without these changes, clothes might keep getting dirtier and dirtier.

Many soaps cause chemical changes that break down dirt and grime.

Burning gasoline in cars is a chemical change.

Chemical changes in batteries release electricity that appliances use.

You rely on the ability of many kinds of material to undergo chemical changes. When you turn the switch on your CD player, for example, chemicals will combine inside batteries. New substances will form. The chemical change will make a small amount of electricity to help you hear your favorite music.

A chemical change between the water and the tablets causes the bubbles.

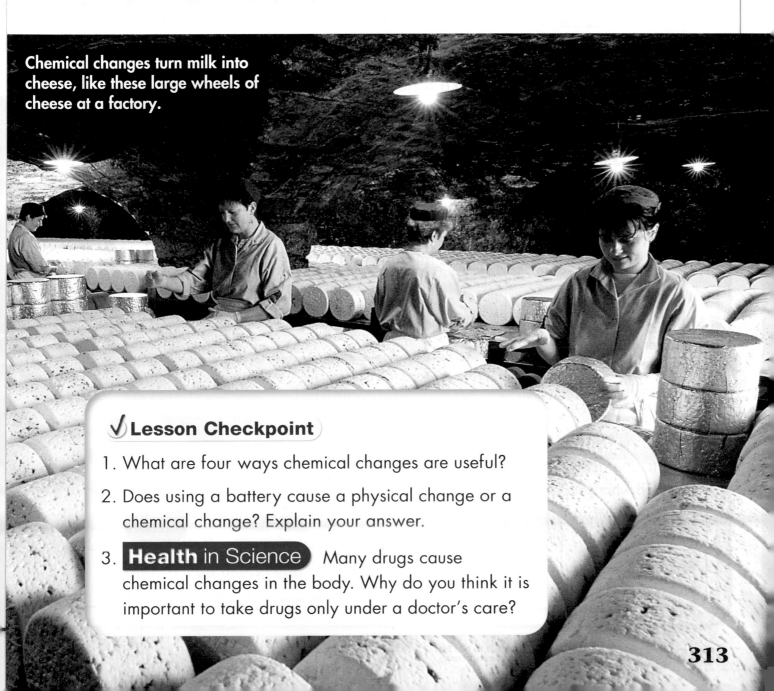

Chemical changes turn milk into cheese, like these large wheels of cheese at a factory.

✓ **Lesson Checkpoint**

1. What are four ways chemical changes are useful?

2. Does using a battery cause a physical change or a chemical change? Explain your answer.

3. **Health** in Science  Many drugs cause chemical changes in the body. Why do you think it is important to take drugs only under a doctor's care?

313

# Firefighter

This firefighter is teaching students about safety.

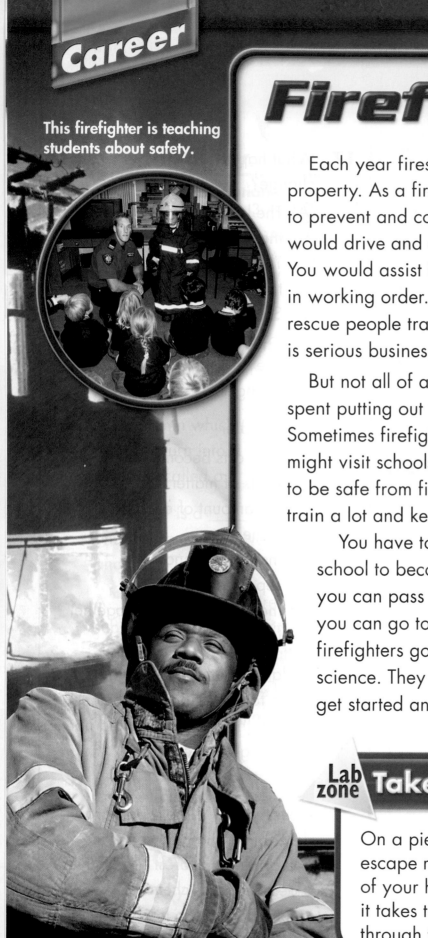

Each year fires kill people and destroy property. As a firefighter, you would work to prevent and control these disasters. You would drive and operate special trucks. You would assist in keeping them clean and in working order. You would learn ways to rescue people trapped in fires. Saving lives is serious business!

But not all of a firefighter's time is spent putting out fires and saving people. Sometimes firefighters teach the public. They might visit schools and show students how to be safe from fire at home. They also must train a lot and keep in good health.

You have to graduate from high school to become a firefighter. Then, if you can pass a physical and written test, you can go to firefighter training. Some firefighters go to college and study fire science. They learn a lot about how fires get started and how they spread.

## Lab zone Take-Home Activity

On a piece of paper, design escape routes from each area of your house. Record the time it takes to move from each area through the proper exit.

# Chapter 12

# Forces and Motion

## You Will Discover

- different ways to describe position and motion.
- how force affects motion.
- how simple machines work.

online
**Student Edition**
sfsuccessnet.com

# How do forces cause motion and get work done?

position

motion

speed

relative position

322

gravity

# Chapter 12 Vocabulary

force

friction

magnetism

work

# Exercising in Space

Do you like to exercise? Running, playing ball, and bicycling are exercises that have motion, speed, and force. But you don't have to be moving to exercise your muscles. Pushing against a wall may not do any work, but the pushing force you use exercises your muscles.

On Earth, the force of gravity helps you exercise. That's because every time you lift your legs or arms, you have to lift them against the force of gravity. So, you have to give your arms and legs force, and that's good exercise. Suppose you are an astronaut aboard the Space Shuttle or the International Space Station. You do not feel the tug of gravity. The very high speed it takes to stay in orbit around the Earth is the reason. It reduces the effect of gravity to zero. You float around the cabin. This makes exercising in space harder than on Earth. Imagine trying to push against a wall on the shuttle. It just sends you off in another direction!

**Astronauts have to wear weights on the treadmill used in space.**

The cycle machine exercises the heart, legs, and arms.

Without exercise, your muscles and bones get weaker. Astronauts in space must exercise every day to keep their muscles and bones healthy.

Special exercise machines had to be built for space. One kind of machine is like an exercise bicycle. Another machine is like a treadmill. The third kind of machine is like a rowing machine that pushes and pulls on muscles. Astronauts have to be strapped to the machines so they don't float away. Then they put on weights so they can exercise their muscles.

Information learned about muscles and bones in space has helped people on Earth know more about keeping healthy. Many gyms on Earth have exercise machines based on those designed for space. This is just another example of how things developed for use in space can help us here on Earth.

Muscles and bones are made stronger by using the resistance machine.

**Lab zone** **Take-Home Activity**

On a piece of paper, design a machine, using pulleys and levers, that allows you to exercise one or more parts of your body.

# The Wright Brothers

Orville and Wilbur Wright were inventors who changed the world. They had been making and selling bicycles. Stories of flying machines, however, got their attention.

The Wright brothers studied forces that affect the motion of aircraft. They knew about the forces that keep a craft in the air and pull the craft down. They also knew about the forces that move the craft forward and slow the craft's motion.

In 1902 they used their skills to build a successful glider. The Wright brothers became the first people to design, build, and fly a craft that could be successfully controlled by a pilot in the air.

Orville and Wilbur's next step was to design and build an aircraft that could fly using an engine. They had to build a gasoline engine that didn't weigh too much. Yet it had to provide enough force to move the craft in the air. In 1903, the brothers made the first controlled flight in an aircraft with an engine.

## Lab zone Take-Home Activity

Ask each family member to design and build a paper plane. Have a contest to see which plane flies the farthest and the longest.

# Chapter 13
# Energy

## You Will Discover

- different forms of energy.
- how energy changes from one form to another.
- how energy travels.

online
**Student Edition**
sfsuccessnet.com

353

# How does energy change form?

reflect

kinetic energy

potential energy

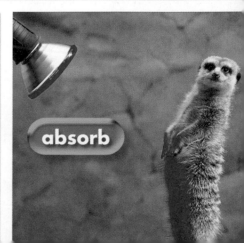

absorb

354

# Chapter 13 Vocabulary

electric charge

electric current

electric circuit

refract

thermal energy

355

# Lab zone Directed Inquiry

## Explore Can electricity produce light and heat?

**Materials**

safety goggles

2 pieces of wire

flashlight bulb
and holder

battery and
battery holder

thermometer

### Process Skills

To help
**communicate**
clearly, scientists
use sketches,
diagrams, and
drawings.

**What to Do**

Wear safety goggles.

**1** Make an electric circuit.

**2** **Observe** the light.

The bulb of the thermometer should touch the light bulb.

**3** Use a thermometer to observe heat. First, record the temperature you observe on the thermometer. Next, place the bulb of the thermometer against the light bulb for 1 minute. Then, record the temperature.

### Explain Your Results

Explain the procedure. Name 2 forms of energy you **observed**. Describe where each was used or produced. Draw and label a diagram or sketch to help **communicate** your ideas.

Is every part of the circuit needed? Use your drawing to help predict, investigate, and describe what would happen if one part of your circuit were missing.

# How to Read Science

## TARGET SKILL Main Idea and Details

- To find the topic of a paragraph, ask who or what the paragraph is about.

- To find the **main idea** in a paragraph, ask "What is the one important idea that all the sentences tell about?"

- To find supporting **details** in a paragraph, ask "Which sentences give information that supports the main idea?"

**Science Article**

### Heating Homes

Energy heats your home. The energy comes from fuel that is burned. Some people heat their homes with natural gas. Some people burn wood to heat their homes. Other people use electricity. The electric company burns coal to make electricity. Gas, coal, and wood are natural resources. They come from Earth.

### Apply It!

You can use a graphic organizer to **communicate** the **main idea and details.** Use one like this to show supporting details from the Science Article.

**Main Idea**

Detail          Detail          Detail

## 🔊 You Are There!

The Sun is shining brightly, but the air outside is cold. You stomp your feet and rub your hands together to warm them. You're looking forward to going inside and warming up. Maybe you'll listen to some music or play a DVD. How many different forms of energy will you use by the end of the day?

💿 AudioText 🔊

## Lesson 1

# What is energy?

*The main source of energy on Earth is the Sun. Energy takes many forms. Energy can be stored and can change form.*

### Energy

Energy is the ability to do work or to cause change. Remember that work is done when a force makes an object move. You already know about the effects of the Sun's energy. Its warmth makes Earth a place in which we can live. The Sun's light energy makes plants grow. The Sun's energy also causes winds to blow and water to move through the water cycle.

**How many things in this kitchen use energy?**

We use many forms of energy in addition to the forms that come directly from the Sun. Electrical energy runs just about everything in this kitchen. Sound energy comes out of your CD player. Chemical energy in fuel runs the engine of a car. The mechanical energy of the car's motion gets you to the store. How do all these forms of energy come about?

1. **✓ Checkpoint** What are two forms of energy that Earth gets from the Sun?

2. **Writing in Science** **Descriptive** Write a paragraph in your **science journal** about the forms of energy you observe or use on your way to school.

## Stored Energy

The skier uses energy that is stored in the body to ski across the snow. Stored energy is **potential energy.** It has the ability to change into another kind in order to do work or cause a change.

Fuels, such as oil, coal, natural gas, and gasoline, are other sources of potential energy. The energy stored in these fuels comes from sunlight. Long ago, plants used energy from sunlight to make food. After the plants died, they turned to a kind of fossil that we use as fuel. When we burn fuels, we release the potential energy within them to do work.

Every time you use batteries, you also release potential energy. The stored energy in food, fuels, and batteries is chemical energy.

Position or height stores another kind of potential enery. This energy is gained from gravity. The skier standing at the top of the hill has potential energy. So does a car at the top of a roller coaster and a playground swing at its highest point.

The standing skier has potential energy.

Gasoline contains the stored energy of living things that died long ago.

Batteries store energy as chemical energy.

360

## Energy of Motion

Potential energy can change to kinetic energy. **Kinetic energy** is the energy of motion. When a car burns gasoline, for instance, potential energy stored in the gasoline changes to kinetic energy. The car moves. Look at the picture of the standing skier. When he pushes off, he goes down the hill. He's in motion. Potential energy stored in the skier's position at the top of the hill changes to kinetic energy. The force of gravity pulls him down the hill.

Many sources of energy are renewable. After a day of skiing, the skier can replace the energy he used by eating food. The skier can climb the hill again. You have learned that some sources of energy are not renewable. We cannot easily replace gasoline, natural gas, and other "fossil" fuels.

As the skier slides down the hill, potential energy changes to kinetic energy.

### ✓ Lesson Checkpoint

1. What are two kinds of potential energy?

2. Give two examples of potential energy and kinetic energy that you see every day.

3. **Main Idea and Details** Use a graphic organizer. What is the main idea of the paragraph at the top of this page? What details support it?

## Lesson 2

# How does energy change form?

*Energy comes in different forms. Energy can change from one form to another. When energy changes form, some energy is given off as heat. People change energy into forms they can easily use, such as electricity.*

Living things, such as this dwarf lemur, change chemical energy in food to energy of motion and heat.

## Changing Forms of Energy

Energy changes into more useful forms all the time. For example, your body stores potential energy as chemical energy. The chemical energy stored in your body changes to kinetic energy as you move.

## Using Energy

You can't use the kinetic energy of your moving arm to make a light bulb burn bright. But you can use this kinetic energy to flip a light switch. This, in turn, helps change electrical energy to light energy. Most light bulbs also get hot. Some of the electrical energy changes to a kind of energy felt as heat. Energy cannot change completely from one form to another. Some energy is always given off in the form of heat.

Electrical energy changes to kinetic energy as the cable car moves along the track.

## Forms of Energy

| Chemical | Mechanical | Electrical | Light | Thermal |
|---|---|---|---|---|
|  |  |  |  |  |
| This energy holds the particles of matter together, such as in food. Eating food is the way we get energy. | This is the energy of moving objects. The moving parts in our machines and playground equipment have this kind of energy. | This energy can pass through wires made of special metal. We use this kind of energy to power appliances in our homes. | We see the Sun's energy in this form. Plants make food with light energy. We also change other forms of energy into light so we can see. | This kind of energy makes particles of matter move faster. We feel this energy as heat. |

People also use machines to change forms of energy. The cable car in the picture changes electrical energy to mechanical energy. The electric toothbrush in the picture stays in a base that has an electric cord that plugs into an outlet. The electrical energy is stored as chemical energy in the toothbrush's battery. The chemical energy changes back to electrical energy and then to mechanical energy when the toothbrush is turned on.

Chemical energy changes to electrical energy which changes to mechanical energy as the toothbrush moves.

1. ✓**Checkpoint** What form of energy do living things change into mechanical energy and thermal energy?

2. **Math in Science** Food energy is measured in Calories. John eats 2,000 Calories in food in a day. How many Calories does he eat in a week?

## Ways That Energy Travels

Energy can travel from one place to another. A moving object, such as a baseball, carries energy. You feel the energy when you try to catch the ball. You can tell how much energy the ball has by how hard it hits your hand.

Energy can also travel as waves. Have you ever seen waves of water? These waves carry energy as the baseball does. These waves of energy have the same shape as the waves of a moving rope. Look at the rope on the next page. How would you describe it? Notice that parts of the rope take turns going from side to side. Energy causes this effect as it travels from one end of the rope to the other. The rope itself does not travel forward. Light and certain other forms of kinetic energy move as waves.

Waves in water can be as small as the ripples in the bucket below. Waves caused by hurricanes can be huge. How big the wave is depends on how much energy it carries.

Ocean waves carry energy.

**PLOP!**

The energy from the falling drop moves in waves across the water. As the waves move away from the source, they lose strength.

364

## Parts of a Wave

You can measure the amount of energy that a wave carries. Look again at the waving rope. One way to measure a wave's energy is by measuring the distance from the midpoint of the wave. The bottom of the wave is called a *trough*. The top of the wave is called a *crest*. Waves with greater distance from the midpoint have more energy. Waves with lesser distance have less energy.

Another way to measure a wave's energy is by measuring the length of the wave. The length of a wave can be the distance from the top of one crest to the top of the next crest. Shorter waves have more energy. Longer waves have less energy.

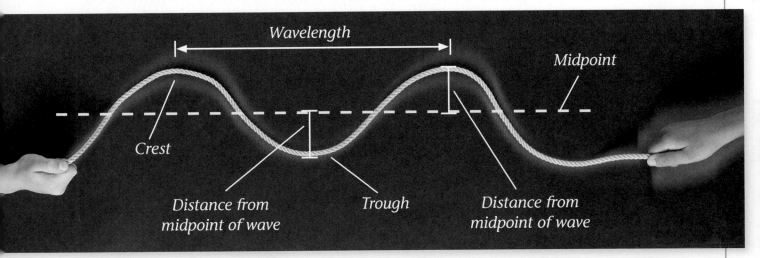

Wavelength

Midpoint

Crest

Distance from midpoint of wave

Trough

Distance from midpoint of wave

### ✓ Lesson Checkpoint

1. Name two types of energy that travel in waves.

2. What happens to energy as it travels away from the source?

3. **Main Idea and Details** Read the paragraph at the top of this page. Use a graphic organizer. What is the main idea? What are the supporting details?

Moving a loose rope from side-to-side on a table makes energy move forward along the rope in the form of waves. The rope itself does not travel forward.

## Lesson 3

# What is heat energy?

*Matter contains thermal energy. Thermal energy travels through objects and space as heat. Heat travels from warm objects to cool ones until they are both at the same temperature.*

### Heat Energy

Matter is made of very small, moving particles. Each particle of matter is moving because it has energy. The sun's rays feel warm on your skin, for instance. The sun's rays warm matter by making its particles move faster. The energy of moving particles is called **thermal energy.** Thermal energy is the total energy of all the particles in matter.

Thermal energy moves as heat from a warmer object to a cooler object. Put a spoon into a hot drink. Heat travels from the drink through the cooler spoon. In a short time, the top of the spoon will feel warm. Once the drink and the spoon reach the same temperature, the flow of energy stops.

**What will happen to the spoon after it is in the hot liquid for a while?**

**The fish is in a bag of water at room temperature. It waits for the clean, cold tank water to warm up. Why will the temperature of both soon be the same?**

## Sources of Heat

When energy is changed from one form to another, at least some heat is given off. The burner coils below the pot change electrical energy to heat. Burning matches, wood, and natural gas are examples of chemical changes that give off heat. You notice friction when you rub your hands together to warm them. The friction caused by rubbing gives off heat. Every time energy moves, there is heat.

## OUCH!

Be careful! The chemical change that happens when a match is lit is a source of heat.

1. ✓**Checkpoint** What are four different kinds of heat sources?

2. **Writing** in Science **Expository** Write a paragraph in your **science journal** to explain how energy travels to the vegetables in the pot.

The heat in the water spreads through the frozen vegetables. The temperature is becoming the same throughout the pot.

## Effects of Heat on Matter

Heat energy affects matter. Think about a cup of liquid water. At 0°C (32°F), however, the water has too little thermal energy to stay in its liquid state. At 0°C, water is a solid like the ice cube stack in the picture.

What happens when you add heat to ice? When the temperature of the air surrounding ice is above 0°C, ice starts to melt and become a liquid. That is what's happening to the ice cubes.

You can measure the effect of heat on matter. To do this, you could chart the time that ice takes to melt. Look again at the stack of ice cubes. At 9 A.M. you put the ice cubes where the temperature remains steady at a certain point above freezing. At 9:15 A.M. what do you observe? Heat moves from the air into the ice. How could you measure the amount of ice that has melted? At 9:30 A.M. what do you observe? Record the time when all the ice is melted. Measure the volume of melted ice. Calculate the amount of time it takes for a certain amount of ice to melt in air of a certain temperature. The time is a rough measure of the change caused by heat energy.

This device is keeping a room at 79.2°F. What would happen if you turned it off and the temperature outside dropped to 50°F?

How is the change from ice to liquid water related to a change in temperature?

9 A.M.

9:15 A.M.

9:30 A.M.

368

If more heat is added to water, water evaporates. It becomes the invisible gas called water vapor. At a temperature of 100°C (212°F), heat makes liquid water change in another way. Heat makes the water boil. Look at the bubbling flask of water. Heat at the bottom of the flask makes water expand. Expand means to get bigger. The liquid water expands enough to evaporate and become a hot gas. Very hot bubbles of this gas float to the water's surface. These bubbles break open and release a cloud of hot water droplets.

At 100°C (212°F) heat makes liquid water change in a special way.

## Toast Time!

How has heat energy changed this piece of bread?

### ✔ Lesson Checkpoint

1. What is the main source of heat on Earth?

2. What causes matter to be in a solid, liquid, or gas state?

3. **Writing** in Science

   **Descriptive** In your **science journal,** write a paragraph that describes how a campfire keeps campers warm on a cold night.

Burning fuels, such as the gas in this gas lamp, can produce light as well as heat.

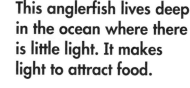

Electricity in heat lamps makes heat and light. A heat lamp is keeping this meerkat warm.

# What is light energy?

*Light is a form of energy. We can see some of the ways that light behaves. Light affects some of the properties of matter.*

## Sources of Light

The Sun is our main source of energy. The Sun's energy travels from the Sun to Earth as waves. The waves have different amounts of energy. We can see or feel the effects of only some of these waves. Light is energy that we can see.

Chemical changes are another source of light. Burning is a chemical change. Candles, campfires, and matches, for instance, give off light as they burn. The lamp in the picture gives off light as the gas burns. The anglerfish's tentacle gives off light too. Chemical changes in the fish's body produce light.

This anglerfish lives deep in the ocean where there is little light. It makes light to attract food.

Electricity is also a source of light. It makes the wire in a light bulb get so hot that it glows and gives off light. Most sources of light are also sources of heat. Heat lamps are used to keep things warm.

## The Path of Light

Light travels from its source in straight lines in all directions. Light will continue to travel in this way until it is stopped by an object. Light will not bend or turn corners in order to get around objects. That is why objects that block light's path cause shadows. Shadows are areas behind the objects that are not getting direct light. The length of the shadow depends on the angle of the light. The shadows you have cast may have been taller than you really are!

1. ✓**Checkpoint** Name three sources of light energy.

2. **Writing** in Science **Narrative** Write a paragraph in your **science journal** telling about the light sources you have seen today. Include what caused the light.

Why do these tables and chairs make shadows in the sunlight?

## How Light Changes

When light hits some objects, much of it can pass through them. These objects do not block all the light. That's why you can see through a window and a clear glass of water.

All objects **reflect** light. This means light bounces off the object and goes in a different direction. Some objects reflect light better than others. Their surfaces are very flat and smooth. All the light that reflects off the surface travels together in the same direction. A mirror reflects light. The light bounces back to your eyes. The smooth lake also reflects light.

What is happening to light in the water droplets in the picture? The droplets **refract,** or bend, the light. When refraction causes the light to bend, the light changes direction. Objects can look different from the way they usually appear. The droplets refract light from the flowers. As the light rays bend, tiny images of the flower form. The lens in a telescope can make big images of small objects. The lens in each of your eyes refracts light too.

The trees are reflected in the smooth water of the lake.

Each water droplet refracts light. A tiny image of the flower forms.

Light refracts because it passes through different materials at different speeds. Light passing through air slows down when it enters water. This causes the straw in the glass to look broken.

Sometimes refraction causes light to separate into its many colors. Then you see a rainbow. Water droplets in the air over a sprinkler refract light in the same way.

Light is made up of different colors. When light hits objects, they **absorb**, or take in, some of the light. They reflect the rest. Different objects absorb and reflect different colors of light. If an object looks red in sunlight, it is reflecting red light and absorbing the other colors of light. If an object looks white, it is reflecting all the colors of sunlight. If an object looks black, it is absorbing all the colors of sunlight. Dark objects feel hot in sunlight. A lot of absorbed sunlight turns to heat.

Water causes light to refract, so the straw looks broken.

### ✓ Lesson Checkpoint

1. What is the main source of light on Earth?

2. How does a shadow form?

3. **Writing in Science** **Narrative**
   Write a story about light in your **science journal.** Use examples of light being absorbed, reflected, and refracted. Brainstorm with others what your story might include.

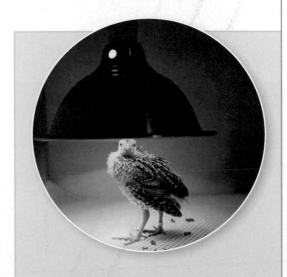

## Effects of Light

Objects can change light. They can reflect, refract, or absorb it. For instance, in sunlight, this chicken looks mostly white. In turn, light can change objects. How is this green light changing the white chicken?

373

# What is electrical energy?

*Matter is made of particles that have electric charges. Electric charges can move as electrical energy through a closed circuit.*

## Electric Charges

All matter is made up of small particles that have electric charges. An **electric charge** is a tiny amount of energy. Particles have both positive and negative charges. When particles have an equal number of positive and negative charges, they balance each other. The matter has no overall charge. Matter with more negative charges than positive charges has an overall negative charge. Matter with more positive charges than negative charges has an overall positive charge.

A balloon with a balanced charge does not attract the paper pieces.

Lightning is a result of moving electric charges.

374

What happens when matter with a negative charge is near matter with a positive charge? The positive and negative charges attract. The negative charge travels toward matter that has a positive charge. If you get a shock when you touch someone, negative charges have jumped between you and that person. Lightning is the result of a much bigger jump of electric charges. Lightning happens when negative electric charges travel within clouds or between clouds and the ground. Light, heat, and sound energy are given off.

The attraction between positive and negative charges can cause objects to stick together. Charges that are the same can cause objects to push away from each other. Rubbing a balloon on your hair, for instance, causes it to pick up negative charges from your hair. The extra negative charge on the balloon pushes aside the negative charges on one side of a piece of paper. This leaves the side of paper closest to the balloon with a positive charge. The balloon then attracts the positive side of the paper. The paper sticks to the balloon.

Rubbing two balloons on your hair gives both balloons the same charge. The balloons then push apart from each other.

Rubbing the balloon gives it an electric charge. It attracts objects with the opposite charge. It pushes away from objects with the same charge.

1. ✓ **Checkpoint** What causes lightning?

2. **Art** in Science Draw a picture of two balloons that shows what happens when one balloon has a positive charge and the other balloon has a negative charge.

## Electric Currents and Circuits

**Electric current** is the movement of electrical energy or electric charge from one place to another. Lightning is an uncontrolled electric current. Lightning can travel in any direction. To be useful, an electric current must travel in a planned way through wires or other materials. This way, electric current can turn on lights or make a CD player work.

Batteries or an outlet that you can plug a cord into are good sources of electrical energy. The path that a controlled electric current flows through is an **electric circuit.** The path must be unbroken for the energy to flow through it. Find the switch in the picture. The switch is on, or closed, so the circuit is unbroken. Electrical energy can flow through the wires of the circuit. If the switch was off, or open, the current could not flow through the circuit.

**1** Electric current flows along a path from the negative part of the battery.

**2** Electricity flows through the circuit to the positive part of the battery.

**3** On its way, current flows through the bulb. A wire in the bulb gets hot and glows. Electrical energy changes to heat and light energy.

**4** If you lift the lever on the switch, the circuit is broken, or open. The light turns off. Lower the lever and the circuit is closed. The light turns on.

*Energy source*

*Switch*

## How Electrical Energy Changes Form

| | | |
|---|---|---|
| | **Light** | Electricity passes through bulbs of all kinds. Bulbs change electrical energy to light so we can see at night. Some heat is given off. |
| | **Heat** | Electricity passes through coils in heaters. Coils change electrical energy to heat so we can be warm in winter, or cook our food. |
| | **Sound** | Electricity passes around a magnet. The magnet changes electrical energy to vibrations of plastic discs in headphone speakers. Then we can hear music. |
| | **Magnetic Force** | Electricity passes around a huge magnet. The moving electricity makes a magnetic field that attracts metal containing iron to the magnet. The magnet can be used to lift heavy cars. |

We rely on electricity for most of our everyday needs. We therefore spend a great deal of effort changing sources of energy into electricity. We change the power of moving water into electricity. We turn the heat of burning coal into electricity. We even turn sunlight into electricity. What happens to electricity once it gets to our homes? Study the table above. Can you imagine not having electricity?

### ✓ Lesson Checkpoint

1. What is the difference between a controlled and an uncontrolled electric current? Give an example of each.

2. What happens when an electric circuit is open?

3. **Main Idea and Details** Describe the path of electricity through a simple electric circuit.

## Investigate Do freshwater ice and saltwater ice melt the same way?

### Materials

2 cups and masking tape

water and graduated cylinder (or measuring cup)

spoon and salt

2 thermometers

tub with very warm water (for Day 2)

timer or stopwatch (or clock with a second hand)

### Process Skills

By making careful **observations** of ice melting and by **collecting data** and organizing it into a chart, you learned how salt affects the melting of ice.

### What to Do

**2** Label one cup *fresh water*. Add 100 mL of water.

**2** Label the other cup *salt water*. Add 100 mL of water and 1 spoonful of salt. Stir.

**3** Place a thermometer in each cup. Your teacher will put the cups in a freezer overnight.

**4** After the water is frozen, record the temperature in each cup.

**5** Put both cups in a tub of very warm water. **Observe** the temperature in each cup until all the ice in the cup melts. Record the temperature every minute.

*salt water*

*fresh water*

**6** Construct a chart or table to help you **collect** your **data**.

Melting Time of Ice

| Time (minutes) | Temperature of Salt Water (°C) | Temperature of Fresh Water (°C) |
|---|---|---|
| 0 (start) | | |
| 1 | | |
| 2 | | |
| 3 | | |

Make a graph if you think it will better help you interpret the data.

## Explain Your Results

1. You put the cups of ice in warm water. This added energy to the frozen water. Heat moved from the warm water to the ice. How did the temperature in each cup change? Look at your chart. Describe the pattern of change.

2. Based on your **observations**, in which cup did the ice finish melting first?

**Go Further**

How would adding more salt to the water affect how fast the ice would melt? Investigate to find out.

# Math in Science

# Measuring Temperature

**Recording temperature is one way to measure thermal energy. You can use different scales to measure temperature.**

Fahrenheit Scale

Celsius Scale

266°F — 130°C
250 — 248 — 120
230 — 110
212 ← Water boils → 100
200 — 194 — 90
176 — 80
158 — 70
150 — 140 — 60
122 — 50
100 — 104 — 40
86 — 30
68 — 20
50 — 50 — 10
32 ← Water freezes → 0
14 — -10
0 — -4 — -20
-22 — -30
-40 — -40 — -40

180 divisions

100 divisions

Alcohol

Alcohol

Freezing Water

Boiling Water

The Celsius scale is often used in science. The Fahrenheit scale is often used in everyday life, such as reading the temperature outdoors. Sometimes both scales are used.

**Degrees Celsius is written °C. So 40°C is read "forty degrees Celsius."**

**Degrees Fahrenheit is written °F. So 40°F is read "forty degrees Fahrenheit."**

**1** What is the boiling point of water on the Celsius scale? What is the boiling point on the Fahrenheit scale?

**2** What is the freezing point of water on the Celsius scale? What is the freezing point of water on the Fahrenheit scale?

**3** About what is the temperature in degrees Fahrenheit when it is 30°C?

## Lab zone Take-Home Activity

Watch the weather report on TV. Are temperatures given in degrees Fahrenheit, Celsius, or both? Make a list of three cities talked about in the report. Write down their temperatures in degrees Fahrenheit and in degrees Celsius. You can use the thermometers shown here.

# Electrical Engineer

You know your house needs electricity to run smoothly. Have you ever thought about how important providing electricity is during space missions?

Barbara Kenny does. She is an electrical engineer who works for NASA on ways to change other kinds of energy into electricity to run spacecraft.

While in orbit, for example, a spacecraft spends part of its time in sunlight. Solar panels gather light and change it to electricity used to run the ship. The spacecraft spends the rest of its time in the shadow of the Earth where there is no sunlight. How does it get electricity then?

Dr. Kenny designs generators that make electricity. One kind uses a heavy wheel called a flywheel. While in sunlight, motors make this wheel spin quickly. The kinetic energy from spinning is used to generate electricity while the spacecraft is in the dark.

Electrical engineers obtain a college degree.

**Dr. Barbara Kenny is an engineer who works with forms of energy.**

## Lab zone Take-Home Activity

If you were an electrical engineer for NASA, what special kind of electrical equipment would you design? How would it be used?

# Chapter 14
# Sound

## You Will Discover

- how different kinds of sound are produced.
- how sound energy and matter interact.
- how sound travels through different materials.

online
**Student Edition**
sfsuccessnet.com

# How does energy produce the sounds we hear?

vibration

pitch

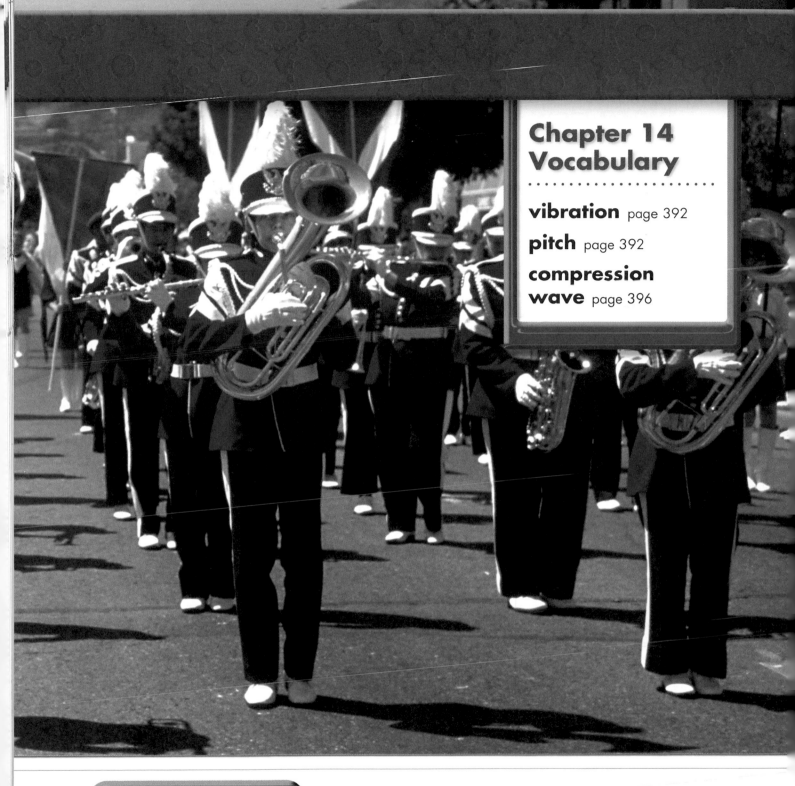

compression wave

## Comparing Density

Matter that has less density than water has buoyancy—it will float in water.

**Idea:** Compare the density of objects with that of water. Use a container of water and a variety of objects.

## Separating Mixtures

The best way to separate a mixture depends on the kinds of matter in the mixture.

**Idea:** Use a variety of mixtures. Demonstrate the best way to separate each mixture.

## Changing Potential to Kinetic Energy

Energy can be stored as potential energy and released as kinetic energy.

**Idea:** Use a wind-up toy to show how the amount of potential energy affects the distance the toy can travel.

## Making Sounds

Sounds vary depending on the way matter vibrates.

**Idea:** Show how sound changes. Stretch rubber bands of varied sizes across the opening of a box.

### Using Scientific Methods

1. Ask a question.
2. State a hypothesis.
3. Identify/control variables.
4. Test your hypothesis.
5. Collect and record your data.
6. Interpret your data.
7. State your conclusion.
8. Go further.

Science Fair Central    More science fair help
sfsuccessnet.com

EC NTL 10 9 8 7 6 5 4 3

# Unit D
# Space and Technology in Indiana

Did you know that the Foucault (foo KOE) Pendulum at the Indiana State Museum never stops swinging? It looks like the path of the pendulum's swing changes. But it is not the pendulum's swing that changes. The floor underneath the pendulum moves because of the rotation of the Earth.

# Field Trip
## Indiana State Museum

You can visit the Indiana State Museum in Indianapolis to see how technology has changed farming. There are horse-drawn plows, steam engines, and gasoline-powered tractors. There are also horse-drawn vehicles, early gasoline-powered cars, and race cars.

Each of the 92 counties in Indiana is represented at the Indiana State Museum. A sculpture outside of the building tells about each county. The chart below tells about the sculptures for four counties.

| County | What the Sculpture Tells |
|--------|--------------------------|
| Crawford | Native Americans used flint from here. |
| Delaware | Glass containers manufactured here. |
| Elkhart | Band instruments manufactured here. |
| Clay | Home to pottery and brick factories. |

## Find out more:

Research to find out more about the Indiana State Museum. Find out more about the sculptures representing Indiana's counties. Then answer these questions:
- What sculpture represents your county? What does it tell about science in Indiana?
- What kinds of technology have been invented or manufactured in your county or in another county in Indiana? Write about how these manufactured goods or technology have changed people's lives.

# Chapter 15
# Patterns in the Sky

## You Will Discover

- what causes day, night, shadows, and seasons.
- why the Moon's shape seems to change.
- what tools help people study stars.

online
**Student Edition**
sfsuccessnet.com

# What patterns do the Earth, Sun, Moon, and stars show?

star

axis

rotation

418

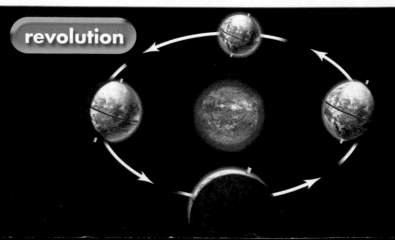

revolution

# Chapter 15 Vocabulary

constellation

phase

telescope

lunar eclipse

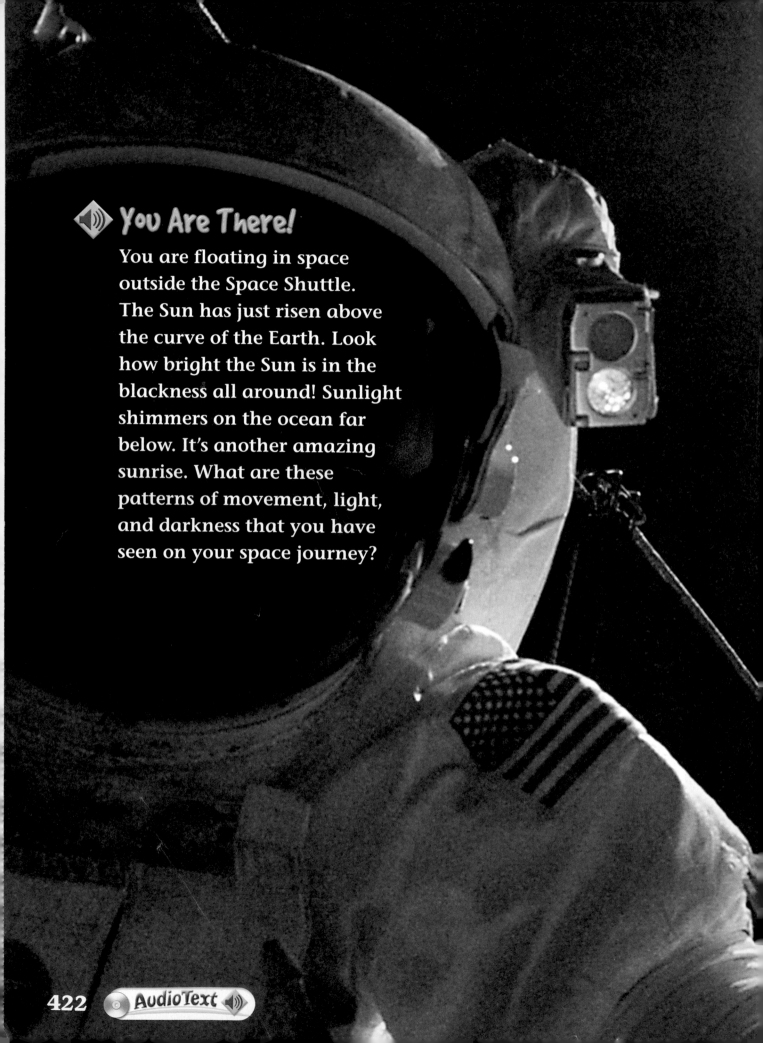

You are floating in space outside the Space Shuttle. The Sun has just risen above the curve of the Earth. Look how bright the Sun is in the blackness all around! Sunlight shimmers on the ocean far below. It's another amazing sunrise. What are these patterns of movement, light, and darkness that you have seen on your space journey?

AudioText 🔊

## Lesson 1

# What are some patterns that repeat every day?

*Every day there is light during the day followed by darkness at night. If the day is sunny, you might notice shadows. Day, night, and shadows are caused by light from the Sun and the movement of Earth.*

## The Sun

You see the Sun in the sky on a sunny day. The Sun is in the sky on cloudy days too. The Sun is a **star**—a giant ball of hot, glowing gases. If you think of a plate that is almost round, the Sun would be in its center. Earth would be between the center and the plate's edge. The Sun is the main source of light and energy for Earth.

Earth is very small compared to the Sun. Like the Sun, Earth is shaped like a ball. Unlike the Sun, Earth does not glow or make its own light. The half of Earth's curved surface facing the Sun is lit by sunlight. The half of Earth's surface facing away from the Sun is not lit by sunlight and is dark.

1. ✓**Checkpoint** What star is the source of light on Earth?
2. 🔄 **Sequence** Describe a pattern on Earth that happens every day.

## Day and Night

If you stand outside, you do not feel as if you are moving. But you are. Earth is always moving. One way it moves is that it spins around an imaginary line. One end of the line would stick out of Earth at the North Pole. The other end of the line would stick out of Earth at the South Pole. This imaginary line around which Earth spins is its **axis.** Find Earth's axis in the drawing below. If you could look down at the North Pole, you might see the Earth spinning or rotating in a counterclockwise direction. This is the opposite direction to the way the hands of a clock move. We could also say that Earth turns from west to east.

Daytime begins when the Sun first appears over the horizon. Although the Sun looks like it rises, it actually stays in the same place. As Earth rotates, this part of Earth is just beginning to face the Sun.

Half of Earth faces the Sun and receives sunlight as Earth spins on its axis.

Earth makes one complete spin on its axis, or **rotation,** every 24 hours. During this time, half of Earth always faces the Sun. That half of Earth has day. The half of Earth that is not facing the Sun has night. As Earth spins, or rotates, a different part of Earth faces the Sun.

Earth rotates at the same speed in the same length of time every day of the year. You may have noticed that the number of hours of sunlight and darkness changes during the year. If you add the hours of sunlight and darkness together during one day and night, you will find they equal 24 hours.

Things are not always as they seem. For instance, think about the Sun's place in the sky throughout the day. The Sun appears to rise in the east, move across the sky, and set in the west. You might think that the Sun moves around Earth. But the Sun only appears to move across the sky. Actually Earth is moving.

The path that the Sun appears to take across the sky is predictable. We can tell ahead of time when the Sun will rise and set.

1. ✓**Checkpoint** What is Earth's axis?

2. **Writing** in Science **Expository** Write a paragraph in your **science journal** that explains how spinning on the Earth's axis causes day and night.

As Earth rotates on its axis, the half of Earth that was in darkness begins to receive sunlight.

Around noon the Sun is at its highest point in the sky.

As Earth continues to rotate, the Sun appears to set in the west. Daytime ends when the Sun disappears below the horizon.

## Shadows

On a hot summer day, you might escape the heat by standing in the shade of a tree. Did you know you are standing in a shadow? As you look out from your spot, you see shadows in other places. Yet other places have no shadows.

You might notice that a shadow forms when light, like sunlight, hits an object. The object stops the light that hits it. You also need a surface on which to see the shadow. The shadow is an area that is not getting direct light. The shadow has about the same shape as the object that blocks the light.

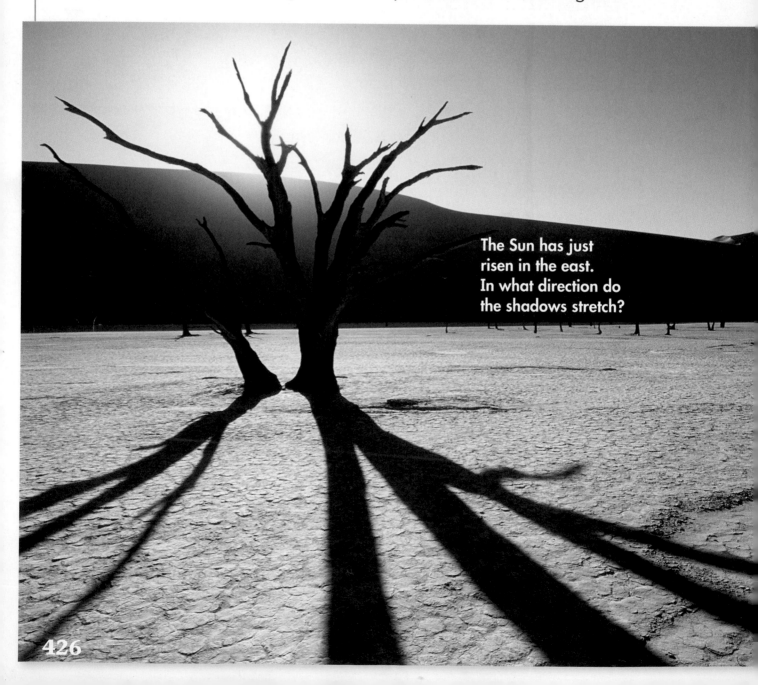

The Sun has just risen in the east. In what direction do the shadows stretch?

West

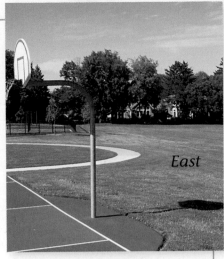
East

Morning        Midday        Afternoon

The length and direction of shadows change during the day. Find the shadows made by the basketball hoop in the pictures. Notice that the morning shadow is long and is in the opposite direction from the Sun in the eastern sky.

As the Sun appears to move higher in the sky, the shadow becomes shorter. Around midday the Sun is at its highest point in the sky. The shadow is very short as seen in the second picture.

As the Sun continues moving across the sky, the shadow becomes longer. Notice the length of the shadow in the third picture. The afternoon shadow stretches in a different direction than the morning shadow did. As the Sun moves toward the horizon in the west, the shadow stretches toward the east. After the Sun sets, there is no sunlight to make shadows.

**How do the length and direction of the shadow cast by this basketball hoop change during the day?**

## ✓ Lesson Checkpoint

1. Explain how each place on Earth has a beginning and an end to daytime.

2. What three things are needed to have a shadow?

3. **Sequence** Describe the pattern of shadows from sunrise to sunset. Include the length and direction of the shadows.

427

## Lesson 2

# What patterns repeat every year?

*Earth's tilt and movement around the Sun cause the seasons. The amount of light and heat Earth receives during different seasons causes seasonal patterns.*

### Earth Moves Around the Sun

You know that Earth rotates on its axis. Earth also moves, or revolves, around the Sun. Find Earth's axis in each part of the diagram. Earth's axis is not straight up and down. It is tilted.

Earth makes one **revolution** when it makes one complete trip around the Sun. One revolution takes one year. As Earth revolves around the Sun, Earth's tilted axis always points in the same direction in space.

### Earth's Position During the Year

The part of Earth pointed toward the Sun receives the most direct sunlight and has warmer temperatures.

### June

The northern half of Earth tilts more toward the Sun. The northern half gets more direct sunlight than the southern half. It is summer in the northern half and winter in the southern half of Earth.

In some places on its path around the Sun, the northern half of Earth is tilted toward the Sun. In other places along its path, the southern half of Earth tilts toward the Sun. The part of Earth that is tilted toward the Sun receives the most direct rays of the Sun and is heated the most. That part of Earth also spends more hours in daylight than in darkness during each 24 hours.

*Equator*

**Direct rays, at the equator, cover less area. The equator is the imaginary line that separates the north and south halves of the Earth. The rays here are more concentrated. They heat Earth more than rays that strike at an angle.**

### March

The northern and southern halves of Earth get about the same amounts of sunlight. Neither pole points toward the Sun or away from it. The northern half is getting warmer, but the southern half is getting cooler.

### December

The northern half of Earth tilts away from the Sun. This tilt causes the northern half of Earth to receive less sunlight and have colder temperatures than the southern half. It is winter in the north, but summer in the south.

### September

As in March, neither end of the axis points toward the Sun or away from the Sun. The northern half of Earth is getting cooler, but the southern half is getting warmer.

1. **✓ Checkpoint** What does Earth revolve around?

2. **Sequence** Describe the pattern of temperature changes during the year in the northern half of Earth. Why does this happen?

# Why does the Moon's shape change?

*The Moon revolves around Earth while Earth revolves around the Sun. These movements and light from the Sun cause the Moon to appear different throughout a month.*

## The Moon and Earth

Did you ever see a full moon rise above the horizon or a half-moon set below it?

Like Earth, the Moon rotates and revolves. It rotates on its axis and revolves around Earth. Unlike Earth, the Moon takes about 27 Earth days to complete one rotation. The Moon completes one revolution of Earth in almost the same time.

**Can you describe how the Earth and Moon move in space?**

**The time the Moon takes to rotate and revolve once is about the same.**

**This photo taken from space shows that the Moon is small compared to Earth.**

The Moon is the closest natural object to Earth. It is 384,000 kilometers (239,000 miles) away. The Moon also is the brightest object in the night sky, but it does not make light. The light you see from the Moon is light from the Sun that shines on the Moon and bounces off.

Notice the sunlight hitting half of Earth and half of the Moon in the picture. Sometimes you can even see the Moon during the day. It does not look as bright as it does at night. Sunlight that reflects off the Moon is only a little brighter than sunlight that passes through the daytime atmosphere. Sometimes you cannot see the Moon at night.

Did you know that we always see the same side of the Moon? We never see the other side from Earth. A spacecraft took the first pictures of the Moon's far side in 1959.

1. ✓**Checkpoint** What are two ways the moon moves? How do these movements affect the appearance of the Moon?

2. **Math in Science** About how many days does it take for the Moon to revolve around the Earth 4 times?

## The Moon and the Sun

On some nights, the Moon looks like a circle of bright light in the night sky. Other nights, you cannot see any part of the Moon, even if the sky is clear. In between these two nights, you can see different amounts of the Moon. How the Moon looks in the sky changes a little each night. The pattern of changes is predictable. And the entire pattern repeats itself about every four weeks or 29 1/2 days.

Each different way that the Moon looks is a **phase** of the Moon. Find some of these phases on the next page. Notice that you can see more and more of the Moon until you see a full Moon. Then you see less and less of the Moon. When you cannot see the Moon at all, the phase is known as a new Moon.

The drawing shows the Moon in different positions in its path around Earth. Notice that half of the Moon is always lighted by sunlight. The lighted half of the Moon cannot always be seen from Earth. The movements of Earth and the Moon cause different amounts of the lighted half of the Moon to be seen from Earth. The amount of the Moon that can be seen from Earth is a phase of the Moon.

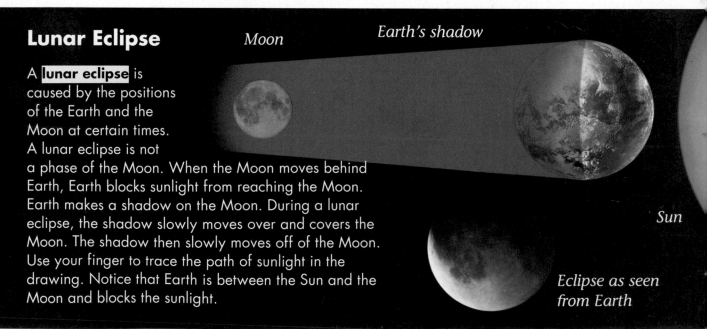

## Lunar Eclipse

A **lunar eclipse** is caused by the positions of the Earth and the Moon at certain times. A lunar eclipse is not a phase of the Moon. When the Moon moves behind Earth, Earth blocks sunlight from reaching the Moon. Earth makes a shadow on the Moon. During a lunar eclipse, the shadow slowly moves over and covers the Moon. The shadow then slowly moves off of the Moon. Use your finger to trace the path of sunlight in the drawing. Notice that Earth is between the Sun and the Moon and blocks the sunlight.

Moon

Earth's shadow

Sun

Eclipse as seen from Earth

*SciLinks* Take It to the Net
sfsuccessnet.com
keyword: lunar eclipse
code: g3p434

# Phases of the Moon

The outer photos show what the Moon looks like from Earth.

The inner ring shows what the Moon looks like from space.

**First Quarter**
About a week after the new Moon, the Moon looks like a half circle.

**Crescent Moon**
As the Moon revolves, we see more and more of its lighted part. A night or two after the new Moon, we see only a small piece of the lighted part of the Moon. You can usually see a crescent Moon shortly after the Sun sets.

**Earth**

**Light**

**Full Moon**
About a week after the First Quarter, we can see all of the lighted part of the Moon. It looks like a circle. After the full Moon, we begin to see less of the Moon each night.

**Third Quarter**

**New Moon**
As the Moon revolves, it gets between the Sun and Earth. The dark half of the Moon faces toward Earth. The lighted half of the Moon faces away from Earth. We cannot see the Moon.

---

## ✓ Lesson Checkpoint

1. How much of the Moon is lighted by sunlight?

2. What position of Earth causes a lunar eclipse?

3. **Sequence** Describe the pattern of the phases of the Moon starting with a full Moon.

**Lesson 4**

# What are star patterns?

*Stars appear to move in the night sky. Telescopes make studying patterns of stars easier.*

## Stars and the Telescope

Think about being outside on a clear, dark night. You see thousands of twinkling stars. You notice that some stars are brighter than others and are easier to see. They all look so small in the sky because they are trillions of miles away. But some of the stars are actually larger than the Sun. Other stars are smaller. The stars that are the farthest away are the dimmest and the hardest to see. You cannot see many stars at all without certain tools to help you.

The camper in the picture is using binoculars to see the stars more clearly. Binoculars and the **telescope** are tools that magnify objects that are far away. They make objects look larger and easier to see. If you use a telescope, you can see many more stars than with your eyes alone.

Find the huge mirror inside the Keck telescope in Hawaii. Telescopes help people see stars that they cannot see with their eyes alone.

Scientists use different kinds of telescopes. The telescope on page 436 and telescopes you might use are similar. These telescopes use tubes, mirrors that make light reflect, and lenses that bend light or refract it. All these parts help bring as much light as possible into the telescope. The result is a larger and clearer view of objects in the sky. Other kinds of telescopes do not collect light. They collect other kinds of waves, such as radio waves.

Binoculars make far-away objects appear larger, brighter, and easier to see.

1. ✓**Checkpoint** What are two tools that can help you see stars?

2. **Art** in Science Draw a picture of some star patterns that you have seen.

## Patterns of Stars

Have you ever spent time looking at stars? You might notice that some of them seem to be in groups that make patterns or shapes. A group of stars that make a pattern is a **constellation.** You can imagine lines drawn between stars. Find the lines drawn in the pictures of the stars on page 439. Many people see a big cup with a handle and a little cup with a handle. This kind of cup is used to dip water. These patterns are the Big Dipper and the Little Dipper. The Big Dipper is a part of the constellation Ursa Major (the Big Bear). The stars of the Little Dipper make up the constellation Ursa Minor (the Little Bear).

People living in ancient times saw the shapes of animals, people, and objects in star patterns. They made up stories about the constellations and gave them names. Some of these names are still used today. You might have heard of the constellation Orion. When people living in ancient Greece saw the stars of Orion, they saw a hunter.

The stars that make up a constellation look like they are close together in space. They really are very far apart. Some of the stars are much farther away than others. If you looked at the same stars from far away in space, they would not make the same pattern.

The picture on the right shows how stars appear to move across the sky at night. Like the Sun, stars really do not move this way. They look like they move across the sky because Earth is rotating on its axis. The patterns of stars also change with Earth's seasons. Notice that the Big Dipper and Little Dipper are in different positions in the sky. As Earth revolves around the Sun, constellations are in different parts of the night sky. You can find constellations more easily if you find the North Star. The stars look like they rotate around the North Star.

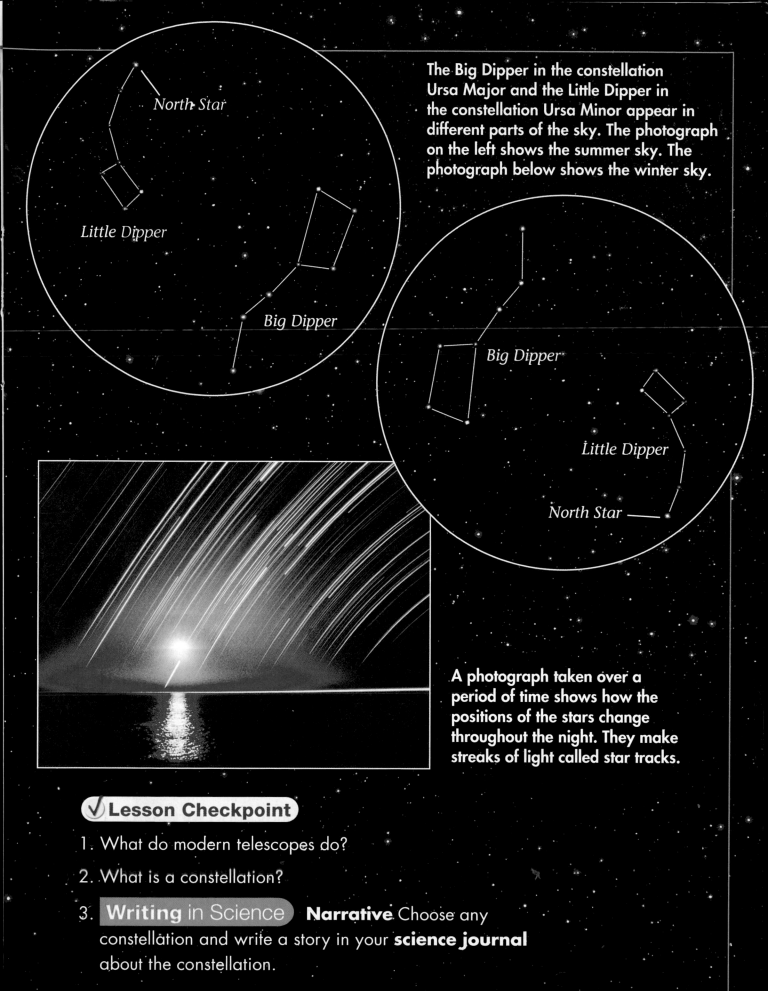

*North Star*

*Little Dipper*

*Big Dipper*

The Big Dipper in the constellation Ursa Major and the Little Dipper in the constellation Ursa Minor appear in different parts of the sky. The photograph on the left shows the summer sky. The photograph below shows the winter sky.

*Big Dipper*

*Little Dipper*

*North Star*

A photograph taken over a period of time shows how the positions of the stars change throughout the night. They make streaks of light called star tracks.

✓ **Lesson Checkpoint**

1. What do modern telescopes do?

2. What is a constellation?

3. **Writing** in Science **Narrative** Choose any constellation and write a story in your **science journal** about the constellation.

# Math in Science

# Comparing Times of Sunrises and Sunsets

As Earth revolves around the Sun, the amount of sunlight hitting different parts of Earth changes each day. The Sun looks like it rises above the horizon and sets below the horizon at different times. In the northern half of Earth, the Sun rises a little earlier and sets a little later each day from January to late June. The days slowly have more daylight hours and fewer hours of darkness. The pattern is reversed in the southern half of Earth.

e Tools    Take It to the Net
sfsuccessnet.com

The chart below shows the pattern in the times of sunrise and sunset for four days during the year.

| Sunrise and Sunset Standard Times for a City in the Northern Half of Earth | | |
| --- | --- | --- |
| Date | Sunrise | Sunset |
| March 21 | 5:52 A.M. | 6:05 P.M. |
| June 21 | 5:16 A.M. | 8:29 P.M. |
| September 21 | 6:38 A.M. | 6:49 P.M. |
| December 21 | 7:15 A.M. | 4:23 P.M. |

## Comparing Times

Use the chart to answer the following questions.

**1** How many hours and minutes of daylight are there on March 21?

**2** Which day has the most hours of daylight?

**3** Which day has the fewest hours of daylight?

**4** During which month would the southern half of the Earth have its longest day? Explain.

**Lab zone Take-Home Activity**

Find the times of sunrise and sunset in your area daily for the next week. Compare the times and decide if the days are getting longer or shorter.

# Chapter 15 Review and Test Prep

## Use Vocabulary

| | |
|---|---|
| **axis** (page 424) | **revolution** (page 428) |
| **constellation** (page 438) | **rotation** (page 424) |
| **lunar eclipse** (page 434) | **star** (page 423) |
| **phase** (page 434) | **telescope** (page 436) |

Use the vocabulary word from the list above that best completes each sentence.

**1.** A(n) _____ is a giant ball of hot, glowing gases.

**2.** Earth spins on its _____.

**3.** Earth makes one complete _____ every 24 hours.

**4.** Earth makes one complete _____ around the Sun every year.

**5.** A(n) _____ of the Moon is the way the moon looks in the sky.

**6.** A(n) _____ happens when Earth's shadow moves across the Moon.

**7.** A(n) _____ magnifies objects that are far away.

**8.** The Big Dipper is part of a(n) _____.

## Explain Concepts

**9.** Explain what causes the phases of the Moon.

**10.** Explain what causes constellations to move across the sky at night.

**11.** On March 1, sunrise is at 6:25 A.M. and sunset is at 5:42 P.M. On March 30, sunrise is at 5:36 A.M. and sunset is at 6:15 P.M. Which day has the most daylight?

### Process Skills

**12.** **Infer** What would happen to daytime and nighttime if Earth did not spin on its axis?

**13.** **Infer** You notice that the shadow made by a pole outside your window has been getting longer. What does this tell you about the time of day? Explain your answer.

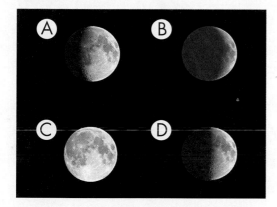

**14.** Draw the images of the Moon phases in the boxes below in the order that they would appear in the sky. Start with picture B.

## Test Prep

Choose the letter that best completes the statement or answers the question.

**15.** A Full Moon can be seen about once every

(A) night.

(B) month.

(C) season.

(D) year.

**16.** You can see many more stars if you use a

(F) calendar.

(G) microscope.

(H) telescope.

(I) hand lens.

**17.** What season does the southern half of Earth have if Earth's north axis is tilted toward the Sun?

(A) spring

(B) summer

(C) fall

(D) winter

**18.** Which of the following is closest to Earth?

(F) Moon

(G) Sun

(H) stars

(I) constellations

**19.** Explain why the answer you chose for Question 18 is best. For each of the answers you did not choose, give a reason why it is not the best choice.

**20.** **Writing** in Science

**Expository** Write a paragraph that describes the patterns of light and temperatures in different seasons.

**44**

# The Hubble Space Telescope

You can use a telescope to make stars and other objects in space easier to see. Imagine how many stars you could see with a telescope 13.2 meters (43.5 feet) long and 4.2 meters (14 feet) wide. Imagine it weighing 11,000 kilograms (24,000 pounds)—about the size of a school bus. You would not be taking it over to a friend's house to look at stars. A telescope this size would not fit in a car, but it did fit in a Space Shuttle.

In 1990, NASA launched the Hubble Space Telescope. The Hubble stays in space about 600 kilometers (375 miles) above Earth. It revolves around Earth every 97 minutes.

The Hubble collects information from space and sends it to scientists on Earth every day. It provides detailed images of Mars and Pluto. It helps scientists understand more about Uranus and Neptune. The Hubble also has helped scientists learn about objects outside our solar system. It provides information about black holes, quasars, and the birth and death of stars.

**An astronaut works on the Hubble Space Telescope.**

The Hubble Telescope was made in a way that makes it easy to repair and update. Since it has been launched, astronauts have made missions to the Hubble to keep it working well. During space walks, astronauts have replaced parts that have worn out. Astronauts also have added parts so that the Hubble always has the newest technology. Each servicing mission adds four to five years to the working life of the Hubble.

This image of the ant nebula, a dying star, was taken by the Hubble Space Telescope.

The solar panels provide power to the telescope.

## Lab zone Take-Home Activity

If you have Internet access at home or at the library, go to the NASA Web site (http://hubblesite.org) and look at images from the Hubble.

# Galileo
## 1564–1642

Galileo was born in Italy in 1564. He studied medicine and mathematics at a university in Italy. He later became the head of the math department at another university.

Galileo became known for inventing science tools and experimenting. One of the tools he is most famous for is a better telescope. When he heard that someone had invented a tool that could magnify objects, he went to work to improve the telescope. Galileo soon had a telescope that could magnify objects twenty times.

Galileo pointed his telescope toward space and made many discoveries. He found that the Moon has craters. Galileo saw four moons revolving around Jupiter and different phases of Venus.

Galileo used his observations to show that Earth revolves around the Sun. Most people during that time believed that the Sun revolved around Earth. Galileo's experiments and observations challenged beliefs of the time and added to the knowledge of science.

## Lab zone Take-Home Activity

Look up the work of Galileo. Describe other observations he made. Tell what his experiments led him to say about patterns in the sky.

# Chapter 16
# The Solar System

## You Will Discover

- how the Sun makes heat and light.
- how the planets move in space.
- what is special about each planet.

online
**Student Edition**
sfsuccessnet.com

**Web Games**
Take It to the Net
sfsuccessnet.com

# How are the planets in the solar system alike and different?

solar system

planet

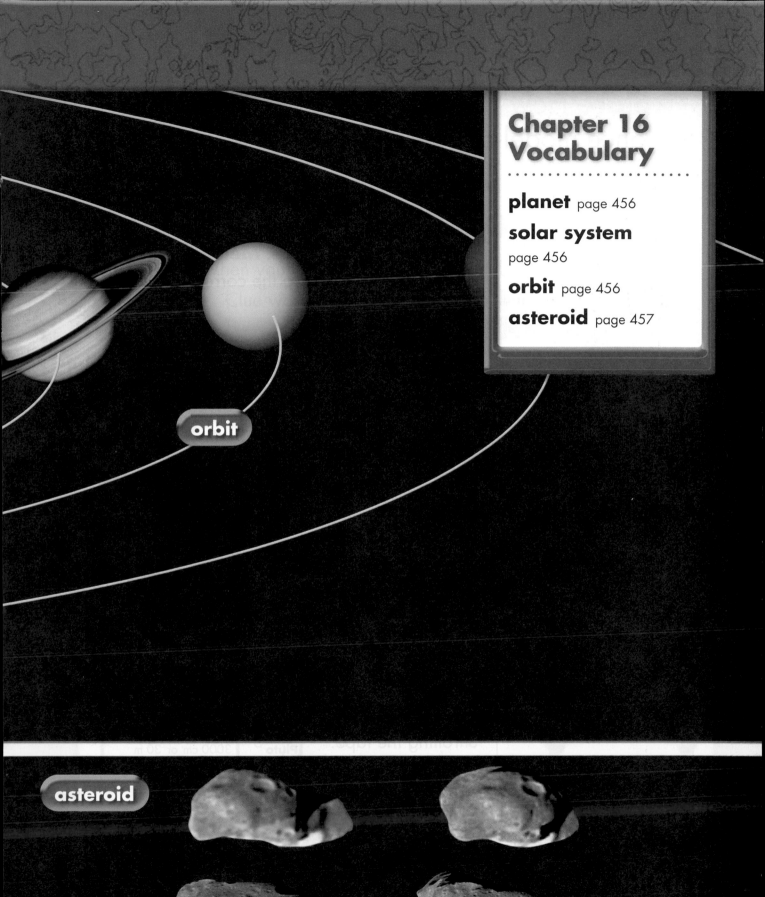

**planet** page 456

**solar system** page 456

**orbit** page 456

**asteroid** page 457

orbit

asteroid

Don't look at it! The Sun has a great amount of energy. You should never look directly at it. The Sun is the fiery center of our solar system. This huge ball of energy holds our solar system together. But what's going on underneath its surface?

## Lesson 1

# What are the parts of the solar system?

*The solar system includes the Sun, the planets, and other objects that travel around it. The Sun gives off energy that moves out in all directions through space.*

### The Sun

The Sun is a ball of hot, glowing gases called plasma. It is a star. The Sun looks larger and brighter than stars you see at night because it is a lot closer to Earth. The other stars in the sky look small because they are so far away.

How big is the Sun? In a word—huge! It is 109 times as wide as Earth, or wider than the length of 15,000,000 football fields! In fact, the Sun is large enough to hold one million Earths inside it!

The temperature on the surface of the Sun is 5,500°C. The center is millions of degrees hot. It's so hot that gas particles that have a positive charge collide and join. This releases a lot of energy. Energy that travels from the Sun through space includes sunlight.

1. ✓ **Checkpoint** Why is the Sun so bright and hot?

2. **Art** in Science   Draw a tiny circle to represent Earth. Then use information from this page to decide how big to draw the Sun.

The Sun is much nearer to Earth than other stars.

## Uranus, Neptune, and Pluto

Like Jupiter and Saturn, Neptune and Uranus are gas giants. Pluto is the only outer planet that is not made of gas and does not have rings.

Uranus is the seventh planet from the Sun. It is smaller than Saturn or Jupiter but about 4 times the size of Earth. It takes Uranus 84 Earth years to revolve around the Sun just one time. However, Uranus rotates in just 17 Earth hours. Uranus is unlike other planets because it rotates on its side. It has 26 moons.

Neptune is the eighth planet from the Sun. It is only slightly smaller than Uranus. Neptune is so far away from the Sun that its orbit around the Sun takes 165 Earth years. Like the other gas giants, Neptune has strong winds and storms. Neptune looks light blue and has rings that are hard to see. Neptune takes about 16 Earth hours to rotate one time. It has at least 13 moons.

**Like other gas giants, Uranus is surrounded by rings.**

Pluto's moon (shown in the right-hand corner) is named Charon.

The weather on Neptune constantly changes. Light cloud-like bands appear and disappear. Storms are seen as dark spots.

Pluto is usually the ninth planet from the Sun. The atmosphere on Pluto is made of poisonous gases. Pluto is so distant that its orbit around the Sun takes 248 years! Sometimes its orbit takes it closer to the Sun than Neptune. That's because its orbit is at an angle to the orbits of the other planets. Pluto's orbit is also the most oval-shaped of all the planets. And, like other planets, the position of the Sun is not in the center of Pluto's orbit. Pluto takes 6 Earth days to rotate. It is the smallest planet in the solar system. It is smaller than Earth's Moon. Pluto has 1 moon.

## Is It a Planet?

On March 15, 2004, scientists announced the discovery of a planet-like object. It is much farther from the Sun than Pluto is. They called this new object Sedna. It is smaller than Pluto and possibly made of rock and ice. Other small objects have been observed beyond Pluto. These objects and Sedna are sometimes called "planetoids."

### ✓ Lesson Checkpoint

1. Which of the nine planets are outer planets?

2. Which of the outer planets is not a gas giant?

3. ↻ Compare and Contrast On a two column chart list the ways that the inner planets and the gas giants are alike and different.

# Investigate How can a planet's distance from the Sun affect its surface temperature?

A planet's temperature can be affected by its atmosphere, its surface, and other factors. How does a planet's distance from the Sun affect its surface temperature?

## Materials

metric ruler

lamp and
3 thermometers

books

## What to Do

**1** **Make a model** of the Sun and the planets. Place a lamp, books, a metric ruler, and thermometers as shown.

**Be careful!**

The light bulb and parts of the lamp will get hot!

The thermometers that are different distances from the light bulb stand for planets that are different distances from the Sun.

Remove ruler before turning on the lamp!

large books

The lamp stands for the Sun.

### Process Skills

You can use a **model** to help you make accurate **inferences**.

**2** Turn on the lamp.

**❸** Make a data chart like this one. **Collect** the **data** you need to complete the chart.

**❹** Wait 15 minutes. Turn off the lamp. Parts of the lamp will be hot!

**❺** Record the temperature of each thermometer. Make a line graph of your data.

| Effect of Distance on Temperature | |
|---|---|
| Distance from Light Bulb (cm) | Temperature after 15 Minutes (°C) |
| 7 cm | |
| 14 cm | |
| 28 cm | |

**Effect of Distance on Temperature**

Temperature After 15 Minutes (°C) vs. Distance from Bulb (cm)

## Explain Your Results

1. Which thermometer showed the highest temperature? Which showed the lowest temperature?

2. **Infer** Think about your **model**. How does a planet's distance from the Sun affect its surface temperature?

## Go Further

What do you think happens to the temperature on the side of the planet not facing the Sun? Make a plan using a model to help investigate.

# Patterns in Planets

**The distance of a planet from the Sun affects the time needed to revolve around the Sun.**

The first column in the chart below lists the outer planets in the order of their distances from the Sun, from the nearest to farthest. The second column gives the length of time each planet takes to complete one orbit.

### The Outer Planets

| Planet | Revolution Time |
|---|---|
| Jupiter | 12 Earth years |
| Saturn | 29 Earth years |
| Uranus | 84 Earth years |
| Neptune | 165 Earth years |
| Pluto | 248 Earth years |

**Use the chart to answer the questions.**

**1** Which of the outer planets takes the shortest time to revolve around the Sun?

A. Jupiter     B. Saturn     C. Neptune     D. Pluto

**2** How much longer is the revolution time of the outer planet farthest from the Sun than that of the outer planet closest to the Sun?

F. 17 Earth years         G. 83 Earth years

H. 81 Earth years         I. 236 Earth years

**3** What pattern do you see about the distance of a planet from the Sun and the planet's revolution time?

A. Planets closer to the Sun take longer to revolve around the Sun.

B. Planets farther from the Sun take longer to revolve around the Sun.

C. Planets farther from the Sun take a shorter time to revolve around the Sun.

D. The chart shows no pattern.

**Lab zone** **Take-Home Activity**

Choose two tables of information about things in newspapers and magazines. Write down what patterns you see in the tables.

# Computer Engineer

Do you like reading adventure stories about going to distant planets? Most planets are too far away for live astronauts to explore them. NASA sends certain spacecraft without people instead. They carry robots that can explore planets the same way astronauts can. Computer engineers help design the robots.

People such as Dr. Ayanna Howard study ways to use robots called rovers. These machines explore the surfaces of other planets. The rovers use computers to help find answers to problems.

Dr. Howard also tries to interest students in careers in math, science, and engineering. She speaks to students around the world about robots, computers, and technology.

People study in college to become computer engineers. Classes include math, engineering, and computer science.

Dr. Ayanna Howard

Mars
Exploration
Rover

## Lab zone Take-Home Activity

Use objects from your home to make a model of a rover or other robot. Describe the parts of your robot and tell what your robot does. Compare your robot with the ones that explore other planets.

EC NTL 10 9 8 7 6 5 4 3

# Chapter 17
# Science in Our Lives

## You Will Discover

- ways we use science and technology every day.
- ways we use technology to solve problems.

**Discovery Channel School**
**Student DVD**
DISCOVERY SCHOOL

online
**Student Edition**
sfsuccessnet.com

# How does technology affect our lives?

technology

invention

tool

# Chapter 17
# Vocabulary

computer

## Explore Which transport system works best?

### Materials

Possible Water Transport Systems

newspaper

plastic tube

funnel

empty cup and cup with water

### Process Skills

When you **predict**, you use what you have **observed** and what you already know to help tell what will happen.

### What to Do

**1** Examine *Possible Water Transport Systems.* **Predict** which of these systems will always work? Which will never work? Which will trap some water?

**2** Test your predictions. Set up each system.

**3** For each system, pour a half cup of water in the funnel. Have a group member hold the tube in place. **Observe** how well the water flows through the system.

Put down newspaper before you begin.

Repeat each test. This will help make your results more reliable.

### Explain Your Results

1. In what direction does water flow best through a system?

2. Examine the different designs, your **predictions**, and your results. Find a rule that explains the results you **observed**.

# How to Read Science

## Reading Skills

### Sequence

A **sequence** is a series of actions that happen in a certain order.

- Sometimes writers use clue words such as *first, then, next,* and *finally* to signal a sequence.

- When a sequence has a repeating pattern, you can **predict** what comes next.

**Newspaper Article**

## The Wright Brothers Fly!

Kitty Hawk, North Carolina–December 17, 1903. Today, Wilbur and Orville Wright flew their powered airplane. How did they do it? At first, the Wrights watched how birds control their flight. Then they flew kites

 to test their ideas. Next they built gliders to find the right wing shape. Finally, they built an airplane with an engine. The flying machine, called *Flyer I*, became the world's first powered airplane.

### Apply It!

Make a graphic organizer like the one shown. Fill it in to show the **sequence** of events that led to the Wright brother's historic first flight.

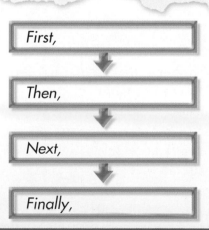

First,

Then,

Next,

Finally,

477

What a beautiful bridge! The arches seem perfectly lined up. It's hard to believe this structure was built by the ancient Romans over 2,000 years ago. The bottom part was used as a road. But the top part was made to carry something completely different. This bridge was part of an amazing system designed to bring water from mountain springs to Roman cities. The ancient Romans, like other people, used technology to solve problems.

**Lesson 1**

# How does technology affect our lives?

*Science helps people understand the way the world works. Technology helps people apply this understanding to solve problems and improve their lives.*

## Finding New Ways

People have always asked questions about the world around them. As they learned new things, they began to use this knowledge. They used it to solve problems and form new ideas. People invented tools to help. A **tool** helps to do work more easily. Tools, in turn, helped people think of new ways of doing things. In other words, they used technology. **Technology** is the use of knowledge to design new tools and new ways to do things. A tool can be as simple as a sewing needle. A tool can be as complicated as a computer.

The invention and use of arches was important technology in ancient Rome. An **invention** is something made for the first time. The Romans needed to get water to their cities. They figured out that an arch with a central stone could support a lot of weight. They used these arches for building bridges and for carrying water to the cities.

The keystone, or central stone wedged at the top, keeps the stones of the arch in place.

1. ✓**Checkpoint** What is technology?

2. **Art** in Science Draw a picture in your **science journal** of two kinds of technology that were not around 100 years ago.

**479**

Roofing and waterproofing

Plumbing

Framing

Heating/cooling

Electrical

## Technology in Your Home

Technology found in a house or apartment is more than a loose bunch of inventions. Different parts of buildings work together as systems, which interact.

For example, when you flush the toilet, you use the plumbing system. This system is made of faucets, drains, sinks, and pipes linked together. Some water in the system passes through a water heater. The electrical system is connected to it. Electricity heats the water. You wouldn't like to take a shower if these systems didn't interact, would you?

In a similar way, the heating and cooling system is made up of many parts that work together. The furnace in some systems burns fuel. Others use electricity. No matter what energy source is used, the heating system needs the electrical system to turn it on and off. In these ways, technology systems interact and work together.

These air conditioning units are part of the cooling system. This system keeps us comfortable during hot summers.

What technology do you see in the frame of the house shown here? Boards are not placed just any old way. House designers know that placing the boards in certain patterns makes the building sturdy. To create the form of something, you need to plan it out in a skillful way.

Now look closely at the particle boards that form part of the wall. They are made of wood chips that have been pressed and glued together. Such wood chips used to be burned. That caused air pollution. New technology now turns those chips into strong boards for buildings.

Particle board is a technology that solves two problems at once. It provides a strong building material and uses waste wood chips that would otherwise be burned.

1. ✓ **Checkpoint** Explain how some technology systems work together in a house.

2. **Writing** in Science

   **Expository** In your **science journal** write a paragraph about two technology systems you would expect to find in a kitchen.

481

## Technology Yesterday, Today, and Tomorrow

A kitchen in the early 1800s did not have electricity. So there was no refrigerator or freezer to keep things cold. People had to chop wood to burn in a stove to cook their food. Preparing meals could take most of the day.

Every few years brought more and more inventions and ideas. Ice boxes made of wood and metal, for example, held blocks of ice that kept food cold. Food could be kept longer without spoiling. Ice boxes were a fantastic technology—until electric refrigerators came along.

Technology has made today's kitchens change in many ways since the 1800s. Microwave ovens cook food in minutes. Electric dishwashers replace the chore of washing dishes by hand.

What do you do with leftovers? Plastic bowls with an airtight seal were invented in 1947.

The non-stick coating on this pan was invented in 1954. How did that make cooking easier?

To hear music not long ago, you played a record with wavy grooves scratched into it. While it spun, a metal needle was dragged along the groove. A machine read the vibrations in the needle. The machine then translated the vibrations into music. In a DVD player, a special beam of light now reads the computer-coded plastic discs. A computer translates what it reads into images on a screen.

This CD player uses a light beam to read and play back the music stored on compact discs.

It's hard to imagine how technology will affect the homes of tomorrow. Some people think that computers will soon run the entire home. Perhaps computer chips in each package of food will tell the oven how to cook it. Refrigerators will be connected to the Internet. The Internet will order food when food supplies are running low.

Will these and other ideas come true? Probably some of them will. One thing is for sure. As long as people continue to learn, technology will change. Who knows what exciting things are in store?

### ✓ Lesson Checkpoint

1. Why was the invention of the arch important technology in ancient Rome?

2. Explain the need for systems in order for technology to work in the home.

3. **Social Studies** in Science  How is a modern kitchen different from a kitchen in the early 1800s?

This DVD player uses a light beam to play back movies recorded on plastic discs.

## Lesson 2

# What are some new technologies?

*Modern technology includes tools that allow us to go far beyond what we can normally see and hear.*

### Tools for Extending Our Senses

Navigators on ships once had to figure out where they were by using math and looking at stars. Now navigators can use a Global Positioning System (GPS). This system relies on space satellites. The satellites send signals. Each ship's GPS computer uses the signals to figure out its location and plot a route.

What if you are hiking in a huge forest? You can use a GPS receiver the size of a cell phone to find your way. Some cars have them too. Farmers also use GPS on their tractors to locate crops that need water, fertilizer, or pesticide.

Cameras in satellites can also make pictures using the infrared light that growing things give off. We can think of this light as heat. These satellites track crops, forests, and grasslands over time. Infrared pictures show which areas are too dry or have a disease. These pictures can also show detailed weather patterns. Forecasters use the pictures to observe and predict the weather.

Satellites with special cameras provide images with many kinds of information.

No more getting lost! Signals from satellites track the exact location of this car.

## Tools for Processing Information

A **computer** stores, processes, and sends electronic information incredibly fast! For instance, computers can rapidly turn countless bits of information about the weather into a weather forecast.

Computer technology is everywhere. A digital watch tells time with a computer chip. Calculators, cameras, and cars all use these chips.

Optical fibers are making computers better. These fibers are thin strands of bendable glass that use light to carry information. The fibers are replacing wires in computer, telephone, and cable television systems. Optical fibers do not get hot like wires. They take up less space. Also, a single fiber can carry more phone calls than hundreds of wires twisted into a fat cable.

Optical fibers (right) in communication systems are replacing copper wires (left).

Small cell phones that you carry are replacing bulky ones fixed in place.

Changing from old, copper wire technology to new fiber optic technology requires a lot of work.

1. ✓ **Checkpoint** Explain how a GPS system helps people know where they are.

2. **Writing in Science** **Expository** Write a paragraph in your **science journal** that tells how technology has affected your life.

485

## Tools for Transporting Materials

Roads are a very important part of our lives. We travel on them to go to work and school. We follow them to pick up and deliver goods. We use them to visit friends and family or just to see the sights.

Fast, safe highways are now in place. Some people call the National Highway System the greatest wonder of the modern world. This system includes all the major highways that go from one state to another. About 80 million trucks carry the nation's supplies on over 260,000 kilometers (160,000 miles) of national highways. About 120 million cars carry passengers from place to place.

The United States began to build the National Highway System so that military vehicles like this one could move quickly over great distances.

Did you ever wonder how complex highway systems are designed? That's the job of highway engineers.

A wheel tractor-scraper is just one of many inventions needed to build roads.

Trains began to transport goods on railroads long before trucks began to transport goods on freeways.

Big tools are needed for building big highways. First, earthmoving machines like the tractor-scraper in the picture lay out the new road. Then workers lay down sand, crushed stone, and concrete or asphalt. Finally, workers paint markings and put up traffic signs.

Roads are not the only pathways over which people and things move. People and freight use railroads and planes such as the ones shown.

The first transportation system in the United States was the nation's rivers. Today, boats push barges loaded with freight over the same rivers. Technology will always help get people and things from place to place.

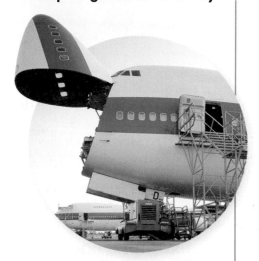

Planes are now the fastest way to carry cargo. Cargo planes can carry loads that weigh 100,000 kg.

1. ✔Checkpoint Why is a modern roadway system important?

2. **Technology** in Science Use the Internet to view maps of the National Highway System. Then plan a trip across the country using the maps.

Using powerful tugboats has improved our nation's river transportation system.

Microwave ovens today are small and easy to use. A special tool sends microwaves into the chamber where food is placed. These waves of energy cause water particles in the food to vibrate. Thermal energy quickly builds, heating the food.

## Unexpected Uses

Sometimes technology becomes useful in unplanned ways. For example, back in 1946 Percy Spencer was working to improve radar. He was testing a light bulb that used microwave energy. Microwaves are a form of radiation, like visible light and invisible radio waves.

One day Spencer stood near the tube. He noticed that a candy bar in his pocket melted. Curious, he put popcorn kernels near the microwave energy. They rapidly popped into fluffy pieces.

Spencer realized that if microwaves could quickly cook popcorn, they could quickly cook other foods, too. He made a drawing that led to the first microwave oven. Technology that was first designed for radar is a great help to those who eat in a hurry!

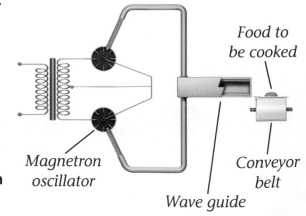

Food to be cooked

Magnetron oscillator

Wave guide

Conveyor belt

**This design by Percy Spencer explains how the first microwave oven would work. The first oven weighed 750 pounds and cost $5,000.**

Will you watch TV today? Television sets and computers started out using glass tubes to display the picture. But these tubes cannot be made to be very big. Glass is heavy and breaks easily in big screens. Now TV screens are huge. How could this happen? New technology makes the difference. In 1970, James Fergason invented the first modern LCD screen. LCD stands for liquid crystal display. Electricity causes each fluid crystal to act like the shutter in a camera. The crystals either block the light or allow the light to pass through. This causes an image on the screen. Screens using these crystals do not need heavy glass. They are light in weight. They are also flat, as the picture shows.

DVD players that you can carry show movies on tiny LCD screens.

A screen made of glass is shaped like a box. But this LCD screen is flat. Computers using LCD screens do not take up a lot of desk space.

## ✓ Lesson Checkpoint

1. What did Percy Spencer accidentally discover that microwaves could do?

2. What does a computer do?

3. **Writing** in Science Why was it important for Percy Spencer to keep asking questions after his candy bar melted? Answer this question in a paragraph in your **science journal.**

## Lesson 3

# How does technology help us get energy?

*Technology has changed the way we get energy. But most of the energy sources we use today cause problems for the environment. We can use technology to develop cleaner energy sources.*

**Mills used to grind grain into flour. Others drove machinery that made things.**

## Using Energy

Plop in a DVD, pop some popcorn in the microwave, and you're set to watch a movie. But be sure everything is plugged in! Today we take our electrical energy for granted. In the past it wasn't so easy.

Before engines and electricity, people relied on wind and water as sources of energy. Water-powered mills like the one shown were built next to rivers. The force of flowing water turned a big wheel. At a sawmill, for instance, the wheel turned a series of rods, gears, and belts. This caused saws to cut wood.

**Moving water makes the parts in this lawn sprinkler spray water in different directions.**

The force of water runs a modern lawn sprinkler. Study the diagram shown. First, the hose sends water into the sprinkler. The moving water has kinetic energy to do work. Water then turns a waterwheel. Next, the waterwheel turns wheel and axle gears. The gears slowly rock the spray arm back and forth. Finally, water from the spray arm waters the lawn.

Windmills were also used to do work. As you might guess, windmills use the energy of moving air instead of water as a power source. The windmill in the picture is still used today. The turning blades move gears in a small box. The gears move a rod up and down. This pumps water from under the ground.

There are good and bad things connected with using windmills and water mills. They do not pollute the air or water. However, water mills can only work along a river. Both wind and water are renewable energy resources. But they don't supply enough power for all our needs.

1. ✔ **Checkpoint** What renewable sources of energy have people used for centuries to generate power?

2. **Sequence** Use a graphic organizer and describe the steps of how a modern water sprinkler works.

Windmills like this one use wind energy to pump water.

## Producing Electricity

We still use waterwheel technology inside hydroelectric power dams. These dams are built on rivers that back up behind the dam to form reservoirs. Study the diagram. The deep water stores potential energy. To release this energy to do work, gates let water rush into the power station. The kinetic energy of the flowing water then spins the blades of waterwheels in turbines. The spinning axle of each turbine drives a generator to make electricity. The electricity is used for power in cities.

Hydroelectric power does not produce much pollution. Since it depends on water, it also is a renewable energy source. But dams can affect fish that travel up the rivers on which the dams are built. The large lake behind the dam floods land, which then changes the environment. There also is a danger of more flooding if a dam breaks.

Generators like this one in a hydroelectric dam change the energy of flowing water into electricity.

Below each generator, the energy of moving water becomes the energy of moving blades in a turbine.

Axle turns to drive generator.

Water pushes against blades, causing the waterwheel to spin.

Water enters from reservoir.

**Turbine**

Water goes out to stream below dam.

Another way to change energy into electricity is by burning coal, oil, or natural gas. The heat from burning this fuel is used to boil water. Boiling water makes steam. Pressure from steam turns wheels of turbines that drive electricity generators.

This technology is a solution to the problem of producing enough electricity for everyone. But this is an example of how technology can create problems too. Burning fuel for electric generators can pollute the air. Burning fuels to move cars also pollutes the air. People are working on ways to use technology to make cars and generators that pollute less.

## Map Fact

Herbert Hoover Dam sits on the Colorado River that divides Arizona and Nevada. It was completed in 1936. Hoover Dam is one of the largest dams in the world.

1. ✓**Checkpoint** How are cars a helpful and a harmful example of technology?
2. **Social Studies** in Science Use the library to learn more about how Hoover Dam on the Colorado River was built.

## Future Sources of Energy

Our energy needs seem to keep growing. How will we meet these needs in the future? Many people are working to answer that question.

Solar energy is one answer. This energy comes directly from the Sun's rays. Panels, like the ones in the picture, gather the Sun's rays. Each panel has lots of small solar cells spread across it. The cells work together to provide enough power to be useful. Solar energy is a major source of electricity in desert areas where there are many days of sunshine.

Solar panels concentrate the Sun's rays. This energy is changed into electricity.

New technology is making solar energy cheaper to use. Many people put panels on the roofs of their houses. Instead of making electricity, however, they make hot water. First, water runs through small tubes. Next, the energy of the Sun's rays is changed into heat when the panels absorb the rays. Then the heat warms the water in the tubes. Finally, the heated water flows into a container that stores the hot water until it's time to take a shower.

Solar energy warms water in this household appliance.

Wind rotates the arms of these windmills to generate electricity.

Wind energy also holds promise. Thousands of windmills like the ones above have already been set up in areas where the wind blows strong and often. To change enough kinetic energy of wind into electrical energy, the blades must be huge. Some blade wheels are wider than a football field is long! Computer technology can sense changing wind conditions. Motors then make shifts in the direction and angle of the blades. Doing this makes the most use of the wind for making the most electricity. These wind farms produce a lot of electricity for the surrounding community.

1. **√ Checkpoint** What two renewable energy resources might meet more of our energy needs in the future?

2. **Sequence** List the steps that lead from the energy of sunshine in solar panels to the energy of hot water in a water tank. Use a graphic organizer.

495

## Technology Time Line

Throughout human history, people have made discoveries and inventions to improve their lives.

**312 B.C.**
Rome completes the first aqueducts. Aqueducts brought water to Roman cities.

**3500 B.C.**
People connect wooden planks with other pieces of wood to make wheels.

**1608**
Dutch eyeglass maker Hans Leppershey places lenses in a tube and makes the first telescope. The famous scientist Galileo soon improves this tool and makes important discoveries about space.

**1957**
The Soviet Union launches the first artificial satellite, called *Sputnik 1*. It is only about the size of a basketball but this new piece of technology starts an international race for space.

**1948**
Opening of the Mount Palomar Observatory in California. It allows scientists to collect new data about our galaxy and beyond. Until 1976 it is the world's largest single-mirror telescope.

**1903**
Orville and Wilbur Wright invent the powered airplane. The first flight lasts only 12 seconds but it sparks a whole new wave of inventions that build the airline industry.

**1876**
Alexander Graham Bell invents the telephone. Imagine what life would be like without telephones.

**2004**
Spirit, the Mars expedition rover, prepares to drill into a rock. Will manned expeditions to Mars be soon to come?

**1969**
Astronauts Neil Armstrong and Edwin Aldrin land on the surface of the Moon. The *Apollo 11* astronauts bring moon rocks back to Earth for further study.

### ✓ Lesson Checkpoint

1. What changes in technology have changed the way we get energy?

2. What must we do in order to continue to use non-renewable fuel resources for energy?

3. **Math in Science** Figure the time in years between the Wright's flight, the launch of *Sputnik 1*, and the first Moon landing. How does this show how fast technology is changing?

## Investigate How does a GPS device find your location?

GPS, the Global Positioning System, can tell you your location anywhere on the globe—if you have a GPS device. The Global Positioning System uses GPS satellites to help find your location. In this activity, you solve a problem: How does a GPS device find a location?

### Materials

Location of GPS Satellites over North America

metric ruler

3 circle patterns

### What to Do

**1** **Make a model** of how a GPS device finds your location. The GPS device learns you are 2,500 km from satellite A. On this map 5 cm stands for 2,500 km. So, use a circle pattern to draw a circle around satellite A with a 5 cm radius.

| Satellite | Actual Distance from Your Location (km) | Distance on Map from Your Location (cm) |
|---|---|---|
| A | 2,500 km | 5 cm |
| B | 1,500 km | 3 cm |
| C | 2,000 km | 4 cm |

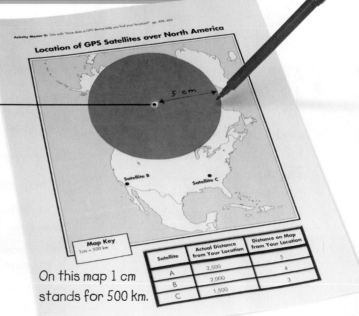

Satellite A

The 5 cm circle shows all the places that are 2,500 km from satellite A. Because you are 2,500 km from satellite A, you must be somewhere on this 5 cm circle.

On this map 1 cm stands for 500 km.

**2** Repeat step 1 for satellites B and C. Use the distances shown in the chart to make 2 more circles. Your location must be on each of these circles too.

**3** Your location is the spot where all the circles meet. Mark an **X** on the map to record your location.

The map scale shows that 1 cm on the map equals 500 km on Earth. When you mark the distances in cm, you are using the scale to help measure distance. An accurate scale is important in producing and using a model of how a GPS device works. If the scale is not accurate, you can not find the correct location.

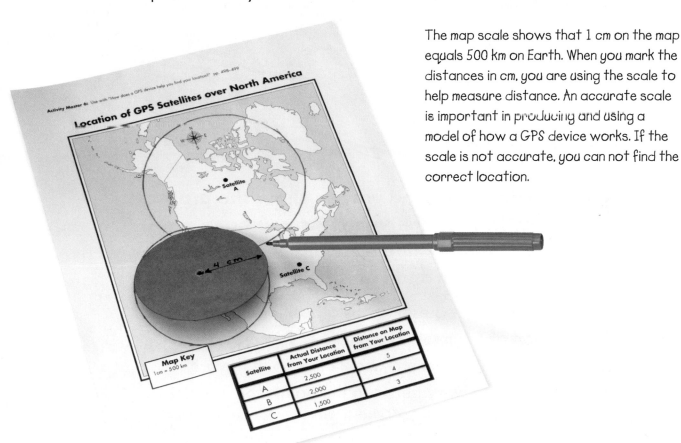

The data for this activity includes the satellite locations, your distance from each satellite, the circles you made, and the **X** you made to show your position.

## Explain Your Results

1. You needed to know your distance from more than 2 satellites in order to find your location. **Infer** why at least 3 satellites were needed.

2. Describe the scale on this map and tell how you used it to **measure** distance. Why was the scale important in this **model** of how a GPS device finds a location?

**Go Further**

What would happen if the three satellites were in different places? Use a map to find a new GPS location, or investigate other questions you may have.

# Technology
## Through the Years

Using a time line is a good way to show the progress of technology through the years. As you have seen, a time line is a number line showing events that took place during a certain span of time.

Any number can be represented as a position on a number line. The position of a number on a number line is important. Since 0.5 is halfway between 0 and 1, the point for 0.5 (or 1/2) should be halfway between the points for 0 and 1. Notice where 0.25 and 0.75 are placed.

Since 25 is one fourth of 100, the point for 25 should be one fourth of the distance from 0 to 100.

In the same way, on a time line, the point for the year 1950 should be halfway between the points for the years 1900 and 2000. 1925 would be one fourth of that distance. 1975 would be three fourths of the distance from 1900 to 2000.

On grid paper copy the time line above. Count grid squares to place the given points correctly. For each event in the table below, mark a point on your time line. Label each point with the year and the event above the line. The first event is already on the line you copied.

## Transportation Technology

| | Year | Event | | Year | Event |
|---|---|---|---|---|---|
| 1 | 1804 | First steam locomotive | 6 | 1956 | Beginning of National Highway system |
| 2 | 1869 | First railroad tracks laid across the U.S. | 7 | 1969 | First moon-landing by astronauts |
| 3 | 1885 | First gasoline-powered automobile | 8 | 1981 | First space shuttle flight |
| 4 | 1903 | First gasoline-powered airplane | 9 | 1999 | First hot-air balloon flight around the world |
| 5 | 1934 | First diesel train in the U.S. | 10 | 2004 | First privately-funded space flight |

## Lab zone Take-Home Activity

Make a time line that shows how technology has changed over the years. You might choose computers, space travel, or buildings. Use library resources to find important dates and events. Choose what events you want to show.

## Use Vocabulary

| | |
|---|---|
| **computer** (page 485) | **technology** (page 479) |
| **invention** (page 479) | **tool** (page 479) |

Use the term from the list above that best completes each sentence.

**1.** An object used to do work is a(n) _____.

**2.** The use of science knowledge to invent tools and new ways of doing things is called _____.

**3.** Something that has been made for the first time is called a(n) _____.

**4.** A(n) _____ stores, processes, and sends information.

## Explain Concepts

**5.** Explain how science and technology are related.

**6.** Describe one of the technology systems found in your school.

**7.** Give two examples of ways technology can be helpful and harmful.

**8.** Compare the good and bad points of windmills and water mills.

**9.** What are some ways you use a computer every day, even if you don't use a desktop computer?

**10.** How is an LCD screen an improvement over glass picture tubes in televisions?

**11.** How has Percy Spencer's discovery changed part of our daily lives?

### Process Skills

**12.** **Infer** Why are electricity-generating wind engines found only in wide-open areas?

**13.** **Predict** what could help solve our energy problems in the future.

**14.** **Sequence** Make a graphic organizer like the one shown. Fill it in to show how water can be used to make electricity.

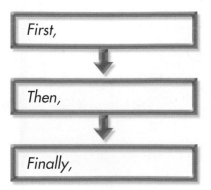

First,

↓

Then,

↓

Finally,

**Test Prep**

**15.** Science and technology can

    (A) help people solve problems.

    (B) sometimes create new problems.

    (C) help people experience new things.

    (D) all of the above

**16.** The heating system in a house connects to the plumbing system when

    (F) the toilet is flushed.

    (G) the microwave oven heats soup.

    (H) the water heater makes some water hot.

    (I) the air conditioning units cool the house.

**17.** What invention do both DVD and CD players use to make images or sound?

    (A) a camera that takes pictures of infrared light

    (B) a tool that shines a light beam on plastic discs

    (C) wheels that water pressure turn

    (D) a generator that makes microwaves

**18.** Which of the following is a nonrenewable resource?

    (F) sun

    (G) coal

    (H) wind

    (I) water

**19.** Explain why the answer you chose for Question 15 is best. Explain why you did not choose one of the other answers.

**20.** **Writing** in Science

**Descriptive** Suppose you are living in your town 50 years from now. Brainstorm with a classmate what that would be like. List kinds of technology you might have in your home. Write a paragraph describing some of this technology.

**503**

# Science Teacher

Are you excited about science? How would you like to get students, teachers, and the public excited about science too? Michelle Thaller and Doris Daou, for instance, are Astronomers and Teachers for NASA. They promote the exciting work NASA is doing to help people study space.

Dr. Thaller and Ms. Daou help schoolteachers use NASA materials in their lessons. They appear on television shows. They speak to thousands of students every year. One area of study they teach audiences about is the use of special telescopes. For instance, following Earth in its orbit around the Sun is the Spitzer Space Telescope. Using infrared technology, it takes pictures of stars and solar systems that hide behind vast clouds of gas and dust.

Science teachers go to college and learn about life, earth, physical, and space science. They train in schools like yours to gain experience in teaching students like you.

Dr. Michelle Thaller

Ms. Doris Daou

Spitzer Space Telescope

## Lab zone Take-Home Activity

Find out more about how infrared telescopes work. Describe the difference between pictures taken with visible light and with infrared rays.

# Unit D Test Talk

**Test-Taking Strategies**
Find Important Words
Choose the Right Answer
Use Information from Text and Graphics
▶ Write Your Answer

## Write Your Answer

To answer the following test questions, you need to write your answer. Read the passage and then answer the questions.

The Sun and other stars appear to move across the sky because Earth is moving. Earth rotates, or spins, on its axis. One complete spin, or rotation, takes 24 hours. This rotation and light from the Sun cause the patterns of day, night, and shadows.

Earth also revolves or moves in an orbit around the Sun. One complete trip around the Sun is one revolution. One revolution takes one year. Earth's axis always points in the same direction. As a result, sometimes the northern half of Earth is tilted toward the Sun and receives the most direct sunlight. Sometimes the southern half of Earth is tilted toward the Sun. Earth's tilt and movement around the Sun causes the patterns of seasons.

The Sun is the star at the center of our solar system. Mercury, Venus, Mars, Jupiter, Saturn, Uranus, Neptune, and Pluto are other planets besides Earth that orbit the Sun. These and other objects that revolve around the Sun make up the solar system.

## Use What You Know

To write your answer to each question, you need to read the passage and the test question carefully. Write your answers in complete sentences. Then read your answer to make sure it is complete, correct, and focused.

**1.** What causes the patterns of day, night, and shadows?

**2.** What are two ways that Earth moves?

**3.** Explain how Earth's tilt and revolution cause seasons.

**4.** What are the names of the planets in our solar system?

# Unit D Wrap-Up

## Chapter 15

### What patterns do the Earth, Sun, Moon, and stars show?

- Earth's revolution around the Sun and rotation on a tilted axis cause the patterns of day, night, shadows, seasons, and the movement of stars across the sky.

- Light from the Sun and the revolution of the Moon around Earth cause the patterns of the phases of the Moon and eclipses.

## Chapter 16

### How are the planets in the solar system alike and different?

- The planets in the solar system all rotate on an axis and revolve around the Sun in orbits. The planets are different sizes, different distances from the Sun, and take different amounts of time to rotate and revolve.

- Each planet in the solar system has special features that make it different from the other planets.

## Chapter 17

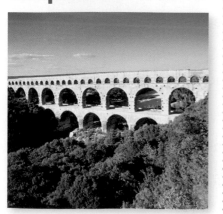

### How does technology affect our lives?

- Technology applies the knowledge gained from science to solve problems and improve our lives.

- Technology helps us to get energy to do work and to develop cleaner energy sources.

## Performance Assessment
### Model a Solar System

Use a large sheet of paper and colored markers to make a model of a solar system that has a star, three planets, and one moon. Describe the parts of the solar system and the patterns your model shows. What is at the center of your model? How are the planets alike and different?

## Read More About Space and Technology!

Look for books like these in the library.

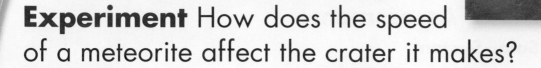

## Experiment How does the speed of a meteorite affect the crater it makes?

**Materials**

safety goggles

copier paper box lid

spoon, marble, cup with flour

metric ruler and meterstick

calculator or computer (optional)

### Process Skills

In an **experiment**, you **identify** the independent and dependent **variables**. You **control** other variables.

### Ask a question.

How does the speed of a meteorite affect the size of the crater it makes?

### State a hypothesis.

If a meteorite is moving faster, then will it make a crater with a width that is smaller than, larger than, or about the same size as a crater made by a slower meteorite? Write your **hypothesis**.

### Identify and control variables.

The marble is a **model** of a meteorite. The flour is a model of the surface the meteorite hits. Use the same marble and the same amount of flour in all tests. These are **controlled variables**.

> Controlled variables are things you need to keep the same if you want a fair test.

The variable you change is the height from which you drop the marble. A marble dropped from a greater height will be moving faster when it hits the flour pile.

> The variable you change is the independent variable.

The variable you will measure is the width of the crater.

> The variable you measure is the dependent variable.

> What are the controlled, independent, and dependent variables?

## Test your hypothesis.

**1** In the center of the box lid, make a flat pile of flour.

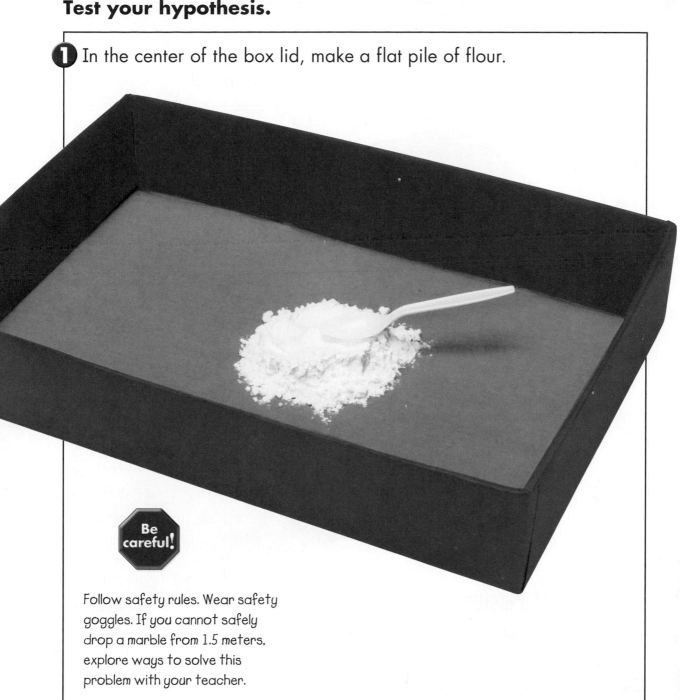

**Be careful!**

Follow safety rules. Wear safety goggles. If you cannot safely drop a marble from 1.5 meters, explore ways to solve this problem with your teacher.

**2** Place the empty flour cup on the floor. Stand above the cup. Close one eye. Aim down at the cup. Drop a marble into the cup. Practice until the marble lands in the cup every time. Then try dropping the marble from 1.5 m above the cup.

**3** Now it is time to make your crater. Drop the marble from a height of 0.5 m (50 cm). Hit the center of the flour pile. Measure the width of the crater.

Select a tool to measure the width of the crater in millimeters.

**4** Remove the marble. Push the pile back together. Repeat steps 3 and 4 twice.

**5** Repeat steps 4 and 5, but drop the marble from 1 m and 1.5 m.

When you repeat your observations and measurements, you can improve their accuracy. Record accurately. Do not change your results because others have different results. Similar investigations seldom turn out exactly the same. However, similar results are expected. Accurate records help scientists learn why there are differences in repeated experiments.

More Lab Activities zone **Take It to the Net** sfsuccessnet.com

## Collect and record your data.

| | Crater Width (mm) | | |
|---|---|---|---|
| | Marble dropped from a height of 0.5 m | Marble dropped from a height of 1 m | Marble dropped from a height of 1.5 m |
| Trial 1 | | | |
| Trial 2 | | | |
| Trial 3 | | | |
| Average | | | |

Your teacher may ask you to use a calculator or a computer with the right software. These tools can help you find the averages and help you graph your data.

## Interpret your data.

Make a bar graph. Study your chart and graph.
What patterns do you see in your data?

**Average Effect of Drop Height on Crater Width**

Crater Width (mm): 50, 45, 40, 35, 30, 25, 20, 15, 10, 5, 0

Drop Height (m): 0.5, 1, 1.5, 2

Discuss your observations with others.

## State your conclusion.
Describe your results. Compare your hypothesis with your results.
**Communicate** your conclusion.
Explain the effect of drop height on crater width.

## Go Further
Interpret your data to predict the effect of dropping the marble from other heights. Use your model system to check your prediction.

# Science Fair Projects

## Using Scientific Methods

1. Ask a question.
2. State your hypothesis.
3. Identify/control variables.
4. Test your hypothesis.
5. Collect and record your data.
6. Interpret your data.
7. State your conclusion.
8. Go further.

## Observing Patterns of Daylight

The Sun appears to rise in the east and set in the west.

**Idea:** Use a calendar and a watch with a second hand to observe and record the time the Sun rises and sets every day for two months.

## Planet-Size Models

One way that planets in the solar system are different is their size.

**Idea:** Use a metric ruler and posterboard to make models that demonstrate the size of the Sun and each of the planets.

## Inventing

People use their knowledge to design new tools and new ways to do things that solve problems and improve their lives.

**Idea:** Use your knowledge to invent a tool or a way to do something to make a job easier.

EC NTL 109876543

# Metric and Customary Measures

The metric system is the measurement system most commonly used in science. Metric units are sometimes called SI units. SI stands for International System because these units are used around the world.

These prefixes are used in the metric system:

kilo- means *thousand*
1 kilometer equals 1,000 meters
milli- means one-*thousandth*
1,000 millimeters equals 1 meter
centi- means *hundredths*
100 centimeters equals 1 meter

## Length and Distance
One meter is longer than 1 foot.

*1 meter*

*1 foot*

## Area

square
centimer

square
inch

## Volume
One liter is greater than 4 cups.

*1 liter*

*1 cup*

## Mass
One kilogram is greater than 1 pound.

*1 pound*

*1 kilogram*

## Temperature
Water freezes at 0°C or 32°F.
Water boils at 100°C or 212°F.

# Glossary

The glossary uses letters and signs to show how words are pronounced. The mark ′ is placed after a syllable with a primary or heavy accent. The mark ′ is placed after a syllable with a secondary or lighter accent.

To hear these words pronounced, listen to the AudioText CD.

**absorb** (ab sôrb′) to take in (p. 373)

**adaptation** (ad′ ap tā′ shən) trait that helps a living thing survive in its environment (p. 48)

**asteroid** (as′tə roid′) a small chunk of rock that orbits around the Sun (p. 457)

**atmosphere** (at′mə sfir) the blanket of air and gases that surround the Earth (p. 176)

**atom** (at′əm) one of the tiny particles that make up all of matter (p. 282)

**axis** (ak′sis) an imaginary line around which Earth spins (p. 424)

**blizzard** (bliz′ərd) a winter storm with very low temperatures, strong winds, heavy snowfall, and blowing snow (p. 183)

**buoyancy** (boi′ən sē) force exerted on an object that is immersed in a gas or liquid that tends to make it float (p. 286)

**carnivore** (kär′nə vôr) living things that hunt other animals for food (p. 106)

**cause** (kȯz) why something happens (p. 277, 311)

**change of state** (chānj uv stāt) physical change that takes place when matter changes from one state to another (p. 304)

**chemical change** (kem′ə kəl chānj) a change that causes one kind of matter to become a different kind of matter (p. 311)

**classifying** (klas′ə fī′ing) to arrange or sort objects, events, or living things according to their properties (p. 244)

**collecting data** (kə lek′ ting dā′ tə) to gather observations and measurements into graphs, tables or charts (p. 26)

**communicating** (kə myü′ nə kāt′ ing) using words, pictures, charts, graphs, and diagrams to share information (p. 324)

**community** (kəm myü′ nə tē) all the populations that live together in the same place (p. 74)

**compare** (kəm pâr′) to show how things are alike (p. 5, 245, 389, 453)

**competition** (kom′ pə tish′ən) struggle that happens when two or more living things need the same resource (p. 110)

**compression wave** (kəm presh′ən wāv) wave that has spaces where particles are squeezed together and spaces where particles are spread apart (p. 396)

**computer** (kəm pyü′ tər) tool which stores, processes, and gets electronic information (p. 485)

**conclusion** (kən klü′ zhən) decision reached after considering facts and details (p. 101)

**condensation** (kon′ den sā′ shən) the changing of a gas into a liquid (p. 157)

**coniferous tree** (kō nif′ər əs trē) does not lose its needle-like leaves in the fall (p. 16)

**conservation** (kon′ sər vā′ shən) the saving and wise use of natural resources (p. 250)

**constellation** (kon′ stə lā′ shən) a group of stars that make a pattern or shape (p. 438)

**consumer** (kən sü′ mər) living things that eat food (p. 106)

**contrast** (kən trast′) to show how things are different (p. 5, 245, 389, 453)

**core** (kôr) the innermost layer of Earth (p. 223)

**crust** (krust) the outermost layer of Earth (p. 223)

**decay** (di kā′) to break down, or rot (p. 118, 206)

**deciduous** (di sij′ü əs) loses its leaves in the fall and grows new ones in the spring (p. 14)

**decomposer** (dē′kəm pō′zər) a living thing that breaks down waste and things that have died (p. 118)

**density** (den′sə tē) measure of the amount of matter in a certain amount of space (p. 286)

**desert** (dez′ərt) an ecosystem that gets less than 25 cm of rainfall a year (p. 78)

**details** (di tālz′) individual pieces of information that support a main idea (p. 69, 357)

**disease** (də zēz′) the name we give an illness (p. 126)

**earthquake** (ėrth′kwāk′) a shaking of Earth's crust caused by sudden, shifting movements in the crust (p. 228)

**ecosystem** (ē′kō sis′təm) all the living and nonliving things that interact with each other in a given area (p. 72)

**effect** (ə fekt′) what happens as the result of a cause (p. 149, 277)

**electric charge** (i lek′trik chärj) tiny amount of energy in the particles of matter (p. 374)

**electric circuit** (i lek′trik sėr′kit) the path that a controlled electric current flows through (p. 376)

**electric current** (i lek′trik kėr′ənt) the movement of an electric charge from one place to another (p. 376)

**element** (el′ə mənt) matter that has only one kind of atom (p. 282)

**energy** (en′ ər jē) the ability to do work or to cause a change (p. 359)

**environment** (en vī′rən mənt) everything that surrounds a living thing (p. 71)

**equator** (i kwā′ tər) the imaginary line that separates the north and south halves of Earth (p. 429)

**erosion** (i rō′ zhən) the movement of weathered materials (p. 232)

**estimating and measuring** (es′tə māt ing and mezh′ər ing) to tell what you think an object's measurements are and then to measure it in units (p. 210)

**evaporation** (i vap′ ə rā′ shən) the changing of a liquid into a gas (p. 157)

**experiment** (ek sper′ə ment) to formulate and test a hypothesis using a scientific method (p. 140)

**explore** (ek splôr′) to study a scientific idea in a hands-on manner (p. 36)

**extinct** (ek stingkt′) no longer lives on Earth (p. 23)

**food chain** (füd chān) the movement of energy from one type of living thing to another (p. 108)

**food web** (füd web) the flow of energy between food chains which ties a community together (p. 108)

**force** (fôrs) a push or a pull (p. 332)

**forming questions and hypotheses** (fôrm′ing kwes′chənz and hī poth′ə sēz′) to think of how you can solve a problem or answer a question (p. 140)

**fossil** (fos′ əl) remains or mark of a living thing from long ago (p. 22)

**friction** (frik′ shən) a contact force that opposes the motion of an object (p. 333)

**gas** (gas) the form of matter which has no shape, has particles that are not connected to each other, and takes up whatever space is available (p. 281)

**germinate** (jėr′ mə nāt) begins to grow (p. 20)

**germs** (jėrmz) small living things that include bacteria and viruses, many of which can cause illness (p. 126)

**grassland** (gras′ land′) land ecosystem that has many grasses and few trees (p. 76)

**gravity** (grav′ə tē) a non-contact force that pulls objects toward each other (p. 336)

**groundwater** (ground′ wȯ′ tər) water that has slowly made its way through soil and then collects in spaces between underground rock; it is brought to the surface by digging wells (p. 155)

**habitat** (hab′ə tat) the place where a living thing makes its home (p. 72)

**heat** (hēt) the transfer of thermal energy from one piece of matter to another (p. 366)

**herbivore** (ėr′bə vôr) living things that eat only plants (p. 106)

**hibernate** (hī′bər nāt) to spend winter resting; body systems slow down in order to save energy (p. 52)

**hurricane** (hėr′ə kān) a huge, strong storm that forms over the ocean (p. 182)

**identifying and controlling variables** (ī den′tə fī ing and kən trōl′ ing vâr′ē ə bəlz) to change one thing, but keep all the other factors the same (p. 40)

**igneous rock** (ig′nē əs rok′) rock that forms when melted earth materials cool and harden (p. 200)

**inclined plane** (in klīnd′ plān) a slanting surface that connects a lower level to a higher level (p. 340)

**inference** (in′fər əns) a conclusion based on facts, experiences, observations, or knowledge (p. 173)

**inferring** (in fėr′ ing) to draw a conclusion or make a reasonable guess based on what you have learned or what you know (p. 100)

**inherited** (in her′it əd) passed on from parent to offspring (p. 48)

**interpreting data** (in tėr′prit ing dā′tə) to use the information you have collected to solve problems or answer questions (p. 26)

**invention** (in ven′ shən) something that has been made for the first time (p. 479)

**investigate** (in ves′ tə gāt) to solve a problem or answer a question by following an existing procedure or an original one (p. 26)

**investigating and experimenting** (in ves′ tə gāt ing and ek sper′ə ment ing) to plan and do an investigation to test a hypothesis or solve a problem (p. 508)

**kinetic energy** (ki net′ik en′ər jē) energy of motion (p. 361)

**landform** (land′ fôrm) a natural feature on the surface of Earth's crust (p. 224)

**larva** (lär′ və) stage in an insect's life after it hatches from the egg (p. 45)

**lava** (lä′ və) hot, molten rock on Earth's surface (p. 226)

**lever** (lev′ər) a simple machine used to lift and move things (p. 341)

**life cycle** (līf sī′kəl) the stages through which an organism passes between birth and death (p. 44)

**light** (līt) a form of energy that can be seen (p. 370)

**liquid** (lik′wid) matter that does not have a definite shape but takes up a definite amount of space (p. 280)

**loam** (lōm) soil that contains a mixture of humus and mineral materials of sand, silt, and clay (p. 209)

**lunar eclipse** (lü′nər i klips′) Earth's shadow moving across the Moon (p. 434)

**magma** (mag′mə) hot, molten rock that forms deep underground (p. 226)

**magnetic** (mag net′ik) having the property to pull on, or attract, metals that have iron in them (p. 337)

**magnetism** (mag′nə tiz′əm) a non-contact force that pulls objects containing iron (p. 337)

**main idea** (mān ī dē′ə) what a paragraph is about; the most important idea (p. 69, 357)

**making operational definitions** (māk′ ing op′ə rā′ shən əl def′ə nish′ənz) to define or describe an object or event based on your own experience (p. 68)

**making and using models** (māk′ ing and yüz′ ing mod′lz) to make a model from materials or to make a sketch or a diagram (p. 36)

**mantle** (man′tl) the middle layer of Earth (p. 223)

**mass** (mas) amount of matter (p. 284)

**matter** (mat′ər) anything that takes up space and has mass (p. 279)

**metamorphic rock** (met′ ə môr′ fik rok′) rock that forms when existing rock is changed by heat and pressure (p. 200)

**migrate** (mī′ grāt) to move to another place to find better climate, food, or a mate (p. 52)

**mineral** (min′ ər əl) natural material that forms from nonliving matter (p. 199)

**mixture** (miks′ chər) two or more kinds of matter that are placed together but can be easily separated (p. 306)

**Moon** (mün) the natural satellite that orbits around Earth (p. 432)

**Moon phase** (mün fāz) the way the Moon looks because of the amount of the lit side of the Moon that can be seen from Earth at the same time (p. 434)

**motion** (mō′shən) a change in the position of an object (p. 327)

**natural resources** (nach′ ər əl ri sôrs′əz) natural materials, such as soil, wood, water, air, oil, or minerals, that living things need (p. 247)

**nonrenewable resources** (non ri nü′ə bəl ri sôrs′ əz) resource that cannot be replaced once it is used up (p. 248)

**nutrient** (nü′ trē ənt) thing plants need in order to grow (p. 206)

**observing** (əb zėrv′ ing) using your senses to find out about objects, events, or living things (p. 4)

**omnivore** (om′ nə vôr′) living things that eat plants and other animals for food (p. 106)

**orbit** (ôr′ bit) the path of any object in space that revolves around another object in space (p. 456)

**periodic table** (pir′ē od′ik tā′bəl) an arrangement of elements based on their properties (p. 283)

**physical change** (fiz′ ə kəl chānj) a change that makes matter look different without becoming a new substance (p. 303)

**pitch** (pich) how high or low a sound is (p. 392)

**planet** (plan′it) a large body of matter that revolves, or travels, around any star (p. 456)

**pollinate** (pol′ ə nāt) move pollen from the part of a flower that makes pollen to the part of a flower that makes seeds (p. 15)

**pollution** (pə lü′ shən) waste materials that make the environment dirty (p. 124)

**population** (pop′ yə lā′ shən) all the living things of the same kind that live in the same place at the same time (p. 74)

**position** (pə zish′ ən) the location of an object (p. 327)

**potential energy** (pə ten′shəl en′ ər jē) the energy something has because of its position (p. 360)

**precipitation** (pri sip′ə tā′ shən) water that falls to Earth as rain, hail, sleet, or snow (p. 159)

**predator** (pred′ə tər) a consumer that hunts other animals for food (p. 107)

**predicting** (pri dikt′ ing) to tell what you think will happen (p. 162)

**pressure** (presh′ər) force per unit area that is applied to a substance (p. 281)

**prey** (prā) any animal that is hunted by others for food (p. 107)

**producer** (prə dü′sər) living things that make their own food (p. 106)

**property** (prop′ər tē) something about matter that you can observe with one or more of your senses (p. 279)

**pulley** (pùl′ē) a machine that changes the direction of motion of an object to which a force is applied (p. 343)

**pupa** (pyü′pə) stage in an insect's life between larva and adult (p. 45)

**recycle** (rē sī′kəl) treat or process something so it can be used again (p. 254)

**reflect** (ri flekt′) to bounce off of (p. 372)

**refract** (ri frakt′) to bend (p. 372)

**relative position** (rel′ə tiv pə zish′ən) a change in an object's position compared to another object (p. 329)

**renewable resource** (ri nü′ ə bəl ri sôrs′) resource that is endless like sunlight, or that is naturally replaced in a fairly short time, such as trees (p. 247)

**resource** (ri sôrs′) See Natural Resources, Renewable Resources, Nonrenewable Resources

**revolution** (rev′ə lü′ shən) one complete trip around the Sun (p. 428)

**rock** (rok) natural, solid, nonliving material made of one or more minerals (p. 199)

**rotation** (rō tā′ shən) one complete spin on an axis (p. 425)

**scientific method** (sī′ ən tif′ik meth′əd) organized ways of finding answers and solving problems (p. xxvi)

**sedimentary rock** (sed′ə men′tər ē rok′) rock that forms when small pieces of earth materials collect and become bound together (p. 200)

**seed leaf** (sēd lēf) part of a seed that has stored food (p. 20)

**seedling** (sēd′ ling) a new, small plant that grows from a seed (p. 20)

**sequence** (sē′kwəns) the order in which events take place (p. 37, 221, 421, 477)

**soil** (soil) the part of Earth's surface consisting of humus and weathered rock in which plants grow (p. 206)

**solid** (sol′id) matter that has a definite shape and takes up a definite amount of space (p. 280)

**solar system** (sō′lər sis′təm) the Sun, the nine planets and their moons, and other objects that revolve around the Sun (p. 456)

**solution** (sə lü′shən) a mixture in which one or more substances dissolves in another (p. 308)

**speed** (spēd) the rate at which an object changes position (p. 330)

**star** (stär) a massive ball of hot gases that produces its own light (p. 423)

**states of matter** (stāts uv mat′ər) the forms of matter – solid, liquid, and gas (p. 304)

**summarize** (sum′ə rīz′) to cover the main ideas or details in a sentence or two (p. 325)

**Sun** (sun) our star; a huge ball of hot, glowing gases (p. 424)

**system** (sis′təm) a set of parts that interact with one another (p. 8)

**technology** (tek nol′ə jē) the use of science knowledge to invent tools and new ways of doing things (p. 479)

**telescope** (tel′ə skōp) a tool that gathers lots of light and magnifies objects that are far away and makes faint stars easier to see (p. 436)

**thermal energy** (thėr′məl en′ər jē) the total kinetic energy of all the particles that make up matter (p. 366)

**tool** (tül) an object used to do work (p. 479)

**tornado** (tôr nā′ dō) a rotating column of air that touches the ground and causes damage with its high winds (p. 182)

**trait** (trāt) a feature passed on to a living thing from its parents (p. 40)

**tundra** (tun′drə) land ecosystem that is cold and dry (p. 80)

**vertebrate** (ver′tə brit) animal with a backbone (p. 40)

**vibration** (vī brā′shən) a very quick back-and-forth movement (p. 392)

**volcano** (vol kā′nō) an opening in the Earth's crust from which hot, melted material erupts (p. 226)

**volume** (vol′yəm) amount of space matter takes up (p. 285)

**water cycle** (wȯ′tər sī′kəl) the movement of water from Earth's surface into the air and back again (p. 158)

**water vapor** (wȯ′tər vā′pər) water in the form of an invisible gas in the air (p. 154)

**weather** (weŦH′ər) what it is like outside including temperature, wind, clouds, and precipitation (p. 175)

**weathering** (weŦH′ər ing) any process that changes rocks by breaking them into smaller pieces (p. 230)

**wetland** (wet′land′) low land ecosystem that is covered by water at least part of the time during the year; marshes and swamps are wetlands (p. 86)

**wheel and axle** (wēl and ak′səl) a simple machine made of a wheel and a rod joined to the center of the wheel (p. 342)

**work** (werk) what happens when a force moves an object over a distance (p. 338)

# Index

This index lists the pages on which topics appear in this book. Page numbers after a *p* refer to a photograph or drawing. Page numbers after a *c* refer to a chart, graph, or diagram.

**Earth,** p424, 424–425, p425, 453, p456, 457, 458, p458
  axis of, 424
  changes from erosion, 232–233
  extremes on, c460, p461
  fossils and, 56
  Hubble Space Telescope and, 446
  layers of, 223–225
  life on, 460–461, p460–461
  lunar eclipse and, 434
  Moon and, 432–433
  plates on, 461
  rotation of, 425, 459
  seasons and, 428–429, p428–429
  shapes on surface of, 224, p224, p225
  size of, 459
  water on, 148, 154, p154

**Earthquake,** 228, p228
  damage from, 229, p229
  measuring, c236, 236–237

**Earthworm,** p206

**Echo,** 399

**Eclipse,** p419, 434, p434

**Ecosystem,** 71–75
  desert, p78, 78–79, p79
  forest, 82–83, p83
  freshwater, 86, p86, p87
  grasslands, 76–77, p77
  groups within, 74, p75
  parts of, 72, c72
  saltwater, 88, p89
  tropical forest, 84, p85
  tundra, p80, 80–81, p81
  water, 86–89

**Egg**
  animal growth and, 44
  butterfly, p44
  frog, p46

**Electrical energy,** 359, c363, 367, p374, 374–377, p375, p376, c377

**Electrical Engineer,** 384

**Electric charge,** p354–355, 374–375

**Electric circuit,** p355, p376, 376–377, c377

**Electric current,** p355, 376, p376, 376–377, c377

**Electricity,** p370
  form changed by, c377
  in home, 480, p480
  light from, 371
  past and present technology and, 482
  producing, p492, 492–493, p493
  in space missions, 384
  water for, 152, p153

**Element,** p274, 282, p282, 283, p283

**Energy,** 354, 357, p357, 359, p359
  changing form by, 362–363
  electrical, p374, 374–377, p375, p376, c377
  from food, 123
  in food web, 108
  forms of, c363
  from fuels, 248
  future sources of, 494–495, p494–495
  heat, p366, 366–369, p367, p368, p369
  light, 370–373
  for living things, 106–109
  of motion, 361
  for new and recycled goods, p255
  sound and, 386, 398

  sources of, 490
  technology and, 490–495
  travel of, 364–365, p364–365
  in waves, 365

**Environment,** 71
  of California redwood tree, p73
  change in, 114–117
  clean, p121
  healthy for people, 120–123
  living things return to, 116
  patterns of change in, 118–119

**Epedocles,** p283

**Equator,** 429

**Erosion,** p219, 232–233, p233, 234–235

**Eruption,** 221, p221

**Estimating and Measuring,** 172, 210, 211, 269, 290, 291, 414, 452

**Evaporation,** p146, 157, 158, p159, 309, 369

**Everglades,** 86, p86

**Evergreen trees.** See Coniferous trees

**Exercise,** p124, 124–125

**Exercising in Space,** 350–351, p350–351

**Exhaust,** 179

**Experiment.** See Full Inquiry, Experiment

**Experimenting.** See Investigating and Experimenting

**Explore.** See Directed Inquiry, Explore

**Hurricane,** 115, *p*170, 182, *p*183

**Hydroelectric power,** 492, *p*492, *p*493

**Hyena,** 111, *p*111

**Hygrometer,** 177, *p*177

**Hypotheses, Forming Questions and,** 140, 268, 412, 508

**Ice,** 155, *p*155, 305, *p*305, 311
heating of, 368, *p*368, 369

**Identifying and controlling variables,** 140, 268, 508

**Igneous rock,** *p*194, 200, 201, *p*201
copper in, *c*205
volcanoes and, *p*227

**Illness,** 126

**Imprint,** 58–59

**Inclined plane,** 340, *p*340

**Indianapolis weather,** *p*186, 186–187, *c*187

**Inferences.** *See* Make Inferences

**Inferring,** 30, 59, 62, 94, 100, 128, 129, 148, 162, 163, 166, 172, 188, 196, 215, 239, 259, 262, 276, 294, 300, 318, 345, 348, 382, 402, 403, 406, 407, 441, 444, 467, 499, 502

**Information processing technology,** 485

**Infrared telescopes,** 504

**Inherited,** *p*34, 48

**Inner ear,** *p*400

**Inner planets,** 458–459

**Insects,** *c*42, *p*83
ancient, 55, *p*55
in grasslands, *p*77
in tropical forests, *p*84

**Instincts,** 52, *p*52

**Instruments,** 389, *p*392, 393, *p*393, *p*394, 394–395, *p*395

**Interaction of living things,** *c*103, 103–105

**Internet,** 26, 36, 58, 68, 87, 90, 100, 128, 148, 162, 164, 172, 184, 186, 196, 199, 210, 212, 220, 234, 244, 258, 260, 276, 290, 292, 300, 303, 314, 324, 346, 356, 388, 420, 442, 447, 452, 476, 487

**Interpreting Data,** 26, 27, 90, 91, 94, 133, 184, 185, 235, 291, 415

**Intestines,** *p*122, 123

**Invention,** *p*474, 479

**Invertebrates,** 42, *p*43

**Investigate.** *See* Guided Inquiry, Investigate

**Investigating and Experimenting,** 268, 412, 508

**Iron,** *c*204, *c*205, 248, *c*248, *p*249
in foods, 204
rusting of, 311

**Islands**
erosion and, 232, *p*232

**Joshua Tree National Park,** *p*79

**Journal.** *See* Science Journal

**Jupiter,** 457, 462

**Keck telescope,** *p*436

**Kilogram,** 284

**Kilometer,** 288

**Kinetic energy,** *p*354, 361, *p*361, 363, *c*363, *p*363

**Konza Prairie,** Kansas, *p*77

**Lab Zone,** 4, 26–27, 29, 32, 36, 58–59, 61, 64, 68, 90–91, 93, 96, 100, 128–129, 131, 135, 136, 140–143, 148, 162–163,165, 168, 172, 184–185, 187, 191, 192, 196, 210–211, 213, 216, 220, 234–235, 237, 240, 244, 258–259, 261, 264, 268–271, 276, 290–291, 293, 296, 300, 314–315, 317, 320, 324, 344–345, 347, 351, 352, 356, 378–379, 381, 384, 388, 402–403, 405, 408, 412–415, 420, 440–441, 443, 447, 448, 452, 466–467, 469, 472, 476, 498–499, 501, 504, 508–511; *See also* Activities

# Credits

## Photographs

Every effort has been made to secure permission and provide appropriate credit for photographic material. The publisher deeply regrets any omission and pledges to correct errors called to its attention in subsequent editions.

Unless otherwise acknowledged, all photographs are the property of Scott Foresman, a division of Pearson Education.

Photo locators denoted as follows: Top (T), Center (C), Bottom (B), Left (L), Right (R), Background (Bkgd).

**Front Matter:** iii Daniel J. Cox/Natural Exposures, (T) Getty Images; v ©Frans Lanting/Minden Pictures; vi ©DK Images; vii (R) ©Randy M. Ury/Corbis, (L) ©Breck P. Kent/Animals Animals/Earth Scenes; viii ©Jack Dykinga/Getty Images; xi ©Douglas Peebles/Corbis; xii ©Lloyd Cluff/Corbis; xv ©RNT Productions/Corbis; xxii ©Timothy O'Keefe/Index Stock Imagery; xxiii Getty Images; xxiv (Bkgd) ©Steve Bloom/Getty Images, (C) ©Robert Sullivan/AFP/Getty Images; xxix Getty Images; xxv ©Frank Greenaway/DK Images; xxviii (BL) Getty Images, (CL) ©Dave King/DK Images; xxx ©Comstock Inc.

**Unit Dividers:** Unit A (Bkgd) Getty Images, (CC) Digital Vision; Unit B (Bkgd) ©Kim Heacox/Getty Images, (BC) Getty Images; Unit C (Bkgd) ©Lester Lefkowitz/Getty Images; Unit D (Bkgd) Corbis

**Chapter 1:** 1 (B) ©Wolfgang Kaehler/Corbis, (T, C) Getty Images; 2 (T) ©John Warden/Index Stock Imagery, (BL) ©DK Images, (BL) Getty Images, (BR) ©Nigel Cattlin/Photo Researchers, Inc.; 3 (BL) ©Nigel Cattlin/Holt Studios, (BC) Neg./Transparency no. K13073. Courtesy Dept. of Library Services/American Museum of Natural History, (CR) ©Stone/Getty Images, (Bkgd) ©John Warden/Index Stock Imagery; 6 ©John Warden/Index Stock Imagery; 7 (BR) ©Jim Steinberg/Photo Researchers, Inc., (TR) ©Photographer's Choice/Getty Images; 8 ©DK Images; 9 (CR, TR, BR) ©DK Images, (TC) Getty Images; 10 (R) Silver Burdett Ginn, (TL) Getty Images; 11 ©DK Images; 12 ©Lou Jacobs Jr./Grant Heilman Photography; 13 (TR) ©George Bernard/NHPA Limited, (C) ©DK Images, (CR) ©TH Foto-Werbung/Photo Researchers, Inc., (TR) ©Niall Benvie/Corbis, (BR) ©The Garden Picture Library/Alamy Images; 14 (BL) ©Stone/Getty Images, (BR) ©Jeff Lepore/Photo Researchers, Inc., (TL) ©Peter Smithers/Corbis; 15 (BR) ©DK Images, (TL) Getty Images; 16 (B) ©Carolina Biological/Visuals Unlimited, (TL) Getty Images; 17 (CL) ©M & C Photography/Peter Arnold, Inc., (TR) ©Brad Mogen/Visuals Unlimited, (TC) ©Pat O'Hara/Corbis, (CR) ©Wally Eberhart/Visuals Unlimited, (BR) ©DK Images; 18 (BC) ©Darryl Torckler/Getty Images, (CC) ©Brian Gordon Green/NGS Image Collection, (BC) ©John Poutier/Maxx Images, Inc., (BC) ©Jorg & Petra Wegner/Animals Animals/Earth Scenes, (TL) ©DK Images; 19 (L) ©DK Images, (CR) ©Steve Bloom Images/Alamy Images; 21 (CL) ©DK Images, (CR) Nigel Cattlin/Holt Studios, (BC) ©Kenneth W. Fink/Photo Researchers, Inc., (BC) ©Nigel Cattlin/Photo Researchers, Inc.; 23 (TR) ©Dr. E. R. Degginger/Color-Pic, Inc., (CL) ©John Cancalosi/Peter Arnold, Inc., (TL) Neg./Transparency no. K13073. Courtesy Dept. of Library Services/American Museum of Natural History, (BR) ©David Muench/Muench Photography, Inc, (CR) ©James L. Amos/Corbis; 24 (BL) ©The Natural History Museum, London, (BR, TL) ©DK Images; 26 ©Ed Young/Corbis; 28 (TR) ©Dennis MacDonald/PhotoEdit, (CR) ©Inga Spence/Visuals Unlimited, (CR) ©Steven Emery/Index Stock Imagery, (BR) ©Comstock Inc.; 31 (TL) ©DK Images, (TR) ©Kenneth W. Fink/Photo Researchers, Inc.; 32 (Bkgd) ©MSFC/NASA, (TL, BR) NASA; **Chapter 2:** 33 (B) ©Barbara Von Hoffmann/Animals Animals/Earth Scenes, (Bkgd) ©David Harrison/Index Stock Imagery; 34 (BL) ©David L. Shirk/Animals Animals/Earth Scenes, (T) ©Tom Brakefield/Corbis, (BR) ©Jeff L. Lepore/Photo Researchers, Inc.; 35 (BL) ©Brad Mogen/Visuals Unlimited; 37 (C) ©David Stover/ImageState, (Bkgd) ©Tom Brakefield/Corbis; 38 ©Tom Brakefield/Corbis; 39 (BR) ©Tom Vezo/Nature Picture Library, (BR) ©Zefa/Masterfile Corporation, (BL) ©Taxi/Getty Images, (BC) ©Natural Visions/Alamy Images, (TR) ©Frans Lanting/Minden Pictures; 40 (B) ©Tom Brakefield/Bruce Coleman Inc., (TL) ©Randy M. Ury/Corbis; 41 (CR) ©DK Images, (BC) ©Jim Brandenburg/Minden Pictures, (BR) ©Frans Lanting/Minden Pictures, (CR) Getty Images, (TR) ©Ken Lucas/Visuals Unlimited; 42 ©David Aubrey/Corbis; 43 (TR) ©Danny Lehman/Corbis, (TR) ©Robert Pickett/Corbis, (CR) ©The Image Bank/Getty Images, (BR) ©Brian Rogers/Visuals Unlimited; 44 (TL, TR) ©DK Images, (BR) ©Charles Melton/Visuals Unlimited; 45 (B) ©Brad Mogen/Visuals Unlimited, (T) ©Dick Scott/Visuals Unlimited; 46 (CL) ©Bettmann/Corbis, (BL) ©Keren Su/China Span/Alamy Images, (TL) ©Zefa/Masterfile Corporation; 47 (TR) ©Carolina Biological Supply Company/Phototake, (CL, BL) ©DK Images, (TL) ©Breck P. Kent/Animals Animals/Earth Scenes, (BR) ©Randy M. Ury/Corbis; 48 (BR) ©DK Images, (TR) ©Ken Lucas/Visuals Unlimited, (TL) ©Tony Evans/Timelapse Library/Getty Images; 49 (CL) ©Frans Lanting/Minden Pictures, (TR) ©Kevin Schafer/Corbis, (CR) ©Gary W. Carter/Corbis, (BR) ©DK Images; 50 ©Vittoriano Rastelli/Corbis, (TL) ©Photodisc Green/Getty Images; 51 (TC) ©Rod Planck/Photo Researchers, Inc., (CC) ©James Robinson/Animals Animals/Earth Scenes, (TL) ©Michael Quinton/Minden Pictures, (TR) ©Chris Newbert/Minden Pictures, (CL) ©The Image Bank/Getty Images, (BL) ©Rolf Kopfle/Bruce Coleman Inc., (BC) ©Tim Laman/NGS Image Collection, (BC) ©Suzanne L. & Joseph T. Collins/Photo Researchers, Inc., (CC) ©Steve E. Ross/Photo Researchers, Inc., (TC) ©Ken Wilson/Papilio/Corbis, (CR) ©David Aubrey/Corbis, (BR) ©E. R. Degginger/Bruce Coleman, Inc., (BL) ©Rick & Nora Bowers/Visuals Unlimited; 52 (TR) ©DK Images, (CR) ©George Grall/NGS Image Collection, (BR) ©Jeff L. Lepore/Photo Researchers, Inc., (BR) ©Eric and David Hosking/Corbis, (TL) ©Photodisc Blue/Getty Images; 53 (T) ©Gerry Ellis/Minden Pictures, (B) ©Terry W. Eggers/Corbis; 54 (TL) ©James L. Amos/Photo Researchers, Inc., (B) ©DK Images, (CL) ©Layne Kennedy/Corbis; 55 (TL) ©DK Images, (TR) ©Breck P. Kent/Animals Animals/Earth Scenes; 56 (R) ©Breck P. Kent/Animals Animals/Earth Scenes, (B) Senekenberg Nature Museum/DK Images, (TL) Colin Keates/Courtesy of the Natural History Museum, London/©DK Images; 57 ©Ross M. Horowitz/Getty Images; 58 ©Larry L. Miller/Photo Researchers, Inc.; 60 Digital Vision; 61 ©Masa Ushioda/Visual & Written/Bruce Coleman, Inc.; 63 ©DK Images; 64 (TL) ©Dutheil Didier/SYGMA/Corbis, (BL) ©Reuters/Corbis; **Chapter 3:** 65 (Bkgd) Getty Images, (T) ©Photodisc Green/Getty Images; 66 (T) ©Mark E. Gibson Stock Photography, (BL) ©J. Eastcott/Y. Eastcott Film/NGS Image Collection, (BR) ©Enzo & Paolo Ragazzini/Corbis; 67 (BL) ©Andy Binns/Ecoscene, (BR) ©Jim Zipp/Photo Researchers, Inc., (CR) ©Alan Carey/Photo Researchers, Inc., (TR) ©Steve Kaufman/Corbis; 69 ©Mark E. Gibson Stock Photography; 70 ©Mark E. Gibson Stock Photography; 71 ©Siede Preis/Getty Images; 72 Getty Images; 73 (Bkgd) ©Melissa Farlow/Aurora & Quanta Productions, (TC) ©DK Images, (BC) Kurt Stier/Corbis; 74 (CL) ©Royalty-Free/Corbis, (BL) ©Alan Carey/Photo Researchers, Inc.; 75 (CR) ©Joseph Van Os/Getty Images, (L) ©Kennan Ward/Corbis, (BR) Darren Bennett/Animals Animals/Earth Scenes; 76 ©OSF/Animals Animals/Earth Scenes; 77 (T) ©Enzo & Paolo Ragazzini/Corbis, (BL) ©Jason Edwards/NGS Image Collection, (BR) ©Steve Kaufman/Corbis; 78 (BL) ©Jack Dykinga/Getty Images, (BR) Jerry Young/©DK Images, (TL) ©DK Images; 79 (Bkgd) ©J. Eastcott/Y. Eastcott Film/NGS Image Collection, (TL) Daniel J. Cox/Natural Exposures; 80 (BL) Daniel J. Cox/Natural Exposures, (TL) ©Ed Reschke/Peter Arnold, Inc.; 81 (L) ©Andy Binns/Ecoscene, (TR, CL, CR) Daniel J. Cox/Natural Exposures; 82 ©Tim Laman/NGS Image Collection; 83 (TR) ©Michio Hoshino/Minden Pictures, (TL, BR) ©Jim Brandenburg/Minden Pictures, (BL) ©Jay Dickman/Corbis, (CR) ©David Ulmer/Stock Boston; 84 (CR) ©Roy Toft/NGS Image Collection, (TR) ©Claus Meyer/Minden Pictures, (BR) ©Ken Preston-Mafham/Animals Animals/Earth Scenes, (TL) Alamy; 85 (BL) ©Michael & Patricia Fogden/Minden Pictures, (TL) ©Tui De Roy/Minden Pictures; 86 (B) Daniel J. Cox/Natural Exposures, (TR) ©Jim Zipp/Photo Researchers, Inc., (TL) ©Roy Toft/NGS Image Collection; 87 (Bkgd) Daniel J. Cox/Natural Exposures, (TR) ©Joseph H. Bailey/NGS Image Collection; 88 (TL) ©Medford Taylor/NGS Image Collection, (BR) ©Fred Bavendam/Peter Arnold, Inc.; 89 (TR) ©Mick Turner/PhotoLibrary, (Bkgd) ©Royalty-Free/Corbis; 90 Getty Images; 95 ©Ken Preston-Mafham/Animals Animals/Earth Scenes; 96 ©Bettmann/Corbis; **Chapter 4:** 97 ©M. Colbeck/OSF/Animals Animals/Earth Scenes; 98 (T) ©Stephen Frink/Corbis, (BL) ©Carol Havens/Corbis, (BR) ©K. H. Haenel/Zefa/Masterfile Corporation; 99 (BL) ©D. Robert and Lorri Franz/Corbis, (B) ©Jim Brandenburg/Minden Pictures, (CR) ©Dr. Gopal Murti/Photo Researchers, Inc., (BR) ©Gerald Hinde/ABPL/Animals Animals/Earth Scenes; 101 (CR) ©Richard Walters/Visuals Unlimited, (Bkgd) ©Stephen Frink/Corbis, (BR) ©Bob Marsh/Papilio/Corbis, (CC) ©David Boag/Alamy Images; 102 ©Stephen Frink/Corbis; 103 (CR) Brand X Pictures, (BR) ©Patti Murray/Earth Scenes/Maxx Images, Inc., (CR) ©Laura Sivell/Papilio/Corbis, (TR) Getty Images; 104 (B) ©Richard Kolar/Animals Animals/Earth Scenes, (T) ©Rick Raymond/Index Stock Imagery; 105 (T) ©Michael & Patricia Fogden/Corbis, (TR) ©B. Jones/M. Shimlock/Photo Researchers, Inc.; 106 (BL) ©Chase Swift/Corbis, (BC) ©Carol Havens/Corbis, (BR) ©Frank Blackburn/Ecoscene/Corbis, (TL) ©Hope Ryden/NGS Image Collection; 107 (B) ©D. Robert and Lorri Franz/Corbis, (TL) ©K. H. Haenel/Zefa/Masterfile Corporation, (CL) ©Randy Wells/Corbis, (BL) ©Danny Lehman/Corbis; 108 (TL, BL) Getty Images, (BR) ©Yva Momatiuk/John Eastcott/Minden Pictures, (BC) ©Naturfoto Honal/Corbis, (CL) ©Kevin R. Morris/Corbis; 109 (C) Minden Pictures, (R) ©Claudia Adams/Alamy Images, (BL) ©Tom Brakefield/Corbis; 110 (TL) ©Gerry Ellis/Minden Pictures, (CL) ©Michael & Patricia Fogden/Corbis, (BL) ©Martin Harvey/Photo Researchers, Inc., (TL) ©Photodisc Green/Getty Images; 111 ©Gerald Hinde/ABPL/Animals Animals/Earth Scenes; 112 (T) ©DK Images, (CL) ©Raymond Gehman/Corbis, (BL) ©Scott Camazine/Photo Researchers, Inc.; 113 ©Paal Hermansen/NHPA Limited; 114 (BR) ©Richard H. Johnston/Getty Images, (BL) ©Harry Engels/Photo